Contents

Introduction by Becca Rothfeld   vii

Editor's Note   xv

THE ANATOMY OF LOVE   I

THE ANATOMY OF LOVE

ROBERT BURTON

INTRODUCTION BY
BECCA ROTHFELD

PUSHKIN PRESS CLASSICS

Pushkin Press
Somerset House, Strand
London WC2R ILA

Introduction © Becca Rothfeld, 2026

The Anatomy of Love was first published as 'Partition Three: Love-Melancholy' in *The Anatomy of Melancholy* in England, 1621

First published by Pushkin Press in 2026

ISBN 13: 978-1-80533-333-3

A CIP catalogue record for this title is available from the British Library

The authorised representative in the EEA is eucomply OÜ,
Pärnu mnt. 139b-14, 11317, Tallinn, Estonia,
hello@eucompliancepartner.com, +33757690241

Cover image: *Vanitas Still Life*, Herman Henstenburgh (1667–1726)

Designed and typeset by Tetragon, London
Printed and bound in the United Kingdom by Clays Ltd, Elcograf S.p.A.

Pushkin Press is committed to a sustainable future for our business, our readers and our planet. This book is made from paper from forests that support responsible forestry.

www.pushkinpress.com

1 3 5 7 9 8 6 4 2

PUSHKIN PRESS CLASSICS

THE ANATOMY OF LOVE

'Burton is a rollicking, more-ish writer, from an age that produced the nation's best prose... And not only that, but it's useful: it makes you less melancholy'
NICHOLAS LEZARD, GUARDIAN

'Above all, Burton is a continuously interesting human voice... Every sentence, every quotation has point, can catch and hold the mind'
LONDON REVIEW OF BOOKS

'An enormous survey of human life... which ranks with Chaucer and Dickens, except the characters are books rather than people'
NORTHROP FRYE

ROBERT BURTON (1577–1640) was born to a family of landed gentry in Leicestershire and matriculated at Oxford at the age of 15. He remained there for the rest of his life, and was eventually appointed librarian of Christ Church College. Inspired by his own struggle with melancholy, Burton began research into the subject, eventually amassing the collection of musings and quotations that would become *The Anatomy of Melancholy*. First published in 1621, the work was immensely popular, and was expanded and reprinted five times over the course of Burton's life.

BECCA ROTHFELD is the non-fiction book critic at *The Washington Post*, an editor at *The Point* and the author of the essay collection *All Things are Too Small*. She lives in Washington, DC with her husband, Zach, and her dog, Kafka.

Introduction

Foremost among the causes of melancholy that the seventeenth-century clergyman, scholar and polymath Robert Burton lists in his sprawling masterpiece, *The Anatomy of Melancholy*, are various species of costiveness. Accordingly, many of the remedies he recommends are evacuations: vomiting, bloodletting and, of course, defecating. 'Where nature is defective,' Burton writes, 'art must supply.' Horse leeches, 'applied especially to the hemrods,' are useful. Sometimes, ''tis not amiss to bore the skull with an instrument, to let out the fuliginous vapours.' Emetics—among them hellebore, a plant we now know to be poisonous—are often in order.

But perhaps the best medicine of all is a different sort of release, equally violent but infinitely more diverting. 'I write of melancholy, by being busy to avoid melancholy,' Burton confesses in the *Anatomy*'s novella-length introduction. 'There is no greater cause of melancholy than idleness.' At over a thousand pages, *The Anatomy of Melancholy* is one of the great feats of literary incontinence.

It is nominally organized into three 'partitions', but these sections bleed into each other with such wild abandon that they recall Burton's melancholics, studded with leeches and haemorrhaging at their doctors' hands. The first partition treats the causes of melancholy, the second the disease's cures. The final partition, presented here in its entirety, is devoted to the special case of 'love-melancholy'—but to suggest that even a sentence of Burton's confines itself to a single topic is to underrate his gift for digression. This book is not just about love and its associated agonies, but about beauty, greed, fashion, God, virtue, marriage, jealousy and much else besides. Even a portion of the *Anatomy* is an impressive effusion.

Burton's biography is as cramped and constipated as his work is capacious. He studied, he suffered, and he did little else. Born in 1577 to affluent denizens of the landed gentry, he spent almost all of his life at Oxford. Some hypothesize that a depressive episode explains the unusual length of his undergraduate study, which lasted nine years, but perhaps he was just displaying an early aptitude for prolixity. In any case, after he received his bachelor's degree, he remained at the university for the rest of his life, serving as a fellow and librarian of Christ Church college, as well as rector of a nearby parish. His library contained 1,700 volumes on all manner of subjects, and it was here that his central dramas were staged. The ferment he weathered was internal, much of it intellectual, some of it emotional—the bulk of it reproduced in the pages of the *Anatomy*.

For make no mistake: this book is the work of his life. Aside from a few youthful plays, it is the only thing he ever wrote. And he never stopped writing it: five editions were published during his lifetime, and in each it expanded. Between 1621, when the first edition appeared, and 1651, when a sixth was released after his death, it swelled from around 350,000 words to well over 500,000. 'But I rove,' he chastises himself on more than one occasion. After a long meditation on the mysteries of astronomy ('Who could give reason of this diversity of meteors, that it should rain stones, frogs, mice, etc. ') he pauses to pant, 'I am now gone quite out of sight, I am almost giddy with roving about.'

True to form, he went on revising compulsively from beyond the grave. 'When he died in 1640,' remarks A.D. Nuttall in the *London Review of Books*, 'he left notes behind him for a further revision.'

His opus went on multiplying, practically of its own accord. In the nineteenth century, no fewer than forty-eight editions appeared. It was reissued by Oxford University Press in 1989, by NYRB Classics in 2001—and here I am, introducing another edition. There could be no career more fitting for a work in which 'etc.' appears on nearly every page.

The book's excesses are captivating. The *Anatomy* was a bestseller in its day, and it garnered many eminent admirers in the succeeding centuries. Samuel Johnson was an acolyte. The English Romantics, among them Keats and Coleridge, sang its praises, and Laurence Sterne liked it so much that he plagiarized some of it in *Tristam Shandy*. It has attracted such a diverse assortment of champions because it is as vast and varied as the world. At times, it is jocular, at others, satirical. At one point, Burton calls it a 'confused lump'. It is certainly not the sober medical tract it sometimes pretends to be, in part because the boundaries between the scholarly specialties were more porous in the age of its composition, in part because of its literary ambition, above all because Burton is too commodious to constrain himself to one genre. He is a raconteur, a philosopher, a preacher, a classicist, a proto-psychologist, a dietician, a doctor and a memoirist; he makes forays into astrology, geography, theology, aesthetics and even chemistry. He quotes indefatigably, lapses frequently into Latin and ventures bits of witty verse; sometimes, he provides 'receipts' for potions, including one 'approved medicine against dotage, head-melancholy and other such diseases of the brain' that involves decapitating a ram and stuffing its skull with spices. His digressions have digressions; his references have references. He roves and raves so often that his detours constitute the true meat of his writing: the *Anatomy* is the rare book composed entirely of asides.

*

That Burton cannot settle on a genre is fitting, for his subject is nothing less than every indisposition there is. During the seventeenth century, a succinct and technical definition of melancholy was available. The theory of the humours—according to which our bodies comprise black bile, yellow bile, phlegm and blood—was soon to be superseded by William Harvey's account of circulation, but it had a venerable pedigree, dating back to the Greek and Roman writers of whom Burton was so fond, and it continued to dominate until the dawn of the eighteenth century. Melancholy was black bile, and the disease of melancholia was occasioned by an imbalance of this humour or its incursion into the blood.

Burton avails himself of this definition sometimes, and his account of melancholy can seem remarkably modern. 'We call him melancholy that is dull, sad, sour, lumpish, ill-disposed, solitary, anyway moved or displeased,' he writes of a state that sounds much like depression. Many of his descriptions of dejected melancholics still ring true. 'Such as are melancholy,' he observes, are apt to 'lie in bed whole days, and keep their chambers, to walk alone in some solitary grove'. Many 'cannot put out of their minds the matters they least wish to think of.' Love-melancholics suffer from 'leanness, want of appetite, want of sleep', and the love-melancholy sections of the *Anatomy* are among its best beloved precisely because they describe such a recognizable and enduring cluster of ailments—the pangs of jealousy, the frenzies of infatuation, the terrifying speed with which adoration can devolve into disgust.

But melancholy is also an oddity that encompasses rabies and delusions. One melancholic 'resolved within himself not to piss, for fear he could drown all the town'; another believed he was burping incessantly because he had swallowed a family of frogs. 'Love is a species of melancholy' with an especially confounding array of symptoms. Many lovers 'suffer themselves to be led like an ox to the slaughter', and there are innumerable cases of besotted unfortunates who killed themselves. Worse, some 'do not offer violence to themselves in this rage of lust, but unto others, their nearest and dearest friends'. Sometimes love-melancholy is tantamount to an intellectual defect, a failure to acknowledge or perceive the beloved's deficiencies; sometimes it is a physical illness, an onslaught of agitation so acute that it causes its victims to bleed at the nose. Yet it can be an improving force: infatuated youths have been known to discipline and refine themselves in hopes of impressing their would-be paramours. Ultimately, Burton despairs of cataloguing all the ways that love-melancholy manifests: 'I conclude there is no end of love's symptoms, 'tis a bottomless pit.'

Anatomizing even a subcategory of melancholy, it emerges, is an impossible task. These conceptual difficulties are compounded by the disorder's prevalence, for 'who is not a fool, who is free from melancholy?' The illness afflicts even inanimate things: 'You shall find that kingdoms and provinces are melancholy, cities and families.' Love-melancholy is no less widespread. There is love 'between the vine and the cabbage, between the vine and the olive'. Mirrors ogle the beautiful women who peer into them, and, wonderfully, 'when a drop of Psyche's candle fell on Cupid's shoulder, I think sure it was to kiss it'. The beauty that compels love is a force so powerful that it stops wild animals in their tracks: Burton recalls how a woman condemned 'to be trodden on by wild horses' was saved by the herd's infatuation.

How is an illness so common and so irresistible to be treated? If it is perennial—if, as Burton writes, 'we change language, habits, laws, customs, manners, but not vices, not diseases, not the symptoms of folly and madness'—we might suspect that it is also incurable. The *Anatomy* sometimes takes the pessimistic view, then contradicts itself and offers sundry therapies. Some of these are sensible. Who would deny that it is advisable to keep busy, or take a walk in the woods, or 'impart our misery to some friend, not to smother it up in our own breast'? Other remedies are likely ineffective, but nonetheless familiar in their endearing quackishness, as when Burton quotes several physicians who recommend eating fifty or more eggs a day.

But then we read, 'It is good overnight to anoint the face with hare's blood, and in the morning to wash it with strawberry and cowslip water.' We learn about the curative aspects of certain gemstones; we are told that black magic is effective but nonetheless impermissible for a pious Christian. Melancholy may be due to a bad diet or a poor sleep schedule—but it may also be the work of 'the devil and his ministers'. Dispirited patients are urged to avoid fowl, which is a 'melancholy meat' and warned that 'indulgence in parsnips creates harmful juices'. Love-melancholy can be caused by the climate in 'hot and southern countries' or the consumption of 'lascivious meats'. The various cures for infatuation are among the most unpleasant in Burton's repertoire: one author whom he cites '"would have [lovers] soundly whipped, or, to cool their courage, kept in prison", and there fed with bread and water till they acknowledge their error and become of another mind'. It is almost as if Burton hopes to discourage us from seeking the cure to so agreeable a malady.

Indeed, he is clear from the first that he hopes to discourage us from reading the *Anatomy* at all. In the first partition, he counsels 'him that is actually melancholy not to read this tract of Symptoms, lest he disquiet or make himself for a time worse and more melancholy than he was before'. But he has already established that all of us are melancholy to a greater or lesser degree. Who, then, can read the *Anatomy* safely?

But perhaps its dangers are a perverse boon, for not only is love-melancholy often seductively pleasant, it is also the very stuff of our life. 'Love is that salt that seasoneth all our harsh and dull labours,'

Burton writes grudgingly. Without it, we would not be what we are: 'He who does not feel the power of love is either a stone or an animal. He is not a man but a block, a very stone.' If this is a disease, it is congenital, and its symptoms often sound very much like some of our most vaunted therapies—very much, that is, like those antic evacuations that we were supposed to drink hellebore and other potions to induce. When love proceeds unchecked, 'it is a wandering, extravagant, a domineering, a boundless, an irrefragable, a destructive passion'. It consumes everything in its wake. It is avid and immoderate. It is, in a word, isomorphic with the *Anatomy*, which takes the form of both the disease and the therapy. This is an iatrogenic document, one bound to cause the very disorder that it purports to cure. But it is also, paradoxically, medicinal. Who would not wish to witness and undergo such glorious evacuations? Such paroxysms of unrestraint, mania, madness, extravagance, etc.?

BECCA ROTHFELD

Editor's Note

This edition presents the third partition of *The Anatomy of Melancholy* in its entirety, without expurgation or abridgement. The text of *Partition Three: Love-Melancholy* has, however, been prepared in such a way as to make it easier for the modern reader to navigate. The long strings of references to tomes inaccessible to all but rare book scholars, with which Burton frequently interrupted his wonderfully textured prose, have been eliminated. So have the bracketed Latin originals of quotations which were already translated in the text, and the elaborate division of Partition, Section, Member and Subsection, confusing when taken out of the context of the wider work. Some contemporary punctuation has been allowed to intrude, with inverted commas marking speech, and the occasional paragraph break not found in the original. We have been inspired by earlier editors, principally Daniel George in his 1962 edition for the New English Library. There are no doubt objections to be made on the grounds of academic rigour and respect for the author – but Burton's intent, as he makes clear himself throughout the *Anatomy*, is to provide solace and amusement, and our aim has simply been to remove the barriers that might prevent today's reader from finding both in this wonderful, one-of-a-kind book.

THE
ANATOMY
OF LOVE

Preface

There will not be wanting, I presume, one or other that will much discommend some part of this treatise and object that it is too light for a divine, too comical a subject to speak of love-symptoms, too phantastical, and fit alone for a wanton poet, a feeling young lovesick gallant, an effeminate courtier, or some such idle person. And 'tis true they say: for by the naughtiness of men it is so come to pass as Caussinus observes that the very name of love is odious to chaster ears; and therefore some again, out of an affected gravity, will dislike all for the name's sake before they read a word, dissembling with him in Petronius, and seem to be angry that their ears are violated with such obscene speeches, that so they may be admired for grave philosophers and staid carriage. They cannot abide to hear talk of love-toys, or amorous discourses; in their outward actions averse, and yet in their cogitations they are all out as bad, if not worse than others.

> *Lucretia blushed and hid my book—*
> *To read it again when Brutus is not there.*

But let these cavillers and counterfeit Catos know that, as the Lord John answered the queen in that Italian Guazzo, an old, a grave, discreet man is fittest to discourse of love matters, because he hath likely more experiences, observed more, hath a more staid judgement, can better discern, resolve, discuss, advise, give better cautions and more solid precepts, better inform his auditors in such a subject, and by reason of his riper years sooner divert. Besides there is nothing here to be excepted at; love is a species of melancholy, and a necessary part of this my treatise, which I may not omit; I must and will perform my task. And that short excuse of Mercerus for his edition of Aristaenetus shall be mine: If I have spent my time ill to write, let not them be so idle as to read. But I am persuaded it is not so ill spent, I ought not to excuse or repent myself of this subject, on which many grave and worthy men have written whole volumes....

A company of stern readers dislike the second of the Aeneids, and tax Virgil's gravity, for inserting such amorous passions in an heroical subject; but his commentator justly vindicates the poet's worth, wisdom, and discretion in doing as he did. Castalio [Castiglione] would not have young men read the Canticles, because to his thinking it was too light and amorous a tract, a Ballad of Ballads, as our old English translation hath it. He might as well forbid the reading of Genesis, because of the loves of Jacob and Rachel, the stories of Shechem and Dinah, Judah and Tamar; reject the Book of Numbers for the fornications of the people of Israel with the Moabites; that of Judges for Samson and Delilah's embracings; that of the Kings, for David and Bathsheba's adulteries, the incest of Amnon and Tamar, Solomon's concubines, etc., the stories of Esther, Judith, Susanna, and many such. Dicaearchus, and some other, carp at Plato's majesty, that he would vouchsafe to indite such love-toys: among the rest, for that dalliance with Agatho.

For my part, saith Maximus Tyrius, a great Platonist himself, I do not only admire, but stand amazed to read that Plato and Socrates both should expel Homer from their city because he writ of such light and wanton subjects as Vulcan's net, Mars' and Venus' fopperies before all the gods; because Apollo fled when he was persecuted by Achilles, the gods were wounded and ran whining away, as Mars that roared louder than Stentor, and covered nine acres of ground with his fall; Vulcan was a summer's day falling down from heaven, and in Lemnos Isle brake his leg, etc., with such ridiculous passages: whenas both Socrates and Plato, by his testimony, writ lighter themselves.

What can be more absurd than for grave philosophers to treat of such fooleries, to admire Autolycus, Alcibiades, for their beauties as they did, to run after, to gaze, to dote on fair Phaedrus, delicate Agatho, young Lysis, fine Charmides? Doth this become grave philosophers? Thus peradventure Callias, Thrasymachus, Polus, Aristophanes, or some of his adversaries and emulators might object; but neither they nor Anytus and Meletus, his bitter enemies, that condemned him for teaching Critias to tyrannize, his impiety for swearing by dogs and plane-trees, for his juggling sophistry, etc., never so much as upbraided him with impure love, writing or speaking of that subject; and therefore without question, as he concludes, both Socrates and Plato in this are justly to be excused. But suppose they had been a little overseen, should divine Plato be defamed? No; rather, as he said of Cato's drunkenness, if Cato were drunk, it should be no vice at all to be drunk. They reprove Plato then, but without cause (as Ficinus pleads); for all love is honest and good, and they are worthy to be loved that speak well of love.

Being to speak of this admirable affection of love (saith Valleriola), there lies open a vast and philosophical field to my discourse, by which many lovers become mad: let me leave my more serious meditations, wander in these philosophical fields, and look into those pleasant groves of the Muses, where with unspeakable variety of flowers we may make garlands to ourselves, not to adorn us only, but with their pleasant smell and juice to nourish our souls, and fill our minds desirous of knowledge, etc. After a harsh and unpleasing discourse of melancholy, which hath hitherto molested your patience and tired the author, give him leave to recreate himself in this kind after his laborious studies, since so many grave divines and worthy men have without offence to manners, to help themselves and others, voluntarily written of it. Heliodorus, a bishop, penned a love story of Theagenes and Chariclea, and when some Catos of his time reprehended him for it, chose rather, saith Nicephorus, to leave his bishopric than his book. Aeneas Sylvius, an ancient divine, and past forty years of age, as he confesseth himself, indited that wanton history of Euryalus and Lucretia. And how many superintendents of learning could I reckon up, that have written of light phantastical subjects!

Give me leave then to refresh my Muse a little, and my weary readers, to expatiate in this delightsome field, to season a surly discourse with a more pleasing aspersion of love matters. 'Tis good to sweeten our life with some pleasing toys to relish it, and, as Pliny tells us, most of our students love such pleasant subjects. Though Macrobius teach us otherwise, that those old sages banished all such light tracts from their studies to nurses' cradles, to please only the ear; yet out of Apuleius I will oppose as honourable patrons, Solon, Plato, Xenophon, Hadrian, etc., that as highly approve of these treatises. On the other side methinks they are not to be disliked, they are not so unfit. I will not peremptorily say, as one did, I will tell you such pretty stories, that foul befall him that is not pleased with them. I will not press you with my pamphlets, or beg attention, but if you like them you may. Pliny holds it expedient, and most fit, to season our works with some pleasant discourse; and there be those, without question, that are more willing to read such toys than I am to write.

'Let me not live,' saith Aretine's Antonia, 'if I had not rather hear thy discourse than see a play!' No doubt but there be more of her mind, ever have been, ever will be, as Jerome bears me witness: A far greater part had rather read Apuleius than Plato. Tully himself confesseth he could not understand Plato's Timaeus, and therefore cared less for it; but every schoolboy hath that famous testament of Grunnius Corocotta Porcellus at his fingers' ends. The comical poet made this his only care and sole study, to please the people, tickle the ear, and to delight; but mine earnest intent is as much to profit as to please; and these my writings, I hope, shall take like gilded pills, which are so composed as well to tempt the appetite and deceive the palate as to help and medicinally work upon the whole body; my lines shall not only recreate but rectify the mind.

I think I have said enough; if not, let him that is otherwise minded remember that of Apuleius Madaurensis; he was in his life a philosopher (as Ausonius apologizeth for him), in his epigrams a lover, in his precepts most severe; in his epistle to Caerellia a wanton. Annianus, Sulpicius, Evenus, Menander, and many old poets besides, did write Fescennines, Atellanes, and lascivious songs, yet were they chaste, severe, and upright livers....

But I presume I need not, as Socrates in Plato, cover his face when he spake of love, or blush and hide mine eyes, as Pallas did in her hood, when she was consulted by Jupiter about Mercury's marriage. It is no such lascivious, obscene, or wanton discourse; I have not offended your chaster ears with anything that is here written, as many French and Italian authors in their modern language of late have done. 'Tis not scurrile this, but chaste, honest, most part serious, and even of religion itself....

Thus much I have thought good to say by way of preface, lest any man should blame in me lightness, wantonness, rashness, in speaking of love's causes, enticements, symptoms, remedies, lawful and unlawful loves, and lust itself. I speak it only to tax and deter others from it, not to teach, but to show the vanities and fopperies of this heroical or Herculean love, and to apply remedies unto it. I will treat of this with like liberty as of the rest. Condemn me not, good reader, then, or censure me hardly, if some part of this treatise to thy thinking as yet be too light; but consider better of it. To the pure all things are pure, a naked man to a modest woman is no otherwise than a picture, as Augusta Livia truly said, *honi soit qui mal y pense*. If in thy censure it be too light I advise thee as Lipsius did his reader for some places of Plautus, if they like thee not, let them pass; or oppose that which is good to that which is bad, and reject not therefore all. For to invert that verse of Martial, and with Hierom Wolfius to apply it to my present purpose, some is good, some bad, some is indifferent. I say farther with him yet, I have inserted some things more homely, light, or comical, which I would request every man to interpret to the best, and, as Julius Caesar Scaliger besought Cardan, I beseech thee, good reader, not to mistake me, or misconstrue what is here written. 'Tis a comical subject; in sober sadness I crave pardon of what is amiss, and desire thee to suspend thy judgement, wink at small faults, or to be silent at least; but if thou likest, speak well of it, and wish me good success.

I am resolved, howsoever, boldly to show myself in this common stage, and in this tragi-comedy of love to act several parts, some satirically, some comically, some in a mixed tone, as the subject I have in hand gives occasion, and present scene shall require or offer itself.

I

Love's Beginning, Object, Definition, Division

Love's limits are ample and great, and a spacious walk it hath, beset with thorns, and for that cause, which Scaliger reprehends in Cardan, not lightly to be passed over. Lest I incur the same censure, I will examine all the kinds of love, his nature, beginning, difference, objects, how it is honest or dishonest, a virtue or vice, a natural passion or a disease, his power and effects, how far it extends....

Love, universally taken, is defined to be a desire, as a word of more ample signification; and though Leon Hebraeus [Judah Abravanel], the most copious writer of this subject, in his third dialogue makes no difference, yet in his first he distinguisheth them again, and defines love by desire. Love is a voluntary affection, and desire to enjoy that which is good. Desire wisheth, love enjoys; the end of the one is the beginning of the other; that which we love is present; that which we desire is absent. It is worth the labour, saith Plotinus, to consider well of love, whether it be a god or a devil, or passion of the mind, or partly god, partly devil, partly passion. He concludes love to participate of all three, to arise from desire of that which is beautiful and fair, and defines it to be an action of the mind desiring that which is good. Plato calls it the great devil, for its vehemency, and sovereignty over all other passions, and defines it an appetite by which we desire some good to be present. Ficinus in his comment adds the word fair to this definition: Love is a desire of enjoying that which is good and fair. St Augustine dilates this common definition, and will have love to be a delectation of the heart, for something which we seek to win, or joy to have, coveting by desire, resting in joy. Scaliger taxeth these former definitions, and will not have love to be defined by desire or appetite; for when we enjoy the things we desire, there remains no more appetite: as he defines it, Love is an affection by which we are either united to the thing we love, or perpetuate our union; which agrees in part with Leon Hebraeus.

Now this love varies as his object varies, which is always good, amiable, fair, gracious, and pleasant. All things desire that which is good, as we are taught in the Ethics, or at least that which to them seems to be good; thou wilt wish no harm, I suppose, no ill in all thine actions, thoughts, or desires; thou wilt not have bad corn, bad soil, a naughty tree, but all good: a good servant, a good horse, a good son, a good friend, a good neighbour, a good wife. From this goodness comes beauty; for beauty, grace and comeliness, which result as so many rays from their good parts, make us to love, and so to covet it: for were it not pleasing and gracious in our eyes, we should not seek it. No man loves, saith Aristotle, but he that was first delighted with comeliness and beauty. As this fair object varies, so doth our love; for, as Proclus holds, every fair thing is amiable, and what we love is fair and gracious in our eyes, or at least we do so apprehend and still esteem of it. Amiableness is the object of love, the scope and end is to obtain it, for whose sake we love, and which our mind covets to enjoy. And it seems to us especially fair and good; for good, fair, and unity cannot be separated. Beauty shines, Plato saith, and by reason of its splendour and shining causeth admiration; and the fairer the object is, the more eagerly it is sought. For, as the same Plato defines it, Beauty is a lively shining or glittering brightness, resulting from effused good by ideas, seeds, reason, shadows, stirring up our minds that by this good they may be united and made one.

Others will have beauty to be the perfection of the whole composition, caused out of the congruous symmetry, measure, order, and manner of parts; and that comeliness which proceeds from this beauty is called grace, and from thence all fair things are gracious. For grace and beauty are so wonderfully annexed, so sweetly and gently win our souls, and strongly allure, that they confound our judgement and cannot be distinguished. Beauty and grace are like those beams and shinings that come from the glorious and divine sun, which are diverse, as they proceed from the diverse objects, to please and affect our several senses; as the species of beauty are taken at our eyes, ears, or conceived in our inner soul, as Plato disputes at large in his dialogue on Beauty and, after many sophistical errors confuted, concludes that beauty is a grace in all things, delighting the eyes, ears, and soul itself; so that, as Valesius infers hence, whatsoever pleaseth our ears, eyes, and soul must needs be beautiful, fair, and delightsome to us. And nothing can more please our ears than music, or pacify our minds. Fair houses, pictures, orchards, gardens, fields, a fair hawk, a fair horse is most acceptable unto us; whatsoever pleaseth our eyes and ears, we call beautiful and fair; pleasure belongeth to the rest of the senses, but grace and beauty to these two alone. As the objects vary and are diverse, so they diversely affect our eyes, ears, and soul itself; which gives occasion to some to make so many several kinds of love as there be objects: one beauty ariseth from God, of which and divine love St Dionysius, with many Fathers and neoterics, have written just volumes on the love of God, as they term it, many paraenetical discourses; another from His creatures: there is a beauty of the body, a beauty of the soul, a beauty from virtue, a beauty of martyrs, St Augustine calls it, which we see with the eyes of our mind; which beauty, as Tully saith, if we could discern with these corporeal eyes, would cause admirable affections, and ravish our souls.

This other beauty, which ariseth from those extreme parts, and graces which proceed from gestures, speeches, several motions, and proportions of creatures, men and women (especially from women, which made those old poets put the three Graces still in Venus' company, as attending on her and holding up her train), are infinite almost, and vary their names with their objects, as love of money, covetousness, love of beauty, lust, immoderate desire of any pleasure, concupiscence, friendship, love, good will, etc., and is either virtue or vice, honest, dishonest, in excess, defect, as shall be showed in his place; heroical love, religious love, etc., which may be reduced to a twofold division, according to the principal parts which are affected, the brain and liver: love and friendship, which Scaliger, Valesius, and Melancthon warrant out of Plato, and from that speech of Pausanias, belike, that makes two Venuses and two loves. One Venus is ancient without a mother, and descended from heaven, whom we call celestial; the younger, begotten of Jupiter and Dione, whom commonly we call Venus.

Ficinus, in his comment upon this place, following Plato, calls these two loves two devils, or good and bad angels according to us, which are still hovering about our souls. The one rears to heaven, the other depresseth us to hell; the one good, which stirs us up to the contemplation of that divine beauty for whose sake we perform justice and all godly offices, study philosophy, etc.; the other base, and though bad yet to be respected; for indeed both are good in their own natures: procreation of children is as necessary as that finding out of truth, but therefore called bad, because it is abused, and withdraws our soul from the speculation of that other to viler objects. So far Ficinus.

St Augustine hath delivered as much in effect: Every creature is good, and may be loved well or ill: and two cities make two loves, Jerusalem and Babylon, the love of God the one, the love of the world the other; of these two cities we all are citizens, as by examination of ourselves we may soon find, and of which. The one love is the root of all mischief, the other of all good. So he will have those four cardinal virtues to be naught else but love rightly composed; he calls virtue the order of love, whom Thomas Aquinas following confirms as much, and amplifies in many words. Lucian, to the same purpose, hath a division of his own: One love was born in the sea, which is as various and raging in young men's breasts as the sea itself, and causeth burning lust; the other is that golden chain which was let down from heaven, and with a divine fury ravisheth our souls, made to the image of God, and stirs us up to comprehend the innate and incorruptible beauty to which we were once created. Beroaldus hath expressed all this in an epigram of his:

> *If divine Plato's tenents they be true,*
> *Two Veneres, two loves there be;*
> *The one from heaven, unbegotten still,*
> *Which knits our souls in unity.*
> *The other famous over all the world,*
> *Binding the hearts of gods and men;*
> *Dishonest, wanton, and seducing, she,*
> *Rules whom she will, both where and when.*

This twofold division of love Origen likewise follows, in his Comment on the Canticles, one from God, the other from the devil, as he holds (understanding it in the worse sense), which many others repeat and imitate. Both which (to omit all subdivisions) in excess or defect, as they are abused, or degenerate, cause melancholy in a particular kind, as shall be showed in his place. Augustine, in another tract, makes a threefold division of this love, which we may use well or ill: God, our neighbour, and the world: God above us, our neighbour next us, the world beneath us. In the course of our desires, God hath three things, the world one, our neighbour two. Our desire to God is either from God, with God, or to God, and ordinarily so runs. From God, when it receives from Him, whence, and for which it should love Him; with God, when it contradicts His will in nothing; to God, when it seeks to repose and rest itself in Him. Our love to our neighbour may proceed from him, and run with him, not to him: from him, as when we rejoice of his good safety and well doing; with him when we desire to have him a fellow and companion of our journey in the way of the Lord; not in him, because there is no aid, hope, or confidence in man. From the world our love comes, when we begin to admire the Creator in His works, and glorify God in His creatures; with the world it should run, if, according to the mutability of all temporalities, it should be dejected in adversity, or over-elevated in prosperity; to the world, if it would settle itself in his vain delights and studies.

Many such partitions of love I could repeat, and subdivisions, but lest (which Scaliger objects to Cardan) I confound filthy burning lust with pure and divine love, I will follow that accurate division of Leon Hebraeus betwixt Sophia and Philo, where he speaks of natural, sensible, and rational love, and handleth each apart. Natural love or hatred is that sympathy or antipathy which is to be seen in animate and inanimate creatures, in the four elements, metals, stones, as a stone to his centre, fire upward, and rivers to the sea. The sun, moon, and stars go still round, for love of perfection. This love is manifest, I say, in inanimate creatures. How comes a loadstone to draw iron to it? jet chaff? the ground to covet showers, but for love? No creature, St Jerome concludes, is to be found that doth not love something, no stock, no stone, that hath not some feeling of love. 'Tis more eminent in plants, herbs, and is especially observed in vegetals; as between the vine and elm a great sympathy; between the vine and the cabbage, between the vine and the olive, between the vine and bays a great antipathy; the vine loves not the bay, nor his smell, and will kill him, if he grow near him; the bur and the lentil cannot endure one another, the olive and the myrtle embrace each other in roots and branches if they grow near. Of the love and hatred of planets, consult with every astrologer: Leon Hebraeus gives many fabulous reasons, and moralizeth them withal.

Sensible love is that of brute beasts, of which the same Leon Hebraeus assigns these causes. First, for the pleasure they take in the act of generation, male and female love one another. Secondly, for the preservation of the species, and desire of young brood. Thirdly, for the mutual agreement, as being of the same kind: beautiful to pig, ass to ass, ox to ox, dog to dog; as Epicharmus held, and according to that adage of Diogenianus, one daw sits with another; they much delight in one another's company, ant likes ant and grasshopper, grasshopper, and birds of a feather will gather together. Fourthly, for custom, use, and familiarity, as if a dog be trained up with a lion and a bear, contrary to their natures, they will love each other. Hawks, dogs, horses, love their masters and keepers: many stories I could relate in this kind. Fifthly, for bringing up, as if a bitch bring up a kid; a hen, ducklings; an hedge-sparrow, a cuckoo, etc.

The third kind is, as Leon calls it, rational love, and is proper to men, on which I must insist. This appears in God, angels, men. God is love itself, the fountain of love, the disciple of love, as Plato styles Him; the servant of peace, the God of love and peace; have peace with all men and God is with you. By this love (saith Gerson) we purchase heaven, and buy the Kingdom of God. This love is either in the Trinity itself, for the Holy Ghost is the love of the Father and the Son, etc. (John iii, 35, v, 20, and xiv, 31), or towards us His creatures, as in making the world. Love built cities, invented arts, sciences, and all good things, incites us to virtue and human- ity, combines and quickens; keeps peace on earth, quietness by sea, mirth in the winds and elements, expels all fear, anger, and rusticity; is a round circle still from good to good; for love is the beginner and end of all our actions, the efficient and instrumental cause, as our poets in their symbols, impresses, emblems of rings, square, etc., shadow unto us.

> *If first and last of anything you wit,*
> *Cease: love's the sole and only cause of it.*

Love, saith Leo, made the world, and afterwards, in redeeming of it, 'God so loved the world, that he gave his only begotten son for it' (John iii, 16), 'Behold what love the Father hath showed on us, that we should be called the sons of God' (1 John iii, i). Or by His sweet Providence, in protecting of it; either all in general, or His saints elect and Church in particular, whom He keeps as the apple of His eye, whom He loves freely, as Hosea, xiv, 5, speaks, and dearly respects. Not that we are fair, nor for any merit or grace of ours, for we are most vile and base; but out of His incomparable love and goodness, out of His Divine Nature. And this is that Homer's golden chain which reacheth down from heaven to earth, by which every creature is annexed, and depends on his Creator. He made all, saith Moses, and it was good, and He loves it as good.

The love of angels and living souls is mutual among themselves, towards us militant in the Church, and all such as love God; as the sunbeams irradiate the earth from those celestial thrones, they by their well-wishes reflect on us, there is joy in heaven for every sinner that repenteth; they pray for us, are solicitous for our good, pure guardian angels. Where reigneth charity, sweet desire, joy, and love towards God are also present. Love proper to mortal men is the subject of my following discourse.

II

Love of Men, which varies as his Objects, Profitable, Pleasant, Honest

VALESIUS DEFINES this love which is in men to be an affection of both powers, appetite and reason. The rational resides in the brain, the other in the liver (as before hath been said out of Plato and others); the heart is diversely affected of both, and carried a thousand ways by consent. The sensitive faculty most part overrules reason, the soul is carried hoodwinked, and the understanding captive like a beast. The heart is variously inclined, sometimes they are merry, sometimes sad, and from love arise hope and fear, jealousy, fury, desperation. Now this love of men is diverse, and varies as the object varies by which they are enticed, as virtue, wisdom, eloquence, profit, wealth, money, fame, honour, or comeliness of person, etc. Leon Hebraeus reduceth them all to these three, profitable, pleasant, honest (out of Aristotle, belike), of which he discourseth at large, and whatsoever is beautiful and fair is referred to them, or any way to be desired. To profitable is ascribed health, wealth, honour, etc., which is rather ambition, desire, covetousness, than love. Friends, children, love of women, all delightful and pleasant objects, are referred to the second. The love of honest things consists in virtue and wisdom, and is preferred before that which is profitable and pleasant; intellectual, about that which is honest. St Augustine calls profitable, worldly; pleasant, carnal; honest, spiritual. Of and from all three, result charity, friendship, and true love, which respects God and our neighbour. Of each of these I will briefly dilate, and show in what sort they cause melancholy.

Among all these fair enticing objects, which procure love and bewitch the soul of man, there is none so moving, so forcible as profit, and that which carrieth with it a show of commodity. Health indeed is a precious thing, to recover and preserve which we will undergo any misery, drink bitter potions, freely give our goods; restore a man to his health, his purse lies open to thee, bountiful he is, thankful and beholding to thee; but give him wealth and honour, give him gold, or what shall be for his advantage and preferment, and thou shalt command his affections, oblige him eternally to thee; heart, hand, life, and all is at thy service, thou art his dear and loving friend, good and gracious lord and master, his Maecenas; he is thy slave, thy vassal, most devote, affectioned, and bound in all duty: tell him good tidings in this kind, there spoke an angel, a blessed hour that brings in gain, he is thy creature, and thou his creator, he hugs and admires thee; he is thine for ever. No loadstone so attractive as that of profit, none so fair an object as this of gold; nothing wins a man sooner than a good turn; bounty and liberality command body and soul:

> *Good turns doth pacify both God and men,*
> *And Jupiter himself is won by them.*

Gold of all other is a most delicious object; a sweet light, a goodly lustre it hath; and we had rather see it than the sun. Sweet and pleasant in getting; in keeping; it seasons all our labours, intolerable pains we take for it, base employments, endure bitter flouts and taunts, long journeys, heavy burdens, all are made light and easy by this hope of gain. The sight of gold refresheth our spirits and ravisheth our hearts, as that Babylonian garment and golden wedge did Achan in the camp, the very sight and hearing sets on fire his soul with desire of it. It will make a man run to the Antipodes, or tarry at home and turn parasite, lie, flatter, prostitute himself, swear, and bear false witness; he will venture his body, kill a king, murder his father, and damn his soul to come at it. The mass of gold is fairer than all your Grecian pictures, that Apelles, Phidias, or any doting painter could ever make: we are enamoured with it. All our labours, studies, endeavours, vows, prayers, and wishes are to get how to compass it.

This is the great goddess we adore and worship; this is the sole object of our desire. If we have it, as we think, we are made for ever, thrice happy, princes, lords, etc. If we lose it we are dull, heavy, dejected, discontent, miserable, desperate, and mad. Our estate and well-being ebbs and flows with our commodity; and as we are endowed or enriched, so are we beloved and esteemed: it lasts no longer than our wealth; when that is gone, and the object removed, farewell friendship; as long as bounty, good cheer, and rewards were to be hoped, friends enough; they were tied to thee by the teeth, and would follow thee as crows do a carcass; but when thy goods are gone and spent, the lamp of their love is out, and thou shalt be contemned, scorned, hated, injured. Lucian's Timon, when he lived in prosperity, was the sole spectacle of Greece, only admired; who but Timon? Everybody loved, honoured, applauded him, each man offered him his service, and sought to be kin to him; but when his gold was spent, his fair possessions gone, farewell Timon: none so ugly, none so deformed, so odious an object as Timon, no man so ridiculous on a sudden, they gave him a penny to buy a rope, no man would know him.

'Tis the general humour of the world, commodity steers our affections throughout, we love those that are fortunate and rich, that thrive, or by whom we may receive mutual kindness, hope for like courtesies, get any good, gain, or profit; hate those, and abhor on the other side, which are poor and miserable, or by whom we may sustain loss or inconvenience. And even those that were now familiar and dear unto us, our loving and long friends, neighbours, kinsmen, allies, with whom we have conversed and lived as so many Geryons for some years past, striving still to give one another all good content and entertainment, with mutual invitations, feastings, disports, offices, for whom we would ride, run, spend ourselves, and of whom we have so freely and honourably spoken, to whom we have given all those turgent titles and magnificent elogiums, most excellent and most noble, worthy, wise, grave, learned, valiant, etc., and magnificent beyond measure: if any controversy arise between us, some trespass, injury, abuse, some part of our goods be detained, a piece of land come to be litigious, if they cross us in our suit, or touch the string of our commodity, we detest and depress upon them a sudden: neither affinity, consanguinity, or old acquaintance can contain us.

A golden apple sets all together by the ears, as if a marrow-bone or honeycomb were flung among bears: father and son, brother and sister, kinsmen are at odds: and look what malice, deadly hatred can invent, that shall be done, terrible, dreadful, destructive, cruel, fierce, mutual injuries, desire of revenge, and how to hurt them, him and his, are all our studies.

If our pleasures be interrupt, we can tolerate it; our bodies hurt, we can put it up and be reconciled; but touch our commodities, we are most impatient: fair becomes foul, the Graces are turned to Harpies, friendly salutations to bitter imprecations, mutual feastings to plotting villainies, minings and counterminings; good words to satires and invectives, naught but his imperfections are in our eyes, he is a base knave, a devil, a monster, a caterpillar, a viper, an hog-rubber, etc. The scene is altered on a sudden, love is turned to hate, mirth to melancholy: so furiously are we most part bent, our affections fixed upon this object of commodity, and upon money, the desire of which in excess is covetousness: ambition tyrannizeth over our souls, as I have showed, and in defect crucifies as much as if a man by negligence, ill husbandry, improvidence, prodigality, waste and consume his goods and fortunes, beggary follows, and melancholy, he becomes an abject, odious and worse than an infidel, in not providing for his family.

III

Pleasant Objects of Love

PLEASANT OBJECTS are infinite, whether they be such as have life, or be without life. Inanimate are countries, provinces, towers, towns, cities, as he said, we see a fair island by description, when we see it not. The sun never saw a fairer city, orchards, gardens, pleasant walks, groves, fountains, etc. The heaven itself is said to be fair or foul; fair buildings, fair pictures, all artificial, elaborate, and curious works, clothes, give an admirable lustre; we admire, and gaze upon them, as children do on a peacock; a fair dog, a fair horse and hawk, etc. The Thessalian loves a colt, the Egyptian a bullock, the Lacedaemonian a young dog. Such things we love, are most gracious in our sight, acceptable unto us, and whatsoever else may cause this passion, if it be superfluous or immoderately loved, as Guianerius observes. These things in themselves are pleasing and good, singular ornaments, necessary, comely, and fit to be had; but when we fix an immoderate eye, and dote on them overmuch, this pleasure may turn to pain, bring much sorrow and discontent unto us, work our final overthrow, and cause melancholy in the end.

Many are carried away with those bewitching sports of gaming, hawking, hunting, and such vain pleasures, as I have said; some with immoderate desire of fame, to be crowned in the Olympics, knighted in the field, etc., and by these means ruinate themselves. The lascivious dotes on his fair mistress, the glutton on his dishes, which are infinitely varied to please the palate, the epicure on his several pleasures, the superstitious on his idol, and fats himself with future joys, as Turks feed themselves with an imaginary persuasion of a sensual paradise: so several pleasant objects diversely affect divers men. But the fairest objects and enticings proceed from men themselves, which most frequently captivate, allure, and make them dote beyond all measure upon one another, and that for many respects. First, as some suppose, by that secret force of stars. They do singularly dote on such a man, hate such again, and can give no reason for it. The physicians refer this to their temperament, astrologers to trine and sextile aspects, or opposite of their several ascendants, lords of their genitures, love and hatred of planets; Cicogna to concord and discord of spirits; but most to outward graces.

A merry companion is welcome and acceptable to all men, and therefore, saith Gomesius, princes and great men entertain jesters and players commonly in their courts. But 'tis that similitude of manners which ties the most men in an inseparable link, as if they be addicted to the same studies or disports, they delight in one another's companies, birds of a feather will gather together; if they be of diverse inclinations, or opposite in manners, they can seldom agree. Secondly, affability, custom, and familiarity may convert nature many times, though they be different in manners, as if they be countrymen, fellow-students, colleagues, or have been fellow-soldiers, brethren in affliction, affinity, or some such accidental occasion, though they cannot agree among themselves, they will stick together like burs, and hold against a third; so after some discontinuance, or death, enmity ceaseth: or in a foreign place.

A third cause of love and hate may be mutual offices; commend him, use him kindly, take his part in a quarrel, relieve him in his misery, thou winnest him for ever; do the opposite, and be sure of a perpetual enemy. Praise and dispraise of each other do as much.

Another great tie or cause of love is consanguinity: parents are dear to their children, children to their parents, brothers and sisters, cousins of all sorts, as a hen and chickens, all of a knot: every crow thinks her own bird fairest. Many memorable examples are in this kind, and 'tis monstrous if they do not: a mother cannot forget her child; Solomon so found out the true owner; love of parents may not be concealed, 'tis natural, descends, and they that are inhuman in this kind are unworthy of that air they breathe, and of the four elements; yet many unnatural examples we have in this rank, of hard-hearted parents, disobedient children, of disagreeing brothers, nothing so common. The love of kinsmen is grown cold, many kinsmen (as the saying is) few friends; if thine estate be good, and thou able to requite their kindness, there will be mutual correspondence, otherwise thou art a burden, most odious to them above all others.

The last object that ties man and man is comeliness of person, and beauty alone, as men love women with a wanton eye: which *par excellence* is termed heroical, or love-melancholy. Other loves (saith Piccolomineus) are so called with some contraction, as the love of wine, gold, etc., but this of women is predominant in a higher strain, whose part affected is the liver, and this love deserves a longer explication, and shall be dilated apart in the next section.

IV

Honest Objects of Love

BEAUTY IS the common object of all love, as jet draws a straw, so doth beauty love: virtue and honesty are great motives, and give as fair a lustre as the rest, especially if they be sincere and right, not fucate, but proceeding from true form and an incorrupt judgement; those two Venus' twins, Eros and Anteros, are then most firm and fast. For many times otherwise men are deceived by their flattering Gnathos, dissembling chameleons, outsides, hypocrites that make a show of great love, learning, pretend honesty, virtue, zeal, modesty, with affected looks and counterfeit gestures: feigned protestations often steal away the hearts and favours of men, and deceive them, by outward show of merit, whenas there is no worth or honesty at all in them, no truth, but mere hypocrisy, subtilty, knavery, and the like. As true friends they are, as he that Caelius Secundus met by the highway side; and hard it is in this temporizing age to distinguish such companions, or to find them out.

Such Gnathos as these for the most part belong to great men, and by this glozing flattery, affability, and such-like philters, so dive and insinuate into their favours, that they are taken for men of excellent worth, wisdom, learning, demi-gods, and so screw themselves into dignities, honours, offices; but these men cause harsh confusion often, and as many stirs as Rehoboam's counsellors in a commonwealth, overthrow themselves and others. Tandlerus and some authors make a doubt whether love and hatred may be compelled by philters or characters; Cardan and Marbodius by precious stones and amulets; astrologers by election of times, etc., as I shall elsewhere discuss.

The true object of this honest love is virtue, wisdom, honesty, real worth, and this love cannot deceive or be compelled; to be loved you must be lovable, love itself is the most potent philter, virtue and wisdom, the sole and only grace, not counterfeit, but open, honest, simple, naked; descending from heaven, as our Apostle hath it, an infused habit from God, which hath given several gifts, as wit, learning, tongues, for which they shall be amiable and gracious (Eph. iv, II), as to Saul stature and a goodly presence (1 Sam. ix, I). Joseph found favour in Pharaoh's court (Gen. xxxix) for his person; and Daniel with the princes of the eunuchs (Dan. i, 9). Christ was gracious with God and men (Luke ii, 52). There is still some peculiar grace, as of good discourse, eloquence, wit, honesty, which is the first mover, and a most forcible loadstone to draw the favours and good wills of men's eyes, ears, and affections unto them. When Jesus spake, they were all astonished at his answers (Luke ii, 47), and wondered at his gracious words which proceeded from his mouth.

An orator steals away the hearts of men, and as another Orpheus, he pulls them to him by speech alone: a sweet voice causeth admiration; and he that can utter himself in good words, in our ordinary phrase, is called a proper man, a divine spirit. For which cause belike, our old poets made Mercury the gentleman-usher to the Graces, captain of eloquence, and those Charities to be Jupiter's and Eurymone's daughters, descended from above. Though they be otherwise deformed, crooked, ugly to behold, those good parts of the mind denominate them fair. Plato commends the beauty of Socrates; yet who was more grim of countenance, stern and ghastly to look upon? So are and have been many great philosophers, as Gregory Nazianzen observes, deformed most part in that which is to be seen with the eyes, but most elegant in that which is not to be seen. Aesop, Democritus, Aristotle, Politianus, Melancthon, Gesner, etc., were withered old men, very harsh and impolite to the eye; but who were so terse, polite, eloquent, generally learned, temperate, and modest? No man then living was so fair as Alcibiades, so lovely to the eye, as Boethius observes, but he had a most deformed soul.

Honesty, virtue, fair conditions are great enticers to such as are well given, and much avail to get the favour and good will of men. Abdolonymus in Curtius, a poor man but, which mine author notes, the cause of this poverty was his honesty, for his modesty and continency from a private person (for they found him digging in his garden) was saluted king, and preferred before all the magnificoes of his time, a purple embroidered garment was put upon him, and they bade him wash himself, and, as he was worthy, take upon him the style and spirit of a king, continue his continency and the rest of his good parts. Titus Pomponius Atticus, that noble citizen of Rome, was so fair conditioned, of so sweet a carriage, that he was generally beloved of all good men, of Caesar, Pompey, Antony, Tully, of divers sects, etc. It is worthy of your attention, Livy cries, you that scorn all but riches, and give no esteem to virtue, except they be wealthy withal, Q. Cincinnatus had but four acres, and by the consent of the senate was chosen dictator of Rome.

Of such account were Cato, Fabricius, Aristides, Antonius, Probus, for their eminent worth: so Caesar, Trajan, Alexander, admired for valour, Hephaestion loved Alexander, but Parmenio the king, Titus, mankind's delight, and which Aurelius Victor hath of Vespasian, the darling of his time, as Edgar Etheling was in England, for his excellent virtues: their memory is yet fresh, sweet, and we love them many ages after, though they be dead: he leaves behind a pleasant memory, saith Lipsius of his friend, living and dead they are all one. I have ever loved, as thou knowest (so Tully wrote to Dolabella), Marcus Brutus for his great wit, singular honesty, constancy, sweet conditions;

and believe it, there is nothing so amiable and fair as virtue. I do mightily love Calvisinus (so Pliny writes to Sossius), a most industrious, eloquent, upright man, which is all in all with me: the affection came from his good parts. And, as St Augustine comments on the 84th Psalm, there is a peculiar beauty of justice, and inward beauty, which we see with the eyes of our hearts, love, and are enamoured with, as in martyrs, though their bodies be torn in pieces with wild beasts, yet this beauty shines, and we love their virtues.

The Stoics are of opinion that a wise man is only fair; and Cato contends the same, that the lineaments of the mind are far fairer than those of the body, incomparably beyond them: wisdom and valour, according to Xenophon, especially deserve the name of beauty, and denominate one fair, as Augustine holds, Christian truth is fairer than Grecian Helen. 'Wine is strong, the king is strong, women are strong, but truth overcometh all things' (1 Esdras iii, 10, 11, 12). 'Blessed is the man that findeth wisdom, and getteth understanding; for the merchandise thereof is better than silver, and the gain thereof better than gold; it is more precious than pearls, and all the things thou canst desire are not to be compared to her' (Prov. iii, 13, 14, 15). A wise, true, just, upright, and good man, I say it again, is only fair: it is reported of Magdalen, Queen of France, and wife to Louis XI, a Scottish woman by birth, that walking forth in an evening with her ladies, she spied M. Alanus [Alain Chartier], one of the king's chaplains, a silly, old, hard-favoured man, fast asleep in a bower, and kissed him sweetly; when the young ladies laughed at her for it, she replied that it was not his person that she did embrace and reverence, but, with a Platonic love, the divine beauty of his soul. Thus in all ages virtue hath been adored, admired, a singular lustre hath proceeded from it: and the more virtuous he is, the more gracious, the more admired. No man so much followed upon earth as Christ Himself; and as the Psalmist saith, xlv, 2, He was fairer than the sons of men. Chrysostom,

Augustine, Cassiodore, Jerome interpret it of the beauty of His person; there was a divine majesty in His looks, it shined like lightning and drew all men to it: but Basil, Cyril, Theodoret, Arnobius, etc., of the beauty of His divinity, justice, grace, eloquence, etc., Thomas, of both; and so doth Baradius, and Peter Morales, adding as much of Joseph and the Virgin Mary: she excels all others in beauty, according to that prediction of the Sibyl of Cuma.

Be they present or absent, near us or afar off, this beauty shines, and will attract men many miles to come and visit it. Plato and Pythagoras left their country to see those wise Egyptian priests: Apollonius travelled into Ethiopia, Persia, to consult with the Magi, Brachmanni, gymnosophists. The Queen of Sheba came to visit Solomon; and many, saith Jerome, went out to Spain and remote places a thousand miles, to behold that eloquent Livy. No beauty leaves such an impression, strikes so deep, or links the souls of men closer than virtue. No painter, no graver, no carver can express virtue's lustre, or those admirable rays that come from it, those enchanting rays that enamour posterity, those everlasting rays that continue to the world's end.

Many, saith Favorinus, that loved and admired Alcibiades in his youth, knew not, cared not for Alcibiades a man; but the beauty of Socrates is still the same; virtue's lustre never fades, is ever fresh and green to all succeeding ages, and a most attractive loadstone, to draw and combine such as are present. For that reason, belike, Homer feigns the three Graces to be linked and tied hand in hand, because the hearts of men are so firmly united with such graces. O sweet bands (Seneca exclaims), which so happily combine, that those which are bound by them love their binders, desiring withal much more harder to be bound, and as so many Geryons to be united into one. For the nature of true friendship is to combine, to be like affected, of one mind, as the poet saith, still to continue one and the same. And where this love takes place there is peace and quietness, a true correspondence, perfect amity, a diapason of vows and wishes, the same opinions, as between David and Jonathan, Damon and Pythias, Pylades and Orestes, Nisus and Euryalus, Theseus and Pirithous, they will live and die together, and prosecute one another with good turns, not only living, but when their friends are dead, with tombs and monuments, funeral songs, epitaphs, elegies, inscriptions, pyramids, obelisks, statues, images, pictures, histories, poems, annals, feasts, anniversaries, many ages after (as Plato's scholars did) they will omit no good office that may tend to the preservation of their names, honours, and eternal memory.

He did express his friends in colours, in wax, in brass, in ivory, marble, gold, and silver (as Pliny reports of a citizen in Rome), and in a great auditory not long since recited a just volume of his life. In another place, speaking of an epigram which Martial had composed in praise of him, 'He gave me as much as he might, and would have done more if he could'; though what can a man give more than honour, glory, and eternity? But that which he wrote, peradventure, will not continue, yet he wrote it to continue. 'Tis all the recompense a poor scholar can make his well-deserving patron, Maecenas, friend, to mention him in his works, to dedicate a book to his name, to write his life, etc., as all our poets, orators, historiographers have ever done, and the greatest revenge such men take of their adversaries, to persecute them with satires, invectives, etc., and 'tis both ways of great moment, as Plato gives us to understand. Paulus Jovius, in the fourth book of the life and deeds of Pope Leo Decimus, his noble patron, concludes in these words: 'Because I cannot honour him as other, rich men do, with like endeavour, affection, and piety I have undertaken to write his life; since my fortunes will not give me leave to make a more sumptuous monument, I will perform those rites to his sacred ashes, which a small, perhaps, but a liberal wit can afford.'

But I rove. Where this true love is wanting, there can be no firm peace, friendship from teeth outward, counterfeit, or, for some by-respects, so long dissembled till they have satisfied their own ends, which upon every small occasion breaks out into enmity, open war, defiance, heart-burnings, whispering, calumnies, contentions, and all manner of bitter melancholy discontents. And those men which have no other object of their love than greatness, wealth, authority, etc., are rather feared than beloved; they neither love nor are loved; and howsoever borne, with for a time, yet for their tyranny and oppression, griping, covetousness, currish hardness, folly, intemperance, imprudence, and such-like vices, they are generally odious, abhorred of all, both God and men. Wife and children, friends, neighbours, all the world forsakes them, would fain be rid of them, and are compelled many times to lay violent hands on them, or else God's judgements overtake them: instead of Graces, come Furies. So when fair Abigail, a woman of singular wisdom, was acceptable to David, Nabal was churlish and evil-conditioned; and therefore Mordecai was received when Haman was executed, Haman the favourite, that had his seat above the other princes, to whom all the king's servants that stood in the gates bowed their knees and reverenced.

Though they flourish many times, such hypocrites, such temporizing foxes, and blear the world's eyes by flattery, bribery, dissembling their natures, or other men's weakness, that cannot so apprehend their tricks, yet in the end they will be discerned, and precipitated in a moment: 'Surely,' saith David, 'thou hast set them in slippery places' (Ps. lxxiii, 18); as so many Sejani, they will come down to the Gemonian scales; and, as Eusebius in Ammianus, that was in such authority, be cast down headlong on a sudden. Or put case they escape, and rest unmasked to their lives' end, yet after their death their memory stinks as a snuff of a candle put out, and those that durst not so much as mutter against them in their lives will prosecute their name with satires, libels, and bitter imprecations, they shall have a bad name in all succeeding ages, and be odious to the world's end.

V

Charity composed of all three Kinds,
Pleasant, Profitable, Honest.

BESIDES THIS LOVE that comes from profit, pleasant, honest (for one good turn asks another in equity), that which proceeds from the law of nature, or from discipline and philosophy, there is yet another love compounded of all these three, which is charity, and includes piety, dilection, benevolence, friendship, even all those virtuous habits; for love is the circle equant of all other affections, of which Aristotle dilates at large in his Ethics, and is commanded by God, which no man can well perform, but he that is a Christian, and a true regenerate man. This is 'to love God above all, and our neighbour as ourself'; for this love is a communicating light, apt to illuminate itself as well as others. All other objects are fair, and very beautiful, I confess; kindred, alliance, friendship, the love that we owe to our country, nature, wealth, pleasure, honour, and such moral respects, etc., of which read copious Aristotle in his Morals; a man is beloved of a man, in that he is a man; but all these are far more eminent and great, when they shall proceed from a sanctified spirit, that hath a true touch of religion and a reference to God.

Nature binds all creatures to love their young ones; an hen to preserve her brood will run upon a lion, an hind will fight with a bull, a sow with a bear, a silly sheep with a fox. So the same nature urgeth a man to love his parents, and this love cannot be dissolved, as Tully holds, without detestable offence; but much more God's commandment, which enjoins a filial love, and an obedience in this kind. The love of brethren is great, and like an arch of stones, where if one be displaced, all come down, no love so forcible and strong, honest, to the combination of which, nature, fortune, virtue, happily concur; yet this love comes short of it.

'Tis sweet and honourable to die for one's country, it cannot be expressed, what a deal of charity that one name of country contains. Love of praise and country take the place of pay. The Decii, Horatii, Curii, Scaevola, Regulus, Codrus, sacrifice themselves for their country's peace and good.

> *One day the Fabii stoutly warred,*
> *One day the Fabii were destroyed.*

Fifty thousand Englishmen lost their lives willingly near Battle Abbey, in defence of their country. Aemilius speaks of six senators of Calais, that came with halters in their hands to the King of England to die for the rest. This love makes so many writers take such pains, so many historiographers, physicians, etc., or at least as they pretend, for common safety, and their country's benefit. Friendship is a holy name, and a sacred communion of friends. As the sun is in the firmament, so is friendship in the world, a most divine and heavenly band. As nuptial love makes, this perfects mankind, and is to be preferred (if you will stand to the judgement of Cornelius Nepos) before affinity or consanguinity; the cords of love bind faster than any other wreath whatsoever. Take this away, and take all pleasure, joy, comfort, happiness, and true content out of the world; 'tis the greatest tie, the surest indenture, strongest band, and, as our modern Maro [Spenser] decides it, is much to be preferred before the rest.

> *Hard is the doubt, and difficult to deem,*
> *When all three kinds of love together meet;*

And do dispart the heart with power extreme,
Whether shall weigh the balance down; to wit,
The dear affection unto kindred sweet,
Or raging fire of love to women kind,
Or zeal of friends, combin'd by virtues meet;
But of them all the band of virtuous mind,
Methinks the gentle heart should most assured bind.
For natural affection soon doth cease,
And quenched is with Cupid's greater flame;
But faithful friendship doth them both suppress,
And them with mastering discipline doth tame,
Through thoughts aspiring to eternal fame.
For as the soul doth rule the earthly mass,
And all the service of the body frame,
So love of soul doth love of body pass,
No less than perfect gold surmounts the meanest brass.

A faithful friend is better than gold, a medicine of misery, an only possession; yet this love of friends, nuptial, heroical, profitable, pleasant, honest, all three loves put together, are little worth, if they proceed not from a true Christian illuminated soul, if it be not done for God's sake. 'Though I had the gift of prophecy, spake with tongues of men and angels, though I feed the poor with all my goods, give my body to be burned, and have not this love, it profiteth me nothing' (1 Cor. xiii, 1, 2, 3); 'tis a splendid sin without charity. This is an all-apprehending love, a deifying love, a refined, pure, divine love, the quintessence of all love, the true philosopher's stone; as Augustine infers, he is no true friend that loves not God's truth.

And therefore this is true love indeed, the cause of all good to mortal men, that reconciles all creatures, and glues them together in perpetual amity and firm league, and can no more abide bitterness, hate, malice, than fair and foul weather, light and darkness, sterility and plenty may be together. As the sun in the firmament (I say), so is love in the world; and for this cause 'tis love without an addition, love *par excellence*, love of God, and love of men. The love of God begets the love of man; and by this love of our neighbour the love of God is nourished and increased. By this happy union of love, all well-governed families and cities are combined, the heavens annexed, and divine souls complicated, the world itself composed, and all that is in it conjoined in God, and reduced to one.

This love causeth true and absolute virtues, the life, spirit, and root of every virtuous action, it finisheth prosperity, easeth adversity, corrects all natural encumbrances, inconveniences, sustained by faith and hope, which with this our love make an indissoluble twist, a Gordian knot, an equilateral triangle, 'and yet the greatest of them is love' (1 Cor. xiii, 13), which inflames our souls with a divine heat, and being so inflamed, purged, and so purgeth, elevates to God, makes an atonement, and reconciles us unto Him. That other love infects the soul of man, this cleanseth; that depresses, this rears; that causeth cares and troubles, this quietness of mind; this informs, that deforms our life; that leads to repentance, this to heaven. For if once we be truly linked and touched with this charity, we shall love God above all, our neighbour as ourself, as we are enjoined (Mark xii, 31, Matt, xix, 19), perform those duties and exercises, even all the operations of a good Christian.

This love suffereth long, it is bountiful, envieth not, boasteth not itself, is not puffed up, it deceiveth not, it seeketh not his own things, is not provoked to anger, it thinketh not evil, it rejoiceth not in iniquity, but in truth. It suffereth all things, believeth all things, hopeth all things (1 Cor. xiii, 4, 5, 6, 7); it covereth all trespasses (Prov. x, 12); a multitude of sins (1 Pet. 4); as our Saviour told the woman in the Gospel, that washed His feet, many sins were forgiven her, for she loved much (Luke vii, 47); it will defend the fatherless and the widow (Isa. i, 17); will seek no revenge, or be mindful of wrong (Levit. xix, 18); will bring home his brother's ox if he go astray, as it commanded (Deut. xxii, 1); will resist evil, give to him that asketh, and not turn from him that borroweth, bless them that curse him, love his enemy (Matt, v); bear his brother's burthen (Gal. vi, 7).

He that so loves will be hospitable, and distribute to the necessities of the saints; he will, if it be possible, have peace with all men, feed his enemy if he be hungry, if he be athirst give him drink; he will perform those seven works of mercy, he will make himself equal to them of the lower sort, rejoice with them that rejoice, weep with them that weep (Rom. xii); he will speak truth to his neighbour, be courteous and tender-hearted, forgiving others for Christ's sake, as God forgave him (Eph. iv, 32); he will be like-minded (Phil, ii, 2), of one judgement; be humble, meek, long-suffering (Col. iii), forbear, forget, and forgive (vv. 12, 13, 23), and what he doth shall be heartily done to God, and not to men; be pitiful and courteous (1 Pet. iii), seek peace and follow it. He will love his brother, not in word of tongue, but in deed and truth (1 John iii, 18), and he that loves God, Christ will love him that is begotten of him (1 John v, 1), etc. Thus should we willingly do, if we had a true touch of charity, of this divine love, if we could perform this which we are enjoined, forget and forgive, and compose ourselves to those Christian laws of love. Angelical souls, how blessed, how happy should we be, so loving, how might we triumph over the devil, and have another heaven upon earth!

But this we cannot do; and which is the cause of all our woes, miseries, discontent, melancholy, want of this charity. We do contemn, insult, vex, torture, molest, and hold one another's noses to the grindstone hard, provoke, rail, scoff, calumniate, challenge, hate, abuse (hardhearted, implacable, malicious, peevish, inexorable as we are), to satisfy our lust or private spleen, for toys, trifles, and impertinent occasions, spend ourselves, goods, friends, fortunes, to be revenged on our adversary, to ruin him and his. 'Tis all our study, practice, and business how to plot mischief, mine, countermine, defend and offend, ward ourselves, injure others, hurt all; as if we were born to do mischief, and that with such eagerness and bitterness, with such rancour, malice, rage, and fury, we prosecute our intended designs, that neither affinity nor consanguinity, love nor fear of God or men can contain us: no satisfaction, no composition will be accepted, no offices will serve, no submission; though he shall upon his knees, as Sarpedon did to Glaucus in Homer, acknowledging his error, yield himself with tears in his eyes, beg his pardon, we will not relent, forgive, or forget, till we have confounded him and his, made dice of his bones, as they say, see him rot in prison, banish his friends, followers, and the whole hated tribe, rooted him out and all his posterity.

Monsters of men, as we are, dogs, wolves, tigers, fiends, incarnate devils, we do not only contend, oppress, and tyrannize ourselves, but as so many firebrands we set on and animate others: our whole life is a perpetual combat, a conflict, a set battle, a snarling fit. The goddess Strife is settled in our tents, oppositing wit to wit, wealth to wealth, strength to strength, fortunes to fortunes, friends to friends; as at a sea-fight we turn our broadsides, or as two millstones with continual attrition we fire ourselves, or break one another's backs, and both are ruined and consumed in the end. Miserable wretches, to fat and enrich ourselves, we care not how we get it—how many thousands we undo, whom we oppress, by whose ruin and downfall we arise, whom we injure, fatherless children, widows, common societies, to satisfy our own private lust. Though we have myriads, abundance of wealth and treasure (pitiless, merciless, remorseless, and uncharitable in the highest degree), and our poor brother in need, sickness, in great extremity, and now ready to be starved for want of food, we had rather, as the fox told the ape, his tail should sweep the ground still, than cover his buttocks; rather spend it idly, consume it with dogs, hawks, hounds, unnecessary buildings, in riotous apparel, ingurgitate, or let it be lost, than he should have part of it; rather take from him that little which he hath than relieve him.

Like the dog in the manger, we neither use it ourselves, nor let others make use of or enjoy it; part with nothing while we live; for want of disposing our household and setting things in order, set all the world together by the ears after our death. Poor Lazarus lies howling at his gates for a few crumbs, he only seeks chippings, offals; let him roar and howl, famish, and eat his own flesh, he respects him not. A poor decayed kinsman of his sets upon him by the way in all his jollity, and runs begging bareheaded by him, conjuring by those former bonds of friendship, alliance, consanguinity, etc., uncle, cousin, brother, father. Show some pity for Christ's sake, pity a sick man, an old man, etc., he cares not, ride on: pretend sickness, inevitable loss of limbs, goods, plead suretyship, or shipwreck, fires, common calamities, show thy wants and imperfections, swear, protest, take God and all His angels to witness, thou art a counterfeit crank, a cheater, he is not touched with it, ride on, he takes no notice of it. Put up a supplication to him in the name of a thousand orphans, an hospital, a spital, a prison, as he goes by, they cry out to him for aid, ride on, he cares not, let them eat stones, devour themselves with vermin, rot in their own dung, he cares not. Show him a decayed haven, a bridge, a school, a fortification, etc., or some public work, ride on; 'Good your worship, your honour, for God's sake, your country's sake,' ride on.

But show him a roll wherein his name shall be registered in golden letters and commended to all posterity, his arms set up, with his devices to be seen, then peradventure he will stay and contribute; or if thou canst thunder upon him, as papists do, with satisfactory and meritorious works, or persuade him by this means he shall save his soul out of hell, and free it from purgatory (if he be of any religion), then in all likelihood he will listen and stay; or that he have no children, no near kinsman, heir, he cares for at least, or cannot well tell otherwise how or where to bestow his possessions (for carry them with him he cannot), it may be then he will build some school or hospital in his life, or be induced to give liberally to pious uses after his death.

For I dare boldly say, vainglory, that opinion of merit, and this enforced necessity, when they know not otherwise how to leave, or what better to do with them, is the main cause of most of our good works. I will not urge this to derogate from any man's charitable devotion, or bounty in this kind, to censure any good work; no doubt there be many sanctified, heroical, and worthy-minded men, that in true zeal and for virtue's sake (divine spirits), that out of commiseration and pity extend their liberality, and as much as in them lies do good to all men, clothe the naked, feed the hungry, comfort the sick and needy, relieve all, forget and forgive injuries, as true charity requires; yet most part there is a deal of hypocrisy in this kind, much default and defect.

Cosmo de Medici, that rich citizen of Florence, ingenuously confessed to a near friend of his, that would know of him why he built so many public and magnificent palaces and bestowed so liberally on scholars, not that he loved learning more than others, but to eternize his own name, to be immortal by the benefit of scholars; for when his friends were dead, walls decayed, and all inscriptions gone, books would remain to the world's ends. The lanthorn in Athens was built by Xenocles, the theatre by Pericles, the famous port Piraeus by Themicles, Pallas' Palladium by Phidias, the Parthenon by Callicrates; but these brave monuments are decayed all, and ruined long since, their builders' names alone flourish by mediation of writers. And as he said of that Marian oak, now cut down and dead, no plant can grow so long as that which is set and manured by those ever-living wits. Allon-bachuth, that weeping oak, under which Deborah, Rebecca's nurse, died and was buried, may not survive the memory of such everlasting monuments. Vainglory and emulation (as to most men) was the cause efficient, and to be a trumpeter of his own fame Cosmo's sole intent, so to do good that all the world might take notice of it.

Such for the most part is the charity of our times, such our benefactors, Maecenases, and patrons. Show me among so many myriads a truly devout, a right, honest, upright, meek, humble, a patient, innocuous, innocent, a merciful, a loving, a charitable man! Show me a Caleb or a Joshua! Show a virtuous woman, a constant wife, a good neighbour, a trusty servant, an obedient child, a true friend, etc. Crows in Africa are not so scant. He that shall examine this iron cage wherein we live, where love is cold, Justice fled with her assistants, virtue expelled: all goodness, gone, where vice abounds, the devil is loose, and see one man vilify and insult over his brother, as if he were an innocent or a block, oppress, tyrannize, prey upon, torture him, vex, gall, torment and crucify him, starve him, where is charity?

He that shall see men swear and forswear, lie and bear false witness, to advantage themselves, prejudice others, hazard goods, lives, fortunes, credit, all, to be revenged on their enemies, men so unspeakable in their lusts, unnatural in malice, such bloody designments, Italian blaspheming, Spanish renouncing, etc., may well ask where is charity. He that shall observe so many lawsuits, such endless contentions, such plotting, undermining, so much money spent with such eagerness and fury, every man for himself his own ends, the devil for all; so many distressed souls, such lamentable complaints, so many factions, conspiracies, seditions, oppressions, abuses, injuries, such grudging, repining, discontent, so much emulation, envy, so many brawls, quarrels, monomachies, etc., may well require what is become of charity? when we see and read of such cruel wars, tumults, uproars, bloody battles, so many men slain, so many cities ruinated, etc. (for what else is the subject of all our stories almost, but bills, bows, and guns?), so many murders and massacres, etc., where is charity? Or see men wholly devote to God, churchmen, professed divines, holy men, to make the trumpet of the gospel the trumpet of war, a company of hell-born Jesuits, and fiery-spirited friars, apply the torch to all seditions, as so many firebrands set all the world by the ears (I say nothing of their contentious and railing books, whole ages spent in writing one against another, and that with such virulency and bitterness, and by their bloody inquisitions, that in thirty years, Bale saith, consumed 39 princes, 148 earls, 235 barons, 14,755 commons, worse than those ten persecutions, may justly doubt where is charity?

Are these Christians? I beseech you, tell me. He that shall observe and see these things may say to them as Cato to Caesar, Sure I think thou art of opinion there is neither heaven nor hell. Let them pretend religion, zeal, make what shows they will, give alms, be peace-makers, frequent sermons if we may guess at the tree by the fruit, they are no better than hypocrites, epicures, atheists; with the fool in their hearts they say there is no God.

'Tis no marvel then if being so uncharitable, hard-hearted as we are, we have so frequent and so many discontents, such melancholy fits, so many bitter pangs, mutual discords, all in a combustion, often complaints, so common grievances, general mischiefs, so many calamities to rend the human race, so many pestilences, wars, uproars, losses, deluges, fires, inundations, God's vengeance, and all the plagues of Egypt come not upon us, since we are so currish one towards another, so respectless of God and our neighbours, and by our crying sins pull these miseries upon our own heads. Nay more, 'tis justly to be feared, which Josephus once said of his countrymen Jews, if the Romans had not come when they did to sack their city, surely it had been swallowed up with some earthquake, deluge, or fired from heaven as Sodom and Gomorrah; their desperate malice, wickedness, and peevishness was such.

'Tis to be suspected, if we continue these wretched ways, we may look for the like heavy visitations to come upon us. If we had any sense or feeling of these things, surely we should not go on as we do, in such irregular courses, practise all manner of impieties; our whole carriage would not be so averse from God. If a man would but consider, when he is in the midst and full career of such prodigious and uncharitable actions, how displeasing they are in God's sight, how noxious to himself, as Solomon told Joab (1 Kings ii), 'The Lord shall bring this blood upon their heads'; (Prov. i, 27): Sudden desolation and destruction shall come like a whirlwind upon them, affliction, anguish; The reward of his hand shall be given him (Isa. iii, 11), etc.; They shall fall into the pit they have digged for others (Ps. vii, 15), and when they are scraping, tyrannizing, getting, wallowing in their wealth, 'This night, O fool, I will take away thy soul' (Luke xii, 20), what a severe account they must make; and how gracious on the other side a charitable man is in God's eyes (Matt, v, 7): 'Blessed are the merciful, for they shall obtain mercy'. He that lendeth to the poor, gives to God; and how it shall be restored to them again (Prov. xix, 17); how by their patience and long-suffering they shall heap coals on their enemies' heads (Rom. xii), and he that followeth after righteousness and mercy shall find righteousness and glory (Prov. xxi, 21); surely they would check their desires, curb in their unnatural, inordinate affections, agree among themselves, abstain from doing evil, amend their lives, and learn to do well. 'Behold how comely and good a thing it is for brethren to live together in union: it is like the precious ointment' (Ps. cxxxiii), etc.

How odious to contend one with the other! Why do we contend one and vex one another? behold, death is over our heads, and we must shortly give an account of all our uncharitable words and actions. Think upon it, and be wise.

VI

Heroical Love causing Melancholy.
His Pedigree, Power, and Extent.

I N THE PRECEDENT section mention was made, among other pleasant objects, of this comeliness and beauty which proceeds from women, that causeth heroical, or love-melancholy, is more eminent above the rest, and properly called love. The part affected in men is the liver, and therefore called heroical, because commonly gallants, noblemen, and the most generous spirits are possessed with it. His power and extent is very large, and in that twofold division of love, those two *Veneres* which Plato and some other make mention of, it is most eminent, and par excellence called Venus, as I have said, or love itself. Which although it be denominated from men, and most evident in them, yet it extends and shows itself in vegetal and sensible creatures, those incorporeal substances (as shall be specified), and hath a large dominion of sovereignty over them.

His pedigree is very ancient, derived from the beginning of the world, as Phaedrus contends, and his parentage of such antiquity, that no poet could ever find it out. Hesiod makes Earth and Chaos to be Love's parents, before the gods were born. Some think it is the self-same fire Prometheus fetched from heaven. Plutarch will have Love to be the son of Iris and Favonius; but Socrates in that pleasant dialogue of Plato, when it came to his turn to speak of love in a poetical strain, telleth this tale: When Venus was born, all the gods were invited to a banquet, and among the rest, Porus the god of bounty and wealth; Penia or Poverty came a-begging to the door; Porus, well

43

whittled with nectar (for there was no wine in those days), walking in Jupiter's garden, in a bower met with Penia, and in his drink got her with child, of whom was born Love; and because he was begotten on Venus' birthday, Venus still attends upon him.

Another tale is there borrowed out of Aristophanes: In the beginning of the world, men had four arms and four feet, but for their pride, because they compared themselves with the gods, were parted into halves, and now peradventure by love they hope to be united again and made one. Otherwise thus: Vulcan met two lovers, and bid them ask what they would and they should have it; but they made answer, 'O Vulcan the gods' great smith, we beseech thee to work us anew in thy furnace, and of two make us one; which he presently did, and ever since true lovers are either all one, or else desire to be united.'

The reason why Love was still painted young is because young men are most apt to love; soft, fair, and fat, because such folks are soonest taken; naked, because all true affection is simple and open; he smiles, because merry and given to delights; hath a quiver, to show his power, none can escape; is blind, because he sees not where he strikes, whom he hits, etc. His power and sovereignty is expressed by the poets, in that he is held to be a god, and a great commanding god, above Jupiter himself; a mighty spirit, as Plato calls him, the strongest and merriest of all the gods according to Alcinous and Athenaeus. As Euripides, love is the god of gods and governor of men; for we must all do homage to him, keep an holy day for his deity, adore in his temples, worship his image, and sacrifice to his altar, that conquers all, and rules all.

I had rather contend with bulls, lions, bears, and giants, than with Love; he is so powerful, enforceth all to pay tribute to him, domineers over all, and can make mad and sober whom he list; insomuch that Caecilius, in Tully's Tusculans, holds him to be no better than a fool or an idiot that doth not acknowledge Love to be a great god, that can make sick and cure whom he list. Homer and Stesichorus were both made blind, if you will believe Leon Hebraeus, for speaking against his godhead: and though Aristophanes degrade him, and say that he was scornfully rejected from the council of the gods, had his wings clipped besides, that he might come no more among them, and to his further disgrace banished heaven for ever, and confined to dwell on earth, yet he is of that power, majesty, omnipotency, and dominion, that no creature can withstand him. Cupid rules over the gods too as he listeth, and not even Jupiter can keep him at bay. He is more than quartermaster with the gods; He divides the empire of the sea with Thetis, of the shades with Aeacus, of Heaven with Jupiter and hath not so much possession as dominion.

Jupiter himself was turned into a satyr, shepherd, a bull, a swan, a golden shower, and what not, for love; that as Lucian's Juno right well objected to him, Thou art Cupid whirligig. How did he insult over all the other gods, Mars, Neptune, Pan, Mercury, Bacchus, and the rest! Lucian brings in Jupiter complaining of Cupid that he could not be quiet for him, and the Moon lamenting that she was so impotently besotted on Endymion, even Venus herself confessing as much, how rudely and in what sort of her own son Cupid had used her, being his mother, now drawing her to Mount Ida, for the love of that Trojan Anchises, now to Libanus for that Assyrian youth's sake. And although she threatened to break his bow and arrows, to clip his wings, and whipped him besides on the bare buttocks with her pantofle, yet all would not serve, he was too headstrong and unruly. That monster-conquering Hercules was tamed by him:

Whom neither beasts, nor enemies could tame,
Nor Juno's might subdue, Love quell'd the same.

(OVID)

Your bravest soldiers and most generous spirits are enervated with it. Apollo, that took upon him to cure all diseases, could not help himself of this, and therefore Socrates calls Love a tyrant, and brings him triumphing in a chariot, whom Petrarch imitates in his Triumph of Love, and Fracastorius in an elegant poem expresseth at large, Cupid riding, Mars and Apollo following his chariot, Psyche weeping, etc.

In vegetal creatures what sovereignty love hath, by many pregnant proofs and familiar examples may be proved, especially of palm-trees, which are both he and she, and express not a sympathy but a love passion, as by many observations have been confirmed. Boughs live for love, every tree in turn feels its passion; palms nod their troth, poplar sighs to poplar, plane to plane, and alder murmurs to alder. Constantine gives an instance out of Florentius his Georgics, of a palm-tree that loved most fervently, and would not be comforted until such time her love applied herself unto her; you might see the two trees bend, and of their own accords stretch out their boughs to embrace and kiss each other: they will give manifest signs of mutual love. Ammianus Marcellinus reports that they marry one another, and fall in love if they grow in sight; and when the wind brings the smell to them they are marvellously affected. Philostratus observes as much, and Galen: they will be sick for love, ready to die and pine away, which the husbandmen perceiving, saith Constantine, stroke many palms that grow together, and so stroking again the palm that is enamoured, they carry kisses from the one to the other; or tying the leaves and branches of the one to the stem of the other, will make them both flourish and prosper a great deal better: which are enamoured, they can perceive by the bending of boughs and inclination of their bodies.

If any man think this which I say to be a tale, let him read that story of two palm-trees in Italy, the male growing at Brundusium, the female at Otranto (related by Jovianus Pontanus in an excellent poem, sometime tutor to Alphonsus Junior, King of Naples, his secretary of state, and a great philosopher), which were barren, and so continued a long time, till they came to see one another growing up higher, though many stadiums asunder....

If such fury be in vegetals, what shall we think of sensible creatures? how much more violent and apparent shall it be in them!

> *All kinds of creatures in the earth,*
> *And fishes of the sea,*
> *And painted birds do rage alike;*
> *This love bears equal sway.*

Common experience and our sense will inform us how violently brute beasts are carried away with this passion, horses above the rest. Cupid in Lucian bids Venus his mother be of good cheer, for he was now familiar with lions, and oftentimes did get on their backs, hold them by the mane, and ride them about like horses, and they would fawn upon him with their tails. Bulls, bears, and boars are so furious in this kind, they kill one another; but especially cocks, lions, and harts, which are so fierce that you may hear them fight half a mile off, saith Turberville, and many times kill each other, or compel them to abandon the rut, that they may remain masters in their places; and when one hath driven his corrival away, he raiseth his nose up into the air, and looks aloft, as though he gave thanks to nature, which affords him such great delight. How birds are affected in this kind, appears out of Aristotle; he will have them to sing for joy or in hope of their venery which is to come.

Fishes pine away for love and wax lean, if Gomesius' authority may be taken, and are rampant too, some of them: Peter Gillius tells wonders of a triton in Epirus. There was a well not far from the shore, where the country wenches fetched water; the triton would set upon them and carry them to the sea, and there drown them if they would not yield; so love tyrannizeth in dumb creatures. Yet this is natural for one beast to dote upon another of the same kind; but what strange fury is that, when a beast shall dote upon a man? Saxo Grammaticus hath a story of a bear that loved a woman, kept her in his den a long time and begot a son of her, out of whose loins proceeded many northern kings: this is the original belike of that common tale of Valentine and Orson. Aelian, Pliny, Peter Gillius are full of such relations. A peacock in Leucadia loved a maid, and when she died the peacock pined. A dolphin loved a boy called Hernias, and when he died the fish came on land, and so perished. The like adds Gillius, a dolphin at Puteoli loved a child, would come often to him, let him get on his back, and carry him about, and when by sickness the child was taken away, the dolphin died.

Every book is full (saith Busbequius, the emperor's orator with the Grand Signior, not long since), and yields such instances, to believe which I was always afraid, lest I should be thought to give credit to fables, until I saw a lynx, which I had from Assyria, so affected towards one of my men that it cannot be denied but that he was in love with him. When my man was present the beast would use many notable enticements and pleasant motions, and when he was going, hold him back, and look after him when he was gone, very sad in his absence, but most jocund when he returned: and when my man went from me the beast expressed his love with continual sickness, and after he had pined away some few days, died. Such another story he hath of a crane of Majorca, that loved a Spaniard, that would walk any way with him, and in his absence seek about for him, make a noise that he might hear her, and knock at his door, and when he took his last farewell, famished herself. Such pretty pranks can love play with birds, fishes, beasts: Venus keeps the keys of sky, sea, and earth, and alone retains command of all and, if all be certain that is credibly reported, with the spirits of the air, and devils of hell themselves, who are as much enamoured and dote (if I may use that word) as any other creatures whatsoever. For if those stories be true that are written of incubus and succubus, of nymphs, lascivious fauns, satyrs, and those heathen gods which were devils, those lascivious Telchines, of whom the Platonists tell so many fables, or those familiar meetings in our days, and company of witches and devils, there is some probability for it.

I know that Biarmannus, Wierus, and some others stoutly deny it, that the devil hath any carnal copulation with women, that the devil takes no pleasure in such facts, they be mere phantasies, all such relations of incubi, succubi, lies and tales; but Augustine doth acknowledge it; Erastus, Jacobus Sprenger and his colleagues, etc.; Zanchius, Dandinus, Bodine, and Paracelsus, a great champion of this tenent among the rest, which give sundry peculiar instances, by many testimonies, proofs, and confessions evince it. Hector Boethius, in his Scottish History, hath three or four such examples, which Cardan confirms out of him, of such as have had familiar company many years with them, and that in the habit of men and women.

Philostratus hath a memorable instance in this kind, which I may not omit, of one Menippus Lycius, a young man twenty-five years of age, that going between Cenchreas and Corinth, met such a phantasm in the habit of a fair gentlewoman, which, taking him by the hand, carried him home to her house in the suburbs of Corinth, and told him she was a Phoenician by birth, and if he would tarry with her, he should hear her sing and play, and drink such wine as never any drank, and no man should molest him; but she being fair and lovely would live and die with him, that was fair and lovely to behold. The young man, a philosopher, otherwise staid and discreet, able to moderate his passions, though not this of love, tarried with her awhile to his great content, and at last married her, to whose wedding, among other guests, came Apollonius, who, by some probable conjectures, found her out to be a serpent, a lamia, and that all her furniture was like Tantalus' gold described by Homer, no substance, but mere illusions. When she saw herself descried she wept, and desired Apollonius to be silent, but he would not be moved, and thereupon she, plate, house, and all that was in it, vanished in an instant: many thousands took notice of this fact, for it was done in the midst of Greece.

Sabine, in his Comment on the tenth of Ovid's Metamorphoses, at the tale of Orpheus, telleth us of a gentleman of Bavaria that for many months together bewailed the loss of his dear wife; at length the devil in her habit came and comforted him, and told him, because he was so importunate for her, that she would come and live with him again, on that condition he would be new married, never swear and blaspheme as he used formerly to do; for if he did, she should be gone: he vowed it, married, and lived with her, she brought him children, and governed his house, but was still pale and sad, and so continued, till one day falling out with him, he fell a-swearing; she vanished thereupon, and was never after seen. This I have heard, saith Sabine, from persons of good credit, which told me that the Duke of Bavaria did tell it for a certainty to the Duke of Saxony.

One more I will relate out of Florilegus, an honest historian of our nation, because he telleth it so confidently, as a thing in those days talked of all over Europe. A young gentleman of Rome, the same day that he was married, after dinner with the bride and his friends went a-walking into the fields, and towards evening to the tennis-court to recreate himself; while he played, he put his ring upon the finger of Venus' statue, which was thereby, made in brass; after he had sufficiently played, and now made an end of his sport, he came to fetch his ring, but Venus had bowed her finger in, and he could not get it off; whereupon, loth to make his company tarry, at the present there left it, intending to fetch it the next day or at some more convenient time, went thence to supper, and so to bed. In the night, when he should come to perform those nuptial rites, Venus steps between him and his wife (unseen or felt of her), and told her that she was his wife, that he had betrothed himself unto her by that ring which he put upon her finger. She troubled him for some following nights. He, not knowing how to help himself, made his moan to one Palumbus, a learned magician in those days, who gave him a letter, and bid him at such a time of the night, in such a crossway, at the town's end, where old Saturn would pass by with his associates in procession, as commonly he did, deliver that script with his own hands to Saturn himself; the young man, of a bold spirit, accordingly did it; and when the old fiend had read it he called Venus to him, who rode before him, and commanded her to deliver his ring, which forthwith she did, and so the gentleman was freed.

Many such stories I find in several authors to confirm this which I have said; and though many be against it, yet I, for my part, will subscribe to Lactantius: God sent angels to the tuition of men; but while they lived among us, that mischievous all-commander of the earth, and hot in lust, enticed them by little and little to this vice, and defiled them with the company of women, and to Anaxagoras: Many of those spiritual bodies, overcome by the love of maids, and lust, failed, of whom those were born we call giants. Justin Martyr, Clemens Alexandrinus, Sulpicius Severus, Eusebius, etc., to this sense make a twofold fall of angels, one from the beginning of the world, another a little before the deluge, as Moses teacheth us, openly professing that these genii can beget, and have carnal copulation with women.

At Japan in the East Indies, at this present (if we may believe the relation of travellers), there is an idol called Teuchedy, to whom one of the fairest virgins in the country is monthly brought, and left in a private room, in the church, where she sits alone to be deflowered. At certain times the Teuchedy (which is thought to be the devil) appears to her, and knoweth her carnally. Every month a fair virgin is taken in; but what becomes of the old, no man can tell. In that goodly temple of Jupiter Belus in Babylon there was a fair chapel, saith Herodotus, an eye-witness of it, in which was a brave bed, a table of gold, etc., into which no creature came but one only woman, which their god made choice of, as the Chaldean priests told him, and that their god lay with her himself, as at Thebes in Egypt was the like done of old. So that you see this is no news; the devils themselves, or their juggling priests, have played such pranks in all ages. Many divines stiffly contradict this; but I will conclude with Lipsius, that since 'examples, testimonies, and confessions of those unhappy women are so manifest on the other side, and many even in this our town of Louvain, that it is likely to be so. One thing I will add, that I suppose that in no age past, I know not by what destiny of this unhappy time, have there ever appeared or showed themselves so many lecherous devils, satyrs, and genii, as in this of ours, as appears by the daily narrations and judical sentences upon record.'

VII

How Love tyrannizeth over men.
Love, or Heroical Melancholy,
his definition, part affected.

YOU HAVE HEARD how this tyrant Love rageth with brute beasts and spirits; now let us consider what passions it causeth among men.

How it tickles the heart of mortal men, I am almost afraid to relate, amazed, and ashamed, it hath wrought such stupend and prodigious effects, such foul offences. Love indeed (I may not deny) first united provinces, built cities, and by a perpetual generation makes and preserves mankind, propagates the Church; but if it rage, it is no more love, but burning lust, a disease, frenzy, madness, hell. 'Tis no virtuous habit this, but a vehement perturbation of the mind, a monster of nature, wit, and art. It subverts kingdoms, overthrows cities, towns, families, mars, corrupts, and makes a massacre of men; thunder and lightning, wars, fires, plagues, have not done that mischief to mankind, as this burning lust, this brutish passion. Let Sodom and Gomorrah, Troy, and I know not how many cities bear record; all succeeding ages will subscribe: Helen was not the first petticoat to cause a war. Joanna of Naples in Italy, Fredegunde and Brunhalt in France, all histories are full of these basilisks. Besides those daily monomachies, murders, effusion of blood, rapes, riot, and immoderate expense, to satisfy their lusts, beggary, shame, loss, torture, punishment, disgrace, loathsome diseases that proceed from thence, worse than calentures and pestilent fevers, those often gouts, pox, arthritis, palsies, cramps, sciatica, convulsions, aches, combustions, etc., which torment the body, that feral melancholy which crucifies the soul in this life, and everlastingly torments in the world to come.

Notwithstanding they know these and many such miseries, threats, tortures, will surely come upon them, rewards, exhortations, on the other hand; yet either out of their own weakness, a depraved nature, or love's tyranny, which so furiously rageth, they suffer themselves to be led like an ox to the slaughter; they go down headlong to their own perdition, they will commit folly with beasts, men leaving the natural use of women, as Paul saith, burned in lust one towards another, and man with man wrought filthiness.

Semiramis with a horse, Pasiphae with a bull, Aristo Ephesius with a jenny-ass, Fulvius with a mare; others with dogs, goats, etc., from which conjunctions in earlier days sprang monsters, Centaurs, Silvanuses, and freaks frightful to behold. Not with brutes only, but among themselves men coupled in the sin vulgarly known as sodomy, a vice usual with Orientals, Greeks, Italians, Africans, Asiatics. Hercules had Hylas, Polycletus, Dion, Pirithous, Abderus, and the Phrygian, and even Eurysteus was said to be his minion. Socrates haunted the gymnasium to admire the beauty of the boys, with Philebus and Phaedo as rivals, as Charmides and other dialogues of Plato testify sufficiently. Of his desire for Alcibiades, Socrates said, I would keep silent, indeed it is abhorrent to me, but he is so enticing. Plato himself doted on Agathon, Xenophon on Clinias, Virgil on Alexis, Anacreon on Bathyllus. Of the prodigious lusts of Nero, Claudius and others of infamous memory, censured by Petronius, Suetonius, and others, how much more might be said; it is an ancient vice, to this day practised among the Asiatics, Turks, Italians; it is, so to speak, the Diana of the Romans; in Turkey common everywhere—ploughing the sands, sowing seeds among stones, as the poet hath it.

Even in marriage the unnatural may be practised; no sin more familiar with the Italians, who defend it in many writings. Johannes de la Casa, Bishop Beventius, calling it a holy, a divine act, claims that no otherwise should Venus be used.

Nothing is more common among monks and priests, a passion leading to death or madness. Angelus Politianus, for love of boys, killed himself. Horrible to relate, in our own country, within memory, that destestable sin was rife. In the year 1538 the wise King Henry VIII sent the venerable doctors Thomas Lee and Richard Layton to inspect the monasteries, where they found so many lechers, eunuchs, catamites, pederasts, sodomites, Ganymedes (saith Bale) that each was a new Gomorrah. See Bale for a catalogue of these things. He has it that girls are not able to sleep for fear of necromantic friars.

If such is the case with votaries, monks, and other religious rascals, what can be expected in towns or palaces? Among nobles, in private places, what nastiness? I remain silent about the other monkish turpitudes, the masturbation, etc. Rodericus and Castra report that they scourge each other by turn to excite venery, and employ those who will discover new practices, including the agile Tribidas and Fricatrices, who tease each other, fulfilling Venus even among eunuchs with their artificial aids and incredible tricks. No wonder that in Constantinople a woman, madly in love with another woman and disguised as a man, could go through a form of marriage with her. I omit reference to those Egyptian embalmers who make love to beautiful corpses, and the insane lust of those in love with idols or images. Ovid's fable of Pygmalion is well enough known, as are those of Mundus and Paulina in Hegesippus, and the picture of Atlanta and Helena, so provocative of desire that one wanted to ravish them. Another madly loved the statue of Good Fortune, saith Aelianus. No part of the body is safe from lust, no orifice excepted. Heliogabalus welcomed lust at every opening. Hostius had a mirror made to magnify his virility, acting both male and female in a manner too abominable to mention. True it is what Gryllus in Plutarch objected to in Ulysses. Furthermore, we have not he saith, in our day among men and women such vileness as among your great and famous heroes—Hercules pursuing beardless youths, crazy for his friends, etc. Unable to contain yourselves, you are like overflowing rivers, causing violence, filthiness, all manner of disturbance and confusion, men copulating with goats, swine, and horses, and women inflamed with desire for beasts—hence Minotaurs, Centaurs, Silvanuses, Sphynxes. Nor would I advance the contrary, or uncover other things which it is unseemly for everyone to know, being for the learned only, to whom, like Rodericus, I would wish to address myself. Not for the frivolous or the depraved have I recorded these squalid sins, and I am not prepared to inquire further into such matters.

I come at last to that heroical love, which is proper to men and women, is a frequent cause of melancholy, and deserves much rather to be called burning lust than by such an honourable title. There is an honest love, I confess, which is natural, a secret snare to captivate the hearts of men, a strong allurement of a most attractive, occult, adamantine property and powerful virtue, and no man living can avoid it. And he who has not felt the power of love is not a man but a block, a very stone, either a god or Nebuchadnezzer, he hath a gourd for his head, a pumpkin for his heart, that hath not felt the power of it, and a rare creature to be found, one in an age, whom no maiden's beauty ever affected; for dote we either young or old, and none are excepted but Minerva and the Muses: so Cupid in Lucian complains to his mother Venus, that among all the rest his arrows could not pierce them.

But this nuptial love is a common passion, an honest, for men to love in the way of marriage; as matter seeks form, so does woman man. You know marriage is honourable, a blessed calling, appointed by God himself in Paradise; it breeds true peace, tranquillity, content, and happiness, than which no holier union exists or ever did, as Daphnaeus in Plutarch could well prove, which makes the human race immortal, when they live without jarring, scolding, lovingly as they should do.

> *Thrice happy they, and more than that,*
> *Whom bond of love so firmly ties,*
> *That without brawls till death them part,*
> *'Tis undissolv'd and never dies.*

(HORACE)

As Seneca lived with his Paulina, Abraham and Sarah, Orpheus and Eurydice, Arria and Paetus, Artemisia and Mausolus, Rubenius Celer, that would needs have it engraven on his tomb, he had led his life with Ennea, his dear wife, forty-three years, eight months, and never fell out. There is no pleasure in this world comparable to it, 'tis the highest good of humanity, the delight of men and gods, bountiful Venus; as one holds, there's something in a woman beyond all human delight; a magnetic virtue, a charming quality, an occult and powerful motive. The husband rules her as head, but she again commands his heart, he is her servant, she his only joy and content: no happiness is like unto it, no love so great as this of man and wife, no such comfort as a sweet wife: when they love at last as fresh as they did at first, as Homer brings Paris kissing Helen, after they had been married ten years, protesting withal that he loved her as dear as he did the first hour that he was betrothed. And in their old age, when they make much of one another, saying, as he did to his wife in the poet Ausonius,

> *Dear wife, let's live in love, and die together,*
> *As hitherto we have in all good will:*

Let no day change or alter our affections,
But let's be young to one another still.

Such should conjugal love be, still the same, and as they are one flesh, so should they be of one mind, as in an aristocratical government, one consent, have one heart in two bodies, will and nill the same. A good wife, according to Plutarch, should be as a looking-glass to represent her husband's face and passion: if he be pleasant, she should be merry; if he laugh, she should smile; if he look sad, she should participate of his sorrow, and bear a part with him, and so they should continue in mutual love one towards another.

No age shall part my love from thee, sweet wife,
Though I live Nestor or Tithonus' life.

(PROPERTIUS)

And she again to him, as the bride saluted the bridegroom of old in Rome, Be thou still Caius, I'll be Caia.

' 'Tis a happy state this indeed, when the fountain is blessed,' saith Solomon (Prov. v, 18), 'and he rejoiceth with the wife of his youth, and she is to him as the loving hind and pleasant roe, and he delights in her continually.' But this love of ours is immoderate, inordinate, and not to be comprehended in any bounds. It will not contain itself within the union of marriage, or apply to one object, but is a wandering, extravagant, a domineering, a boundless, an irrefragable, a destructive passion: sometimes this burning lust rageth after marriage, and then it is properly called jealousy; sometimes before, and then it is called heroical melancholy; it extends sometimes to corrivals, etc., begets rapes, incests, murders: Marcus Antonius embraced his sister Faustina, Caracella his stepmother Julia, Nero his mother, Caligula his sisters, Cinyras his daughter Myrrha. But it is confined within no terms of blood, years, sex, or whatsoever else. Some furiously rage before they come to discretion or age. Quartilla in Petronius never remembered she was a maid; and the Wife of Bath, in Chaucer, cracks,

> *Since I was twelve years old, believe,*
> *Husbands at kirk-door had I five.*

Aretine's Lucretia sold her maidenhead a thousand times before she was twenty-four years old. Rahab, that harlot, began to be a professed quean at ten years of age, and was but fifteen when she hid the spies. Generally women begin puberty, as Julius Pollux cites out of Aristophanes, at fourteen years old; then they do offer themselves, and some plainly rage. Leo Afer saith, that in Africa a man shall scarce find a maid at fourteen years of age, they are so forward, and many among us after they come into the teens do not live without husbands, but linger.

What pranks in this kind the middle age have played is not to be recorded, no tongue can sufficiently declare, every story is full of men and women's insatiable lust. They neigh after other men's wives (as Jeremiah v, 8, complaineth) like fed horses, or range like town bulls, ravishers of widows and maids, as many of our great ones do. Solomon's wisdom was extinguished in this fire of lust, Samson's strength enervated, piety in Lot's daughters quite forgot, gravity of priesthood in Eli's sons, reverend old age in the Elders that would violate Susanna, filial duty in Absalom to his stepmother, brotherly love in Amnon towards his sister. Human, divine laws, precepts, exhortations, fear of God and men, fair, foul means, fame, fortunes, shame, disgrace, honour cannot oppose, stave off, or withstand the fury of it, love conquers all. No cord nor cable can so forcibly draw, or hold so fast, as love can do with a twined thread. The scorching beams under the equinoctial, or extremity of cold within the circle

Arctic, where the very seas are frozen, cold or torrid zone cannot avoid or expel this heat, fury, and rage of mortal men.

Of women's unnatural, unsatiable lust, what country, what village doth not complain? Mother and daughter sometimes dote on the same man; father and son, master and servant on one woman. What breach of vows and oaths, fury, dotage, madness, might I reckon up! Yet this is more tolerable in youth, and such as are still in their hot blood; but for an old fool to dote, to see an old lecher, what more odious, what can be more absurd? and yet what so common? Who so furious? Some dote then more than ever they did in their youth. How many decrepit, hoary, harsh, writhen, bursten-bellied, crooked, toothless, bald, blear-eyed, impotent, rotten old men shall you see flickering still in every place? One gets him a young wife, another a courtesan, and when he can scarce lift his leg over a sill, and hath one foot already in Charon's boat, when he hath the trembling in his joints, the gout in his feet, a perpetual rheum in his head, a continuate cough, his sight fails him, thick of hearing, his breath stinks, all his moisture is dried up and gone, may not spit from him, a very child again, that cannot dress himself, or cut his own meat, yet he will be dreaming of, and honing after wenches; what can be more unseemly?

Worse it is in women than men; when she is an old widow, a mother so long since (in Pliny's opinion), she doth very unseemly seek to marry; yet while she is so old a crone, a beldam, she can neither see nor hear, go nor stand, a mere carcass, a witch, and scarce feel, she caterwauls, and must have a stallion, a champion, she must and will marry again, and betroth herself to some young man, that hates to look on her but for her goods, abhors the sight of her; to the prejudice of her good name, her own undoing, grief of friends, and ruin of her children.

But to enlarge or illustrate this power and effects of love is to set a candle in the sun. It rageth with all sorts and conditions of men, yet is most evident among such as are young and lusty, in the flower of their years, nobly descended, high fed, such as live idly and at ease; and for that cause (which our divines call burning lust) this mad and beastly passion, as I have said, is named by our physicians heroical love, and a more honourable title put upon it, noble love, as Savonarola styles it, because noble men and women make a common practice of it, and are so ordinarily affected with it. Avicenna calleth this passion *Ilishi*, and defines it to be a disease or melancholy vexation, or anguish of mind, in which a man continually meditates of the beauty, gesture, manners of his mistress, and troubles himself about it; desiring (as Savonarola adds) with all intentions and eagerness of mind to compass or enjoy her; as commonly hunters trouble themselves about their sports, the covetous about their gold and goods, so is he tormented still about his mistress. Arnoldus Villanovanus, in his book of heroical love, defines it a continual cogitation of that which he desires, with a confidence or hope of compassing it; which definition his commentator cavils at. For continual cogitation is not the *genus*, but a symptom of love; we continually think of that which we hate and abhor as well as that which we love; and many things we covet and desire without all hope of attaining.

Carolus à Lorme, in his Questions, makes a doubt whether this heroical love be a disease: Julius Pollux determines it. They that are in love are likewise sick. Arnoldus will have it improperly so called and a malady rather of the body than mind. Tully, in his Tusculans, defines it a furious disease of the mind; Plato, madness itself; Ficinus, his commentator, a species of madness, for many have run mad for women (1 Esdras iv, 26); but Rhasis, a melancholy passion; and most physicians make it a species or kind of melancholy (as will appear by the symptoms), and treat of it apart; whom I mean to imitate, and to discuss it in all his kinds, to examine his several causes, to show his symptoms, indications, prognostics, effects, that so it may be with more facility cured.

The part affected in the meantime, as Arnoldus supposeth, is the former part of the head for want of moisture, which his commentator rejects. Langius will have this passion sited in the liver, and to keep residence in the heart, to proceed first from the eyes so carried by our spirits, and kindled with imagination in the liver and heart; the liver compels one to love, as the saying is. He strikes right through the liver, as Cupid in Anacreon. For some such cause belike Homer feigns Titius' liver (who was enamoured on Latona) to be still gnawed by two vultures day and night in hell, for that young men's bowels thus enamoured are so continually tormented by love. Gordonius will have the testicles an immediate subject or cause, the liver an antecedent. Fracastorius agrees in this with Gordonius. It causes venereal images, erection, etc., with excessive titillation of the parts, so that until the semen is emitted, adds Guastavinius, there is incessant voluptuousness of sensation.

But properly it is a passion of the brain, as all other melancholy, by reason of corrupt imagination, and so doth Jason Pratensis (who writes copiously of this erotical love) place and reckon it among the affections of the brain. Melancthon confutes those that make the liver a part affected, and Guianerius, though many put all the affections in the heart, refers it to the brain. Ficinus will have the blood to be the part affected. Freitagius supposeth all four affected, heart, liver, brain, blood; but the major part concur upon the brain, 'tis a discorded imagination and both imagination and reason are misaffected; because of his corrupt judgement, and continual meditation of that which he desires, he may truly be said to be melancholy. If it be violent, or his disease inveterate, as I have determined in the precedent partitions, both imagination and reason are misaffected, first one, then the other.

VIII

Causes of Heroical Love, Temperature, full Diet, Idleness, Place, Climate, etc.

O F ALL CAUSES the remotest are stars. Ficinus saith they are most prone to this burning lust that have Venus in Leo in their horoscope, when the Moon and Venus be mutually aspected, or such as be of Venus' complexion. Plutarch interprets astrologically that tale of Mars and Venus; they are commonly lascivious, and if women, queans, as the good wife of Bath confessed in Chaucer:

> *I followed aye mine inclination,*
> *By virtue of my constellation.*

But of all those astrological aphorisms which I have ever read, that of Cardan is most memorable, for which howsoever he is bitterly censured by Marinus Marcennus, a malapert, friar, and some others (which he himself suspected), yet methinks it is free, downright, plain, and ingenuous. In his eighth geniture, or example, he hath these words of himself: 'When Venus and Mercury are in conjunction, Mercury in the ascendant, thoughts of love give me no peace. I am in continuous torment, and since it is not permissible to satisfy my desire, I am lost in the indulgence of fancy.' He also saith, 'the dominion of the Moon and Mercury inclined me to libidinousness.' So far Cardan of himself, and for this he is traduced by Marcennus, whenas in effect he saith no more than what Gregory of Nazianzen of old to Chilo his scholar: 'Visions of women offering themselves, tempting my virtue with marvellous grace and beauty, and though I resisted, yet in my imagination I gathered the flowers of their virginity.'

Those born when Venus is in a masculine sign are prone to venery, when Saturn is in opposition. Ptolemy confirmed these things by experiment. Thomas Campanella, in his remonstrances against amatory madness, may be consulted. The Chiromantics have many conjectures about the girdle of Venus and the mount of Venus.

Physicians divine wholly from the temperature and complexion; phlegmatic persons are seldom taken, according to Ficinus; naturally melancholy less than they, but once taken they are never freed; though many are of opinion flatuous or hypochondriacal melancholy are most subject of all others to this infirmity. Valescus assigns their strong imagination for a cause, Bodine abundance of wind, Gordonius of seed, and spirits or atomi in the seed, which cause their violent and furious passions. Sanguine thence are soon caught, young folks most apt to love, and by their good wills, saith Lucian, would have a bout with everyone they see: the colt's evil is common to all complexions.

Theomnestus, a young and lusty gallant, acknowledgeth (in the said author) and this to be verified in him: 'I am so amorously given, you may sooner number the sea-sands, and snow falling from the skies, than my several loves. Cupid had shot all his arrows at me, I am deluded with various desires, one love succeeds another, and that so soon, that before one is ended, I begin with a second! she that is last is still fairest, and that she is present pleaseth me most: as an hydra's head my loves increase, no Iolaus can help me. Mine eyes are so moist a refuge and sanctuary of love that they draw all beauties to them, and are never satisfied. I am in a doubt what fury of Venus this should be. Alas, how have I offended her so to vex me? what Hippolytus am I?' What Telchin is my genius? or is it a natural imperfection, an hereditary passion?

Another in Anacreon confesseth that he had twenty sweethearts in Athens at once, fifteen at Corinth, as many at Thebes, at Lesbos, and at Rhodes, twice as many in Ionia, thrice in Caria, twenty thousand in all:

> *Canst count the leaves in May,*
> *Or sand i' th' ocean sea?*
> *Then count my loves I pray.*

His eyes are like a balance, apt to propend each way, and to be weighed down with every wench's looks, in his heart a weathercock, his affection tinder, or naphtha itself, which every fair object, sweet smile, or mistress' favour sets on fire. Guianerius refers all this to the hot temperature of the testicles; Ferrandus, a Frenchman, to certain atomi in the seed, 'such as are very spermatic and full of seed'. I find the same in *Aristotle*, until rid of the semen they must burn, as Guastavinius his commentator translates it: for which cause these young men that be strong set, of able bodies, are so subject to it. Hercules de Saxonia hath the same words in effect. But most part, I say, such are aptest to love that are young and lusty, live at ease, stall-fed, free from cares, like cattle in a rank pasture, idle and solitary persons, they must needs play the goat, as Guastavinius recites out of Censorinus.

> *The mind is apt to lust, and hot or cold,*
> *As corn luxuriates in a better mould.*

The place itself makes much wherein we live, the clime, air, and discipline if they concur. In our Mysia, saith Galen, near to Pergamus, thou shalt scarce find an adulterer, but many at Rome, by reason of the delights of the seat. It was that plenty of all things which made Corinth so infamous of old, and the opportunity of the place to entertain those foreign comers; every day strangers came in, at each gate, from all quarters. In that one temple of Venus a thousand whores did prostitute themselves, as Strabo writes, besides Lais and the rest of better note: all nations resorted thither, as to a school of Venus. Your hot and southern countries are prone to lust, and far more incontinent than those that live in the north. The Asiatics are amorous; so are Turks, Greeks, Spaniards, Italians, even all that latitude; and in those tracts, such as are more fruitful, plentiful, and delicious, as Valentia in Spain, Capua in Italy, home of luxury Tully terms it, and (which Hannibal's soldiers can witness) Canopus in Egypt, Sybaris, Phaeacia, Baiae, Cyprus, Lampsacus. In Naples the fruits of the soil and pleasant air enervate their bodies, and alter constitutions: insomuch that Florus calls it a contest between Bacchus and Venus, but Foliot admires it. In Italy and Spain they have their stews in every great city, as in Rome, Venice, Florence, wherein, some say, dwell ninety thousand inhabitants, of which ten thousand are courtesans; and yet for all this, every gentleman almost hath a peculiar mistress; fornications, adulteries, are nowhere so common: how should a man live honest among so many provocations?

Now if vigour of youth, greatness, liberty I mean, and that impunity of sin which grandees take unto themselves in this kind shall meet, what a gap must it needs open to all manner of vice, with what fury will it rage! What will not lust effect in such persons? For commonly princes and great men make no scruple at all of such matters, but with that whore in Spartan they think they may do what they list, profess it publicly, and rather brag with Proculus (that writ to a friend of his in Rome, what famous exploits he had done in that kind) than any way be abashed at it. Nicholas Sanders relates of Henry VIII (I know not how truly), he saw very few pretty maids that he did not desire, and desired fewer whom he did not enjoy: nothing so familiar among them, 'tis most of their business: Sardanapalus, Messalina, and Joan of Naples are not comparable to meaner men and women; Solomon of old had a thousand concubines; Ahasuerus his eunuchs and keepers; Nero his Tigellinus, panders, and bawds; the Turks, Muscovites, Mogors, Xeriffs of Barbary, and Persian Sophies are no whit inferior to them in our times. There is a levy, saith Jovius, throughout of beautiful girls for the emperor; and those whom he leaves the nobles take; they press and muster up wenches as we do soldiers, and have their choice of the rarest beauties their countries can afford, and yet all this cannot keep them from adultery, incest, sodomy, buggery, and such prodigious lusts. We may conclude, that if they be young, fortunate, rich, high-fed, and idle withal, it is almost impossible that they should live honest, not rage, and precipitate themselves into these inconveniences of burning lust.

Idleness overthrows all, love tyrannizeth in an idle person. If thou hast nothing to do, thou shalt be haled in pieces with envy, lust, some passion or other. 'Tis Aristotle's simile, 'As match or touchwood takes fire, so doth an idle person love.' Why was Aegisthus a whoremaster? You need not ask a reason of it. Ismenodora stole Bacho, a woman forced a man, as Aurora did Cephalus: no marvel, saith Plutarch: she was rich, fortunate and jolly, and doth but as men do in that case, as Jupiter did by Europa, Neptune by Amymone. The poets therefore did well to feign all shepherds lovers, to give themselves to songs and dalliances, because they lived such idle lives. For love, as Theophrastus defines it, is an affection of an idle mind, or as Seneca describes it, youth begets it, riot maintains it, idleness nourisheth it, etc., which makes Gordonius, the physician, call this disease the proper passion of nobility. Now if a weak judgement and a strong apprehension do concur, how, saith Hercules de Saxonia, shall they resist? Savonarola appropriates it almost to monks, friars, and religious persons, because they live solitarily, fare daintily, and do nothing: and well he may, for how should they otherwise choose?

Diet alone is able to cause it: a rare thing to see a young man or woman that lives idly and fares well, of what condition soever, not to be in love. Alcibiades was still dallying with wanton young women, immoderate in his expenses, effeminate in his apparel, ever in love, but why? he was over-delicate in his diet, too frequent and excessive in banquets. Lust and security domineer together as St Jerome averreth. All which the Wife of Bath in Chaucer freely justifies:

> *For all so sicker, as cold engendreth hail,*
> *A liquorish tongue must have a liquorish tail.*

Especially if they shall further it by choice diet, as many times those Sybarites and Phaeaces do, feed liberally, and by their good will eat nothing else but lascivious meats. First of all a generous wine, vegetables, beans, roots of all kinds liberally peppered, radishes, lettuce, leeks, onions, nuts, almonds, electuaries, broth, oysters, fish, chickens, testicles of animals, rich sauces, etc. And whatever physicians may prescribe for those suffering from impotence, they have an aphrodisiac in delicacies and sumptuous feasts, honey drinks, exotic fruits, cakes, soups, insinuating sweet wine, all that cuisine or pharmacy has to offer. Thus replete with dishes like those prepared for Chrysis, having primed themselves with snails so as to be capable of Venus, who would not be raging with lust, ready almost to run completely mad? Immoderate drinking provokes lechery, saith Augustine. Wine is the milk of venery, saith Aristophanes. Neither Etna nor Vesuvius is so fiery as young wine-filled bellies. To make the vines flourish Lampsacus was dedicated to Priapus. Bacchus as well as Orpheus charmed Venus. From undiluted wine, taken on an empty stomach, what can we expect but mad fury?

Gomesius includes salt among things that provoke a rage of lust, contending that women are specially affected. Did not Venus herself arise from the sea? Perhaps from this, from the *salt* of the sea, comes the word *salacity*. In the East Indies cubebs soaked in wine are used to incite venery, and surax root by the Africans. China roots have the same effect. An infinity of other things are proposed, but wise physicians warn us, beware lest in the effort to increase virility the opposite ensues.

IX

Other causes of Love-Melancholy,
Sight, Beauty from the face, eyes,
other parts, and how it pierceth.

MANY SUCH CAUSES may be reckoned up, but they cannot avail, except opportunity be offered of time, place, and those other beautiful objects, or artificial enticements, as kissing, conference, discourse, gestures concur, with suchlike lascivious provocations. Kornmannus makes five degrees of lust, out of Lucian belike, which he handles in five chapters, Sight, Converse, Companionship, Kissing, Touch. Sight, of all other, is the first step of this unruly love, though sometimes it be prevented by relation or hearing, or rather incensed. For there be those so apt, credulous, and facile to love that if they hear of a proper man, or woman, they are in love before they see them, and that merely by relation, as Achilles Tatius observes. 'Such is their intemperance and lust, that they are as much maimed by report as if they saw them.'

Callisthenes, a rich young gentleman of Byzance in Thrace, hearing of Leucippe, Sostratus' fair daughter, was far in love with her, and, out of fame and common rumour, so much incensed, that he would needs have her to be his wife. And sometimes by reading they are so affected, as he in Lucian confesseth of himself, 'I never read that place of Panthea in Xenophon but I am as much affected as if I were present with her.' Such persons commonly feign a kind of beauty to themselves; and so did those three gentlewomen in Baldassare Castiglione fall in love with a young man whom they never knew, but only heard him commended: or by reading of a letter; for there is a grace cometh from hearing, as a moral philosopher informeth us, as well from sight; and the species of love are received into the phantasy by relation alone: both senses affect. Sometimes we love those that are absent, saith Philostratus, and gives instance in his friend Athenorodus, that loved a maid at Corinth whom he never saw; we see with the eyes of our understanding.

But the most familiar and usual cause of love is that which comes by sight, which conveys those admirable rays of beauty and pleasing graces to the heart. Plotinus derives love from sight, the eyes are the harbingers of love, and the first step of love is sight, as Lilius Giraldus proves at large; they as two sluices let in the influence of that divine, powerful, soul-ravishing, and captivating beauty, which, as one saith, is sharper than any dart or needle, wounds deeper into the heart; and opens a gap through our ears to that lovely wound, which pierceth the soul itself. 'Through it love is kindled like a fire' (Eccles. ix, 8).

This amazing, confounding, admirable, amiable beauty, than which in all nature's treasure (saith Isocrates) there is nothing so majestical and sacred, nothing so divine, lovely, precious, 'tis nature's crown, gold and glory; if not the highest good, yet frequently triumphing over the highest, whose power hence may be discerned: we contemn and abhor generally such things as are foul and ugly to behold, account them filthy, but love and covet that which is fair.

'Tis beauty in all things which pleaseth and allureth us, a fair hawk, a fine garment, a goodly building, a fair house, etc. That Persian Xerxes, when he destroyed all those temples of the gods in Greece, caused that of Diana to be spared alone for that excellent beauty and magnificence of it. Inanimate beauty can so command. 'Tis that which painters, artificers, orators all aim at, as Erixymachus, the physician in Plato, contends. It was beauty first that ministered occasion to art, to find out the knowledge of carving, painting, building, to find out models, perspectives, rich furnitures, and so many rare inventions. Whiteness in the lily, red in the rose, purple in the violet, a lustre in all things without life, the clear light of the moon, the bright beams of the sun, splendour of gold, purple, sparkling diamond, the excellent features of the horse, the majesty of the lion, the colour of birds, peacock's tails, the silver scales of fish, we behold with singular delight and admiration.

And that which is rich in plants, delightful in flowers, wonderful in beasts, but most glorious in men, doth make us affect and earnestly desire it, as when we hear any sweet harmony, an eloquent tongue, see any excellent quality, curious work of man, elaborate art, or aught that is exquisite, there ariseth instantly in us a longing for the same. We love such men, but most part for comeliness of person; we call them gods and goddesses, divine, serene, happy, etc. And of all mortal men they alone (Calcagninus holds) are free from calumny; we back-bite, wrong, hate renowned, rich, and happy men, we repine at their felicity, they are undeserving, we think, fortune is a stepmother to us, a parent to them. We envy (saith Isocrates) wise, just, honest men, except with mutual offices and kindnesses, some good turn or other, they extort this love from us; only fair persons we love at first sight, desire their acquaintance, and adore them as so many gods: we had rather serve them than command others, and account ourselves the more beholding to them, the more service they enjoin us, though they be otherwise vicious, unhonest, we love them, favour them, and are ready to do them any good office for their beauty's sake, though they have no other good quality beside. As that eloquent Phavorinius breaks out in Stobaeus, 'Speak, fair youth, speak, Autolycus, thy words, are sweeter than nectar; speak, O Telemachus, thou art more powerful than Ulysses; speak, Alcibiades, though drunk, we will willingly hear thee as thou art.' Faults in such are no faults: for when the said Alcibiades had stolen Anytus his gold and silver plate, he was so far from prosecuting so foul a fact (though every man else condemned his impudence and insolency) that he wished it had been more, and much better (he loved him dearly) for his sweet sake.

No worth is eminent in such lovely persons, all imperfections hid; for hearing, sight, touch, etc., our mind and all our senses are captivated. Many men have been preferred for their person alone, chosen kings, as among the Indians, Persians, Ethiopians of old the properest man of person the country could afford was elected their sovereign lord: and so have many other nations thought and done, as Curties observes; for there is a majestical presence in such men; and so far was beauty adored among them that no man was thought fit to reign that was not in all parts complete and super-eminent. Agis, King of Lacedaemon, had like to have been deposed, because he married a little wife: they would not have their royal issue degenerate.

Who would ever have thought that Adrian the Fourth, an English monk's bastard (as Papirius Massovius writes in his life), a poor for-saken child, should ever come to be Pope of Rome? But why was it? As he follows it out of Nubrigensis, for he ploughs with his heifer, he was wise, learned, eloquent, of a pleasant, a promising counte-nance, a goodly, proper man; he had, in a word, a winning look of his own, and that carried it, for that he was especially advanced. So Saul was a goodly person and a fair. Mamiminus elected emperor, etc. Branchus, the son of Apollo, whom he begot of Jance, Succron's daughter (saith Lactantius), when he kept King Admetus' herds in Thessaly, now grown a man, was an earnest suitor to his mother to know his father; the nymph denied him, because Apollo had conjured her to the contrary; yet overcome by his importunity, at last she sent him to his father; when he came into Apollo's presence, reverently kissing the cheeks of the god, he carried himself so well, and was so fair a young man, that Apollo was infinitely taken with the beauty of his person, he could scarce look off him, and said he was worthy of such parents, gave him a crown of gold, the spirit of divination, and in conclusion made him a demigod.

A goddess beauty is, whom the very gods adore; she is love's mistress, love's harbinger, love's loadstone, a witch, a charm, etc. Beauty is a dower of itself, a sufficient patrimony, an ample commendation, an accurate epistle, as Lucian, Apuleius, Tiraquellus, and some others conclude. Beauty deserves a kingdom, saith Abulensis, immortality; and more have got this honour and eternity for their beauty than for all other virtues besides; and such as are fair are worthy to be honoured of God and men. That Idalian Ganymede was therefore fetched by Jupiter into heaven. Hephaestion dear to Alexander, Antinous to Hadrian.

Plato calls beauty for that cause a privilege of nature, nature's masterpiece, a dumb comment; Theophrastus, a silent fraud; still rhetoric, Carneades, that persuades without speech, a kingdom without a guard, because beautiful persons command as so many captains; Socrates, a tyranny, which tyrannizeth over tyrants themselves; which made Diogenes belike call proper women queens, because men were so obedient to their commands. They will adore, cringe, compliment, and bow to a common wench (if she be fair) as if she were a noblewoman, a countess, a queen, or a goddess. Those intemperate young men of Greece erected at Delphi a golden image with infinite cost, to the eternal memory of Phryne the courtesan, as Aelian relates, for she was a most beautiful woman, insomuch, saith Athenaeus, that Apelles and Praxiteles drew Venus' picture from her. Thus young men will adore and honour beauty; nay, kings themselves, I say, will do it, and voluntarily submit their sovereignty to a lovely woman.

'Wine is strong, kings are strong, but a woman strongest' (1 Esdras iii, 10), as Zorobabel proved at large to King Darius, his princes and noblemen. 'Kings sit still and command sea and land, etc., all pay tribute to the king; but women make kings pay tribute, and have dominion over them. When they have got gold and silver they submit all to a beautiful woman, give themselves wholly to her, gape and gaze on her, and all men desire her more than gold or silver, or any precious thing: they will leave father and mother, and venture their lives for her, labour and travel to get, and bring all their gains to women, steal, fight, and spoil for their mistresses' sakes. And no king so strong, but a fair woman is stronger than he is. All things [as he proceeds] fear to touch the king; yet I saw him and Apame his concubine, the daughter of the famous Bartacus, sitting on the right hand of the king, and she took the crown off his head, and put it on her own, and stroke him with her left hand; yet the king gaped and gazed on her, and when she laughed he laughed, and when she was angry he flattered to be reconciled to her.'

So beauty commands even kings themselves; nay, whole armies and kingdoms are captivated together with their kings. And 'tis a great matter, saith Xenophon, and of which all fair persons may worthily brag, that a strong man must labour for his living if he will have aught, a valiant man must fight and endanger himself for it, a wise man speak, show himself, and toil; but a fair and beautiful person doth all with ease, he compasseth his desire without any painstaking: God and men, heaven and earth conspire to honour him; everyone pities him above other, if he be in need, and all the world is willing to do him good.

Chariclea fell into the hand of pirates, but when all the rest were put to the edge of the sword, she alone was preserved for her person. When Constantinople was sacked by the Turk, Irene escaped, and was so far from being made a captive that she even captivated the Grand Seignior himself. So did Rosamund insult over King Henry the Second:

> *I was so fair an object;*
> *Whom fortune made my king, my love made subject;*
> *He found by proof the privilege of beauty,*
> *That it had power to countermand all duty.*
>
> (DANIEL)

It captivates the very gods themselves, even the most austere. The king of the gods for beauty's sake became a bull, a horse, a shower, a swan of gold. And those evil spirits are taken with it, as I have already proved. The barbarians stand in awe of a fair woman, and at a beautiful aspect a fierce spirit is pacified. For whenas Troy was taken, and the wars ended (as Clemens Alexandrinus quotes out of Euripides), angry Menelaus, with rage and fury armed, came with his sword drawn, to have killed Helena with his own hands, as being the sole cause of all those wars and miseries; but when he saw her fair face, as one amazed at her divine beauty, he let his weapon fall, and embraced her besides; he had no power to strike so sweet a creature.

The edge of a sharp sword (as the saying is) is dulled with a beautiful aspect, and severity itself is overcome. Hyperides the orator, when Phryne his client was accused at Athens for her lewdness, used no other defence in her cause, but tearing her upper garment, disclosed her naked breast to the judges, with which comeliness of her body and amiable gesture they were so moved and astonished that they did acquit her forthwith, and let her go. O noble piece of justice! mine author exclaims: and who is he that would not rather lose his seat and robes, forfeit his office, than give sentence against the majesty of beauty? Such prerogatives have fair persons, and they alone are free from danger.

Parthenopaeus was so lovely and fair that when he fought in the Theban wars, if his face had been by chance bare, no enemy would offer to strike at or hurt him, such immunities hath beauty. Beasts themselves are moved with it. Sinalda was a woman of such excellent feature, and a queen, that when she was to be trodden on by wild horses for a punishment, the wild beasts stood in admiration of her person and would not hurt her. Wherefore did that royal virgin in Apuleius, when she fled from the thieves' den in a desert, make such an apostrophe to her ass on whom she rode (for what knew she to the contrary, but that he was an ass?): 'Take me back to my parents, beloved. I shall be grateful to you and honour you for ever, give you the finest food.' She would comb him, dress him, feed him, and trick him every day herself, and he should work no more, toil no more, but rest and play, etc. And besides, she would have a dainty picture drawn, in perpetual remembrance, a virgin riding upon an ass's back, with this motto, A royal virgin riding upon an ass to escape captivity. Why said she all this? why did she make such promises to a dumb beast but that she perceived the poor ass to be taken with her beauty; for he did often kiss her feet as she rode, offer to give consent as much as in him was to her delicate speeches, and besides he had some feeling, as she conceived, of her misery? And why did Theagenes' horse in Heliodorus curvet, prance, and go so proudly, but that sure, as mine author supposeth, he was in love with his master? A fly lighted on Malthius' cheek as he lay asleep; but why? Not to hurt him, as a parasite of his, standing by, well perceived, but certainly to kiss him, as ravished with his divine looks.

Inanimate creatures, I suppose, have a touch of this. When a drop of Psyche's candle fell on Cupid's shoulder I think sure it was to kiss it. When Venus ran to meet her rose-cheeked Adonis, as an elegant poet of ours [Shakespeare] sets her out,

> *The bushes in the way*
> *Some catch her neck, some kiss her face,*
> *Some twine about her legs to make her stay,*
> *And all did covet her for to embrace.*

As Heliodorus holds, the air itself is in love: for when Hero played upon her lute, 'The wanton air in twenty sweet forms danc't after her fingers' (Chapman), and those lascivious winds stayed Daphne (in Ovid) when she fled from Apollo, exposing her limbs as her garments fluttered. Boreas loved Hyacinthus, and Orithyia, Erectheus' daughter of Athens: he took her away by force, as she was playing with other wenches at Ilissus, and begat Zetes and Calais his two sons of her. That seas and waters are enamoured with this our beauty is all out as likely as that of the air and winds; for when Leander swimmed in the Hellespont, Neptune with his trident did beat down the waves, but they

> *Still mounted up, intending to have kissed him,*
> *And fell in drops like tears because they missed him.*
>
> (MARLOWE)

The River Alpheus was in love with Arethusa, as she tells the tale herself in Ovid: As she drifted her green tresses, she related the ancient love of the stream Alpheus. 'I was once a nymph, etc.' When our Thame and Isis meet, the air resounds with kisses, with arms intertwined they hang on each other's neck. Inachus and Peneus, and how many loving rivers can I reckon up, whom beauty hath enthralled!

I say nothing all this while of idols themselves that have committed idolatry in this kind, of looking-glasses that have been rapt in love (if you will believe poets), when their ladies and mistresses looked on to dress them.

> *Though I no sense at all of feeling have,*
> *Yet your sweet looks do animate and save;*
> *And when your speaking eyes do this way turn,*
> *Methinks my wounded members live and burn.*

I could tell you such another story of a spindle that was fired by a fair lady's looks, or fingers, some say, I know not well whether, but fired it was by report, and of a cold bath that suddenly smoked and was very hot when naked Caelia came into it.

But of all the tales in this kind, that is the most memorable of Death himself, when he should have stroken a sweet young virgin with his dart he fell in love with the object. Many more such could I relate which are to be believed with a poetical faith. So dumb and dead creatures dote, but men are mad, stupefied many times at the first sight of beauty, amazed, as that fisherman in Aristaenetus, that spied a maid bathing herself by the sea-side: 'I shook from head to foot, I was dazed and stupefied.' And as Lucian, in his Images, confesses of himself, that he was at his mistress's presence void of all sense, immovable, as if he had seen a Gorgon's head: which was no such cruel monster (as Caelius interprets it), but the very quintessence of beauty, some fair creature, as without doubt the poet understood in the first fiction of it, at which the spectators were amazed. Poor wretches are compelled at the very sight of her ravishing looks to run mad, or make away themselves.

> *They wait the sentence of her scornful eyes;*
> *And whom she favours lives, the other dies.*
>
> (MARLOWE)

Heliodorus brings in Thyamis almost beside himself, when he saw Chariclea first, and not daring to look upon her a second time, for he thought it unpossible for any man living to see her and contain himself. The very fame of beauty will fetch them to it many miles off (such an attractive power this loadstone hath), and they will seem but short, they will undertake any toil of trouble, long journeys, Penia or Atalanta shall not overgo them, through seas, deserts, mountains, and dangerous places, as they did to gaze on Psyche: many mortal men came far and near to see that glorious object of her age, as Paris for Helena, Coraebus to Troy.

King John of France, once prisoner in England, came to visit his old friends again, crossing the seas; but the truth is, his coming was to see the Countess of Salisbury, the nonpareil of those times, and his dear mistress. That infernal god Plutus came from hell itself, to steal Proserpina; Achilles left all his friends for Polyxena's sake, his enemy's daughter; and all the Grecian gods forsook their heavenly mansions for that fair lady, Philo Dioneus' daughter's sake, the paragon of Greece in those days; she was so beautiful that all the gods were rivals for her. They will not only come to see, but as a falconer makes a hungry hawk, hover about, follow, give attendance and service, spend goods, lives, and all their fortune to attain:

> *Were beauty under twenty locks kept fast,*
> *Yet love breaks through, and picks them all at last.*

When fair Hero came abroad the eyes, hearts, and affections of her spectators were still attendant on her

> *So far above the rest fair Hero shined,*
> *And stole away the enchanted gazer's mind.*
>
> (MARLOWE)

When Peter Aretine's Lucretia came first to Rome, and that the fame of her beauty was spread abroad, they came in (as they say) thick and threefold to see her, and hovered about her gates, as they did of old to Lais of Corinth, and Phryne of Thebes, at whose gates lay all Greece. Every man sought to get her love, some with gallant and costly apparel, some with an affected pace, some with music, others with rich gifts, pleasant discourse, multitude of followers; others with letters, vows, and promises, to commend themselves, and to be gracious in her eyes. Happy was he that could see her, thrice happy that enjoyed her company.

Charmides in Plato was a proper young man, in comeliness of person, and all good qualities, far exceeding others; whensoever fair Charmides came abroad, they seemed all to be in love with him (as Critias describes their carriage), and were troubled at the very sight of him; many came near him, many followed him wheresoever he went, as those admirers of beauty did Acontius, if at any time he walked abroad: the Athenian lasses stared on Alcibiades; Sappho and the Mitylenian women on Phaon the fair. Such lovely sights do not only please, entice, but ravish and amaze. Cleonymus, a delicate and tender youth, present at a feast which Androcles his uncle made in the Piraeus at Athens, when he sacrificed to Mercury, so stupefied the guests, Dineas, Aristippus, Agasthenes, and the rest (as Charidemus in Lucian relates it), that they could not eat their meat, they sat all supper-time gazing, glancing at him, stealing looks, and admiring of his beauty.

Many will condemn these men that are so enamoured for fools; but some again commend them for it; many reject Paris' judgement, and yet Lucian approves of it, admiring Paris for his choice; he would have done as much himself, and by good desert in his mind; beauty is to be preferred before wealth or wisdom. Athenaeus holds it not such indignity for the Trojans and Greeks to contend ten years, to spend so much labour, lose so many men's lives for Helen's sake, for so fair a lady's sake. That one woman was worth a kingdom, an hundred thousand other women, a world itself. Well might Stesichorus be blind for carping at so fair a creature, and a just punishment it was. The same testimony gives Homer of the old men of Troy, that were spectators of that single combat between Paris and Menelaus at the Scaean gate, when Helen stood in presence; they said all, the war was worthily prolonged and undertaken for her sake. The very gods themselves (as Homer and Isocrates record) fought more for Helena than they did against the giants.

When Venus lost her son Cupid she made proclamation by Mercury, that he that could bring tidings of him should have seven kisses; a noble reward some say, and much better than so many golden talents; seven such kisses to many men were more precious than seven cities, or so many provinces. One such a kiss alone would recover a man if he were a-dying. Great Alexander married Roxane, a poor man's child, only for her person. 'Twas well done of Alexander, and heroically done; I admire him for it. Orlando was mad for Angelica, and who doth not condole his mishap? Thisbe died for Pyramus, Dido for Aeneas; who doth not weep, as (before his conversion) Augustine did, in commiseration of her estate? she died for him; methinks (as he said) I could die for her.

But this is not the matter in hand; what prerogative this beauty hath, of what power and sovereignty it is, and how far such persons that so much admire and dote upon it are to be justified—no man doubts of these matters; the question is, how and by what means beauty produceth this effect? By sight: the eye betrays the soul, and is both active and passive in this business; it wounds and is wounded, is an especial cause and instrument, both in the subject and in the object. As tears, it begins in the eyes, descends to the breast; it conveys these beauteous rays, as I have said, unto the heart. I saw, I was undone! Mars sees her and immediately desires her. Shechem saw Dinah the daughter of Leah, and defiled her (Gen. xxxiv, 3); Jacob, Rachel (xxix, 17), 'for she was beautiful and fair'; David spied Bathsheba afar off (2 Sam. xi, 2); the Elders, Susanna, as that Orthomenian Strato saw fair Aristoclea, the daughter of Theophanes, bathing herself at that

Hercyne well in Lebadea; and were captivated in an instant. Amnon fell sick for Tamar's sake (2 Sam. xiii, 2). The beauty of Esther was such that she found favour not only in the sight of Ahasuerus, but of all those that looked upon her. Gerson, Origen, and some others contended that Christ Himself was the fairest of the sons of men, and Joseph next unto Him, and they will have it literally taken; His very person was such that He found grace and favour of all those that looked upon Him. Joseph was so fair, that, as the ordinary gloss hath it, they ran to the top of the walls and to the windows to gaze on him, as we do commonly to see some great personage go by: and so Matthew Paris describes Matilda, the Empress going through Cologne. P. Morales the Jesuit saith as much of the Virgin Mary.

Antony no sooner saw Cleopatra, but, saith Appian, he was enamoured on her. Theseus at the first sight of Helen was so besotted that he esteemed himself the happiest man in the world if he might enjoy her, and to that purpose kneeled down and made his pathetical prayers unto the gods. Charicles, by chance espying that curious picture of smiling Venus naked in her temple, stood a great while gazing, as one amazed; at length he brake into that mad passionate speech, 'O fortunate god Mars, that wast bound in chains, and made ridiculous for her sake!' He could not contain himself, but kissed her picture, I know not how oft, and heartily desired to be so disgraced as Mars was. And what did he that his betters had not done before Him? When Venus came first to heaven her comeliness was such that (as mine author saith) all the gods came flocking about, and saluted her, each of them went to Jupiter, and desired he might have her to be his wife. When fair Autolycus came in presence, as a candle in the dark his beauty shined, all men's eyes (as Xenophon describes the manner of it) were instantly fixed on him, and moved at the sight, insomuch that they could not conceal themselves, but in gesture or looks it was discerned and expressed. Those other senses, hearing, touching, may much penetrate and affect, but none so much, none so forcible as sight. Achilles was moved in the midst of a battle by fair Briseis, Ajax by Tecmessa; Judith captivated that great captain Holofernes; Delilah, Samson; Rosamund, Henry the Second; Roxalana, Solyman the Magnificent, etc. A fair woman overcomes fire and sword.

> *Naught under heaven so strongly doth allure*
> *The sense of man and all his mind possess,*
> *As beauty's loveliest bait, that doth procure*
> *Great warriors oft their rigour to suppress,*
> *And mighty hands forget their manliness,*
> *Driven with the power of an heart-robbing eye,*
> *And wrapt in fetters of a golden tress,*
> *That can with melting pleasure mollify*
> *Their harden'd hearts inur'd to blood and cruelty.*
>
> (SPENSER)

Clitiphon ingenuously confesseth, that he no sooner came in Leucippe's presence, but he was wounded at the first sight, his heart panted, and he could not possibly turn his eyes from her. So doth Calasiris in Heliodorus, Isis' priest, a reverend old man, complain, who by chance at Memphis seeing that Thracian Rhodopis, might not hold his eyes off her: 'I will not conceal it, she overcame me with her presence, and quite assaulted my continency which I had kept unto mine old age; I resisted a long time my bodily eyes with the eyes of my understanding; at last I was conquered, and as in a tempest carried headlong.' Xenopithes, a philosopher, railed at women downright for many years together, scorned, hated, scoffed at them; coming at last into Daphnis a fair maid's company (as he condoles his mishap to his friend Demaretus) though free before, was far in love, and quite overcome upon a sudden.

Such another mishap, but worse, had Stratocles the physician, that blear-eyed old man (so Prodromus describes him); he was a severe woman-hater all his life, a bitter persecutor of the whole sex, asps and vipers, he called them, in human shape, he forswore them all still, and mocked them wheresoever he came, in such vile terms that if thou hadst heard him thou wouldst have loathed thine own mother and sisters for his word's sake. Yet this old doting fool was taken at last with that celestial and divine look of Myrilla, the daughter of Anticles the gardener, that smirking wench, that he shaved off his bushy beard, painted his face, curled his hair, wore a laurel crown to cover his bald pate, and for her love besides was ready to run mad. For the very day that he married he was so furious he could not stay till it was night, the meat scarce out of his mouth, without any leave taking, he would needs go presently to bed.

What young man therefore, if old men be so intemperate, can secure himself? Who can say, I will not be taken with a beautiful object, I can, I will contain? No, saith Lucian of his mistress, she is so fair, that if thou dost but see her, she will stupefy thee, kill thee straight, and, Medusa-like, turn thee to a stone; thou canst not pull thine eyes from her, but as an adamant doth iron, she will carry thee bound headlong whither she will herself, infect thee like a basilisk. It holds both in men and women. Dido was amazed at Aeneas' presence, and, as he feelingly verified out of his experience:

> *I lov'd her not as others soberly,*
> *But as a madman rageth, so did I.*

So Musaeus of Leander, and Chaucer of Palamon:

> *He cast his eye upon Emilia,*
> *And therewith he blent and cried ha, ha,*
> *As though he stongen were unto the heart.*

If you desire to know more particularly what this beauty is, how it doth influence, how it doth fascinate (for, as all hold, love is a fascination), thus in brief. This comeliness or beauty ariseth from the due proportion of the whole, or from each several part. For an exact delineation of which, I refer you to poets, historiographers, and those amorous writers, to Lucian's Images and Charidemus, Xenophon's description of Panthea, Petronius' Catalecta, Heliodorus' Chariclea, Tatius' Leucippe, Longus Sophista's Daphnis and Chloe, Theodorus Prodromus his Rhodanthe, Aristaenetus' and Philostratus' Epistles, Baldassare Castiglione, Laurentius, Aeneas Sylvius his Lucretia, and every poet almost, which have most accurately described a perfect beauty, an absolute feature, and that through every member, both in men and women. Each part must concur to the perfection of it; for as Seneca saith, she is no fair woman, whose arm, thigh, etc., are commended, except the face and all the other parts be correspondent. And the face especially gives a lustre to the rest: the face is it that commonly denominates fair or foul: the face is beauty's tower; and though the other parts be deformed, yet a good face carries it, that alone is most part respected, principally valued, and of itself able to captivate.

Glycera's too fair a face was it that set him on fire, too fine to be beheld. When Chaerea saw the singing-wench's sweet looks he was so taken that he cried out, 'O fair face, I'll never love any but her, look on any other hereafter but her; I am weary of these ordinary beauties, away with them!' The more he sees her, the worse he is; as in a burning-glass the sunbeams are re-collected to a centre, the rays of love are projected from her eyes. It was Aeneas' countenance ravished Queen Dido; he had an angelical face.

> *O sacred looks, befitting majesty,*
> *Which never mortal wight could safely see!*

Although for the greater part this beauty be most eminent in the face, yet many times those other members yield a most pleasing grace, and are alone sufficient to enamour. An high brow like unto the bright heavens, white and smooth like the polished alabaster, a pair of cheeks of vermilion colour, in which love lodgeth: love that basks all night on a maid's soft cheeks; a coral lip, a temple of kisses, in which a thousand kisses show, a thousand lurk, the most pleasant seat of the graces; a sweet-smelling flower, from which bees may gather honey: 'Ye honey-gathering bees, come to the lips of my mistress, where roses breathe.' A white and round neck, that milky way; dimple in the chin, black eyebrows, Cupid's bow, sweet breath, white and even teeth which some call the sale-piece, a fine soft round pap, gives an excellent grace, and makes a pleasant valley, between two chalky hills, sisterly little breasts, snowy companions to arouse desire at sight, 'perfect for caresses' (Ovid).

A flaxen hair: golden hair was ever in great account, for which Virgil commends Dido: 'Not yet had Proserpine clipped her golden hair ...' Apollonius will have Jason's golden hair to be the main cause of Medea's dotage on him. Castor and Pollux were both yellow-haired; Paris, Menelaus, and most amorous young men have been such in all ages, sweet and smooth, as Baptista Porta infers, lovely to behold. Homer so commends Helen, makes Patroclus and Achilles both yellow-haired; Venus fair-haired; and Cupid himself was yellow-haired, with bright golden curls, like that neat picture of Narcissus in Callistratus, for so Psyche spied him asleep; Briseis, Polyxena, etc., were all yellow-haired,

> *And Hero the fair,*
> *Whom young Apollo courted for her hair.*
>
> (MARLOWE)

Leland commends Guithera, King Arthur's wife, for a fair flaxen hair; so Paulus Aemilius sets out Clodoveus, that lovely King of France. Synesius holds every effeminate fellow or adulterer is fair-haired: and Apuleius adds that Venus herself, Goddess of Love, cannot delight, though she come accompanied with the Graces, and all Cupid's train to attend upon her, girt with her own girdle, and smell of cinnamon and balm, yet if she be bald or bad-haired she cannot please her Vulcan. Which belike makes our Venetian ladies at this day to counterfeit yellow hair so much, great women to calamistrate [use tongs] and curl it up, to adorn their heads with spangles, pearls, and made flowers; and all courtiers to affect a pleasing grace in this kind. In a word, the hairs are Cupid's nets, to catch all comers, a brushy wood, in which Cupid builds his nest, and under whose shadow all loves a thousand several ways sport themselves.

A little soft hand, pretty little mouth, small, fine long fingers—'tis that which Apollo did admire in Daphne: a straight and slender body, a small foot, and well-proportion leg hath an excellent lustre, on which the whole depends as a temple on its foundations. Clearchus vowed to his friend Amynander in Aristaenetus, that the most attractive part of his mistress, to make him love and like her first, was her pretty leg and foot; a soft and white skin, etc., have their peculiar graces; a cloud is not softer than her lovely breasts.

Though in men these parts are not so much respected; a grim Saracen sometimes, a martial hirsute face pleaseth best; a black man is a pearl in a fair woman's eye, and is as acceptable as lame Vulcan was to Venus; for he, being a sweaty fuliginous blacksmith, was dearly beloved of her, when fair Apollo, nimble Mercury were rejected, and the rest of the sweet-faced gods forsaken. Many women (as Petronius observes) fall for dirty fellows (as many men are more moved with kitchen-wenches, and a poor market-maid, than all these illustrious court and city dames), will sooner dote upon a

slave, a servant, a dirt-dauber, a Brontes, a cook, a player, if they
see his naked legs or arms, or brawny arms, etc., like that huntsman
Meleager in Philostratus, though he be all in rags, obscene and dirty,
besmeared like a ruddle-man, a gipsy, or a chimney-sweeper, than
upon a noble gallant, Nireus, Hephaestion, Alcibiades, or those
embroidered courtiers full of silk and gold. Justin's wife, a citizen of
Rome, fell in love with Pylades a player, and was ready to run mad
for him, had not Galen himself helped her by chance. Faustina the
empress doted on a fencer.

Not one of a thousand falls in love but there is some peculiar
part or other which pleaseth most, and inflames him above the rest.
A company of young philosophers on a time fell at variance which
part of a woman was most desirable and pleased best? some said of
the forehead, some the teeth, some the eyes, cheeks, lips, neck, chin,
etc.; the controversy was referred to Lais of Corinth to decide; but
she, smiling, said they were a company of fools; for suppose they had
her where they wished, what would they first seek?

Yet this notwithstanding, I do easily grant, and none, I think, will
contradict me, all parts are attractive, but especially the eyes, which
are love's fowlers; the shoeing-horns, the hooks of love (as Arandus
will), the guides, touchstone, judges, that in a moment cure madmen
and make sound folks mad, the watchmen of the body; what do they
not? how vex they not? All this is true, and (which Athenaeus and
Tatius hold) they are the chief seats of love, and as James Lernutius
hath facetely expressed in an elegant ode of his:

> *I saw Love sitting in my mistress' eyes*
> *Sparkling, believe it all posterity,*
> *And his attendants playing round about*
> *With brow and arrows ready for to fly.*

Scaliger calls the eyes Cupid's arrows, the tongue, the lightning of love; the paps, the tents: Baldassare Castiglione, the causes, the chariots, the lamps of love:

> *Eyes emulating stars in light,*
> *Enticing gods at the first sight;*

Love's orators, Petronius:

> *O sweet and pretty speaking eyes,*
> *Where Venus, love, and pleasure lies;*

Love's torches, touch-box, naphtha, and matches, Tibullus:

> *Tart Love, when he will set the gods on fire,*
> *Lightens the eyes as torches to desire.*

Leander, at the first sight of Hero's eyes, was incensed, saith Musaeus:

> *Love's torches 'gan to burn first in her eyes,*
> *And set his heart on fire which never dies:*
> *For the fair beauty of a virgin pure*
> *Is sharper than a dart, and doth inure*
> *A deeper wound, which pierceth to the heart*
> *By the eyes, and causeth such a cruel smart.*

Jacob Cornelius brings in Amnon complaining of Tamar:

> *It was thy beauty, 'twas thy pleasing smile,*
> *Thy grace and comeliness did me beguile;*

> *Thy rose-like cheeks and unto purple fair,*
> *Thy lovely eyes and golden knotted hair.*

Philostratus Lemnius cries out on his mistress's basilisk eyes, those two burning glasses, they had so inflamed his soul, that no water could quench it. What a tyranny (saith he) what a penetration of bodies is this! thou drawest with violence, and swallowest me up, as Charybdis doth sailors, with thy rocky eyes: he that falls into this gulf of love can never get out. Let this be the corollary then, the strongest beams of beauty are still darted from the eyes.

> *For who such eyes with his can see,*
> *And not forthwith enamoured be!*

And as men catch dotterels by putting out a leg or an arm, with those mutual glances of the eyes they first inveigle one another. Of all eyes (by the way) black are most amiable, enticing and fairest, which the poet observes in commending of his mistress, notable for wonderful black eyes and black hair, which Hesiod admires in his Alcmena,

> *From her black eyes, and from her golden face,*
> *As if from Venus came a lovely grace*

and Triton in his Milane; 'my black-eyed maid is beautiful.' Homer useth that epithet of ox-eyed in describing Juno, because a round black eye is the best, the sun of beauty, and farthest from black the worse; which Polydore Virgil taxeth in our nation: we have grey eyes for the most part. Baptista Porta puts grey colour upon children, they be childish eyes, dully and heavy. Many commend on the other side Spanish ladies, and those Greek dames at this day, for the blackness of their eyes, as Porta doth his Neapolitan young wives. Suetonius describes Julius Caesar to have been of a black, quick, sparkling eye: and although Averroes will have such persons timorous, yet without question they are most amorous.

Now, last of all, I will show you by what means beauty doth fascinate, bewitch, as some hold, and work upon the soul of a man by the eye. For certainly I am of the poet's mind, love doth bewitch and strangely change us.

> *Love mocks our senses, curbs our liberties,*
> *And doth bewitch us with his art and rings,*
> *I think some devil gets into our entrails,*
> *And kindles coals, and heaves our souls from th'hinges.*

Heliodorus proves at large that love is witchcraft: it gets in at our eyes, pores, nostrils, engenders the same qualities and affections in us as were in the party whence it came. The manner of the fascination, as Ficinus declares it, is thus: Mortal men are then especially bewitched, whenas by often gazing one on the other they direct sight to sight, join eye to eye, and so drink and suck in love between them; for the beginning of this disease is the eye. And therefore he that hath a clear eye, though he be otherwise deformed, by often looking upon him, will make one mad, and tie him fast to him by the eye. Leonard Variuse telleth us that by this interview the purer spirits are infected, the one eye pierceth through the other with his rays, which he sends forth, and many men have those excellent piercing eyes, that, which Suetonius relates of Augustus, their brightness is such, they compel their spectators to look off, and can no more endure them than the sunbeams. Baradius reports as much of our Saviour Christ, and Peter Morales of the Virgin Mary, whom Nicephorus describes likewise to have been yellow-haired, of a wheat colour, but of a most amiable and piercing eye.

The rays, as some think, sent from the eyes, carry certain spiritual vapours with them, and so infect the other party, and that in a moment. I know they that hold sight comes from the images will make a doubt of this; but Ficinus proves it from blear-eyes, that by sight alone make others blear-eyed; and it is more than manifest that the vapour of the corrupt blood doth get in together with the rays, and so by the contagion the spectator's eyes are infected. Other arguments there are of a basilisk, that kills afar off by sight, as that Ephesian did of whom Philostratus speaks, of so pernicious an eye, he poisoned all he looked steadily on: and that other argument, of menstruous women, out of Aristotle's Problems; diseased, Capivaccius adds, and Septalius the Commentator, that contaminate a looking-glass with beholding it. So the beams that come from the agent's heart, by the eyes, infect the spirits about the patients, inwardly wound, and thence the spirits infect the blood. To this effect she complained in Apuleius, 'Thou are the cause of my grief; thy eyes, piercing through mine eyes to mine inner parts, have set my bowels on fire, and therefore pity me that am now ready to die for thy sake.'

Ficinus illustrates this with a familiar example of that Marrhusian Phaedrus and Theban Lycias: 'Lycias he stares on Phaedrus' face, and Phaedrus fastens the balls of his eyes upon Lycias, and with those sparkling rays sends out his spirits. The beams of Phaedrus' eyes are easily mingled with the beams of Lycias', and spirits are joined to spirits. This vapour, begot in Phaedrus' heart, enters into Lycias' bowels: and that which is a greater wonder, Phaedrus' blood is in Lycias' heart, and thence come those ordinary love-speeches, My sweetheart Phaedrus! and mine own self, my dear bowels! And Phaedrus again to Lycias, O my light, my joy, my soul, my life! Phaedrus follows Lycias because his heart would have his spirits; and Lycias follows Phaedrus, because he loves the seat of his spirits; both follow, but Lycias the earnester of the two: the river hath more need of the fountain than the fountain of the river; as iron is drawn to that which is touched with a loadstone, but draws not it again, so Lycias draws Phaedrus.'

But how comes it to pass, then, that a blind man loves, that never saw? We read, in the Lives of the Fathers, a story of a child that was brought up in the wilderness, from his infancy, by an old hermit: now come to man's estate, he saw by chance two comely women wandering in the woods: he asked the old man what creatures they were, he told him fairies; after a while, talking casually, the hermit demanded of him, which was the pleasantest sight that ever he saw in his life? He readily replied, the two fairies he spied in the wilderness. So that, without doubt, there is some secret loadstone in a beautiful woman, a magnetic power, a natural inbred affection, which moves our concupiscence; and, as he sings,

> *Methinks I have a mistress yet to come,*
> *And still I seek, I love, I know not whom.*

'Tis true indeed of natural and chaste love, but not of this heroical passion, or rather brutish burning lust of which we treat; we speak of wandering, wanton, adulterous eyes, which, as Castiglione saith, lie still in wait as so many soldiers, and when they spy an innocent spectator fixed on them, shoot him through, and presently bewitch him: especially when they shall gaze and gloat, as wanton lovers do one upon another, and with a pleasant eye-conflict participate each other's souls.

Hence you may perceive how easily and how quickly we may be taken in love; since at the twinkling of an eye, Phaedrus' spirits may so perniciously infect Lycias' blood. Neither is it any wonder, if we but consider how many other diseases closely, and as suddenly, are caught by infection, plague, itch, scabs, flux, etc. The spirits, taken in, will not let him rest that hath received them, but egg him on; 'the mind seeks the body whence came its love-wound'; and we may manifestly perceive a strange education of spirits, by such as bleed at nose after they be dead, at the presence of the murderer.

X

Artificial Allurements of Love,
Causes and Provocations to Lust,
Gestures, Clothes, Dower, etc.

ATURAL BEAUTY is a stronger loadstone of itself, as you have heard, a great temptation, and pierceth to the very heart; but much more when those artificial enticements and provocations of gestures, clothes, jewels, pigments, exornations, shall be annexed unto it; those other circumstances, opportunity of time and place, shall concur, which of themselves alone were all-sufficient, each one in particular, to produce this effect. It is a question much controverted by some wise men, whether natural or artificial objects be more powerful; but not decided: for my part, I am of opinion that, though beauty itself be a great motive, and give an excellent lustre in beggary, as a jewel on a dunghill will shine and cast his rays, it cannot be suppressed, which Heliodorus feigns of Chariclea, though she were in beggar's weeds: yet, as it is used, artificial is of more force, and much to be preferred.

> *So toothless Aegle seems a pretty one,*
> *Set out with new-bought teeth of Indy bone:*
> *So foul Lycoris blacker than berry*
> *Herself admires, now finer than cherry.*

(MARTIAL)

John Lerius the Burgundian is altogether on my side. For whereas (saith he) at our coming to Brazil, we found both men and women naked as they were born, without any covering, so much as of their privities, and could not be persuaded, by our Frenchmen that lived a year with them, to wear any, many will think that our so long commerce with naked women must needs be a great provocation to lust; but he concludes otherwise, that their nakedness did much less entice them to lasciviousness than our women's clothes. And I dare boldly affirm (saith he) that those glittering attires, counterfeit colours, headgears, curled hairs, plaited coats, cloaks, gowns, costly stomachers, guarded and loose garments, and all those other accoutrements wherewith our countrywomen counterfeit a beauty, and so curiously set out themselves, cause more inconvenience in this kind than that barbarian homeliness, although they be no whit inferior unto them in beauty. I could evince the truth of this by many other arguments, but I appeal (saith he) to my companions at that present, which were all of the same mind.

His countryman Montaigne, in his Essays, is of the same opinion, and so are many others; out of whose assertions thus much in brief we may conclude, that beauty is more beholding to art than nature, and stronger provocations proceed from outward ornaments than such as nature hath provided. It is true that those fair sparkling eyes, white neck, coral lips, turgent paps, rose-coloured cheeks, etc., of themselves are potent enticers; but when a comely, artificial, well-composed look, pleasing gesture, an affected carriage shall be added, it must needs be far more forcible than it was, when those curious needleworks, variety of colours, purest dyes, jewels, spangles, pendants, lawn, lace, tiffanies, fair and fine linen, embroideries, calamistrations, ointments, etc., shall be added, they will make the veriest dowdy otherwise a goddess, when nature shall be furthered by art.

For it is not the eye of itself that enticeth to lust, but an adulterous eye, as Peter terms it (2, ii, 14), a wanton, a rolling, lascivious eye: a wandering eye, which Isaiah taxeth (iii, 16). Christ Himself and the

Virgin Mary had most beautiful eyes, as amiable eyes as any persons, saith Baradius, that ever lived, but withal so modest, so chaste, that whosoever looked on them was freed from that passion of burning lust; if we may believe Gerson and Bonaventure, there was no such antidote against it as the Virgin Mary's face; 'tis not the eye, but carriage of it, as they use it, that causeth such effects. When Pallas, Juno, Venus, were to win Paris' favour for the golden apple, as it is elegantly described in that pleasant interlude of Apuleius, Juno came with majesty upon the stage, Minerva with gravity, but Venus smiling with her gracious graces and exquisite music, as if she had danced, and which was the main matter of all, she danced with her rolling eyes: they were the brokers and harbingers of her suit. So she makes her brags in a modern poet [Daniel]:

> *Soon could I make my brow to tyrannize,*
> *And force the world do homage to mine eyes.*

The eye is a secret orator, the first bawd, the gate of love, and with private looks, winking, glances, and smiles, as so many dialogues, they make up the match many times, and understand one another's meanings before they come to speak a word.

Euryalus and Lucretia were so mutually enamoured by the eye, and prepared to give each other entertainment, before ever they had conference: he asked her good will with his eyes; she met him half-way and gave consent with a pleasant look. That Thracian Rhodopis was so excellent at this dumb rhetoric, that if she had but looked upon anyone almost (saith Calasiris) she would have bewitched him, and he could not possibly escape it. For, as Salvianus observes, the eyes are the windows of our souls, by which as so many channels all dishonest concupiscence gets into our hearts. They reveal our thoughts, and as they say, the face is the index to the mind, but the eye of the countenance: 'Why do you look at me with wanton eyes?' [Buchanan].

I may say the same of smiling, gait, nakedness of parts, plausible gestures, etc. To laugh is the proper passion of a man, an ordinary thing to smile; but those counterfeit, composed, affected, artificial, and reciprocal, those counter-smiles are the dumb-shows and prognostics of greater matters, which they most part use to inveigle and deceive; though many fond lovers again are so frequently mistaken, and led into a fool's paradise. For if they see but a fair maid laugh, or show a pleasant countenance, use some gracious words or gestures, they apply it all to themselves, as done in their favour; sure she loves them, she is willing, coming, etc.

> *When a fool sees a fair maid for to smile,*
> *He thinks she loves him, 'tis but to beguile.*

They make an art of it, as Ovid telleth us:

> *Who can believe? to laugh maids make an art,*
> *And seek a pleasant grace to that same part.*

And 'tis as great an enticement as any of the rest: She makes thine heart leap with a pleasing gentle smile of hers. 'I love Lalage as much for smiling as for discoursing,' saith Horace; as the lover said in Petronius of his mistress, being well pleased, she gave so sweet a smile. It won Ismenias, as he confesseth: 'Ismene smiled so lovingly the second time I saw her, that I could not choose but admire her'; and Galia's sweet smile quite overcame Faustus the shepherd; 'as she caught sight of me, she smiled sweetly.' All other gestures of the body will enforce as much. Daphnis in Lucian was 'a poor tattered wench when I knew her first,' said Crobyle, 'but now she is a stately piece indeed, hath her maids so attend her, brave attires, money in her purse, etc.; and will you know how this came to pass? by setting out herself after the best fashion, by her pleasant carriage, affability, sweet smiling upon all,' etc.

Many women dote upon a man for his compliment only, and good behaviour, they are won in an instant; too credulous to believe that every light, wanton suitor who sees or makes love to them is instantly enamoured, he certainly dotes on, admires them, will surely marry, whenas he means nothing less, 'tis his ordinary carriage in all such companies. So both delude each other by such outward shows; and among the rest, an upright, a comely grace, courtesies, gentle salutations, cringes, a mincing gait, a decent and an affected pace, are most powerful enticers, and which the prophet Isaiah, a courtier himself, and a great observer, objected to the daughters of Zion (iii, 16), 'they minced as they went, and made a tinkling with their feet', to say the truth, what can they not effect by such means?

> *She sets you all afire with her voice,*
> *Her hand, her walk, her breast, her face, her eyes.*

When art shall be annexed to beauty, when wiles and guiles shall concur; for to speak as it is, love is a kind of legerdemain; mere juggling, a fascination. When they show their fair hand, fine foot and leg withal, saith Baldassare Castiglione, they set us a-longing, and so when they pull up their petticoats and outward garments, as usually they do to show their fine stockings, and those of purest silken dye, gold fringes, laces, embroiderings (it shall go hard, but when they go to church, or to any other place, all shall be seen), 'tis but a springe to catch woodcocks; and as Chrysostom telleth them downright, though they say nothing with their mouths, they speak in their gait, they speak with their eyes, they speak in the carriage of their bodies. And what shall we say otherwise of that baring of their necks, shoulders, naked breasts, arms, and wrists? to what end are they but only to tempt men to lust?

> *Pray, why display those milk-white breasts and paps*
> *Without the modesty-piece? 'Tis but to say,*
> *'Ask me, and I surrender.' 'Tis but to*
> *Invite your lovers to the field of love.*
>
> (JOVIANUS PONTANUS)

There needs no more, as Fredericus Matenesius well observes, but a crier to go before them so dressed, to bid us look out, a trumpet to sound, or for defect a sow-gelder to blow:

> *Look out, look out and see*
> *What object this may be*
> *That doth perstringe mine eye;*
> *A gallant lady goes*
> *In rich and gaudy clothes,*
> *But whither away God knows,*

or to what end and purpose? But to leave all these phantastical raptures, I'll prosecute my intended theme.

Nakedness, as I have said, is an odious thing of itself, a cure for love; yet it may be so used, in part, and at set times, that there can be no such enticement as it is:

> *Neither Diana draped nor naked Venus pleases me,*
> *One is too voluptuous, the other not at all.*

David so espied Bathsheba, the elders Susanna: Apelles was enamoured with Campaspe, when he was to paint her naked. Tiberius supped with Sestius Gallus, an old lecher, provided that naked girls waited on them; some say as much of Nero, and Pontus Heuter of Carolus Pugnax. Among the Babylonians, it was the custom of some lascivious queans to dance frisking in that fashion, saith Curtius, and Sardus writes of others to that effect. The Tuscans at some set banquets had naked women to attend upon them, which Leonicus confirms of such other bawdy nations. Nera would have filthy pictures still hanging in his chamber, which is too commonly used in our times, and Heliogabalus, to excite himself, had others performing in his presence. So things may be abused. A servant-maid in Aristaenetus spied her master and mistress through the key-hole merrily disposed; upon the sight she fell in love with her master. Antoninus Caracalla observed his mother-in-law with her breasts amorously laid open; he was so much moved, that he said, 'O that I might!' which she by chance overhearing, replied as impudently, 'Thou mayst do what thou wilt': and upon that temptation he married her: this object was not in cause, not the thing itself, but that unseemly, undecent carriage of it.

When you have all done, the greatest provocations of lust are from apparel; God makes, they say, man shapes, and there is no motive like unto it,

> *Which doth even beauty beautify,*
> *And most bewitch a wretched eye.*

(SIDNEY)

A filthy knave, a deformed quean, a crooked carcass, a maukin, a witch, a rotten post, an hedge-stake may be set out and tricked up that it shall make as fair a show, as much enamour, as the rest; many a silly fellow is so taken. The first snare of lust, one calls it; Bossus, a snare of souls, a fatal reed; the greatest bawd; and with tears of blood to be deplored, saith Matenesius. Not that comeliness of clothes is therefore to be condemned, and those usual ornaments: there is a decency and decorum in this as well as in other things, fit to be used, becoming several persons, and befitting their estates; he is only phantastical that is not in fashion, and like an old image in arras hangings, when a manner of attire is generally received; but when they are so new-fangled, so unstaid, so prodigious in their attires, beyond their names and fortunes, unbefitting their age, place, quality, condition, what should we otherwise think of them? Why do they adorn themselves with so many colours of herbs, fictitious flowers, curious needleworks, quaint devices, sweet-smelling odours, with those inestimable riches of precious stones, pearls, rubies, diamonds, emeralds, etc.? Why do they crown themselves with gold and silver, use coronets and tires of several fashions, deck themselves with pendants, bracelets, earrings, chains, girdles, rings, pins, spangles, embroideries, shadows, rabatoes, versicolour ribands? Why do they make such glorious shows with their scarfs, feathers, fans, masks, furs, laces, tiffanies, ruffs, falls, cauls, cuffs, damasks, velvets, tinsels, cloth of gold, silver tissue? with colours of heavens, stars, planets? the strength of metals, stones, odours, flowers, birds, beasts, fishes, and whatsoever Africa, Asia, America, sea, land, art and industry of man can afford? Why do they use and covet such novelty of inventions, such new-fangled tires, and spend such inestimable sums on them? To what end are those crisped, false hairs, painted faces, as Petronius observes, such a composed gait, not a step awry? Why are they like so many Sybarites, or Nero's Poppaea, Ahasuerus' concubines, so costly, so long a-dressing as Caesar was marshalling his army, or an hawk in pruning? A gardener takes not so much delight and pains in his garden, a horseman to dress his horse, scour his armour, a mariner about his ship, a merchant his shop and shop-book, as they do about their faces, and all those other parts: such setting up with corks, straitening with whalebones; why is it but, as a day-net catcheth larks, to make young men stoop unto them? Philocharus, a gallant in Aristaenetus, advised his friend Polyaenus to take heed of such enticements, for it was the sweet sound and motion of his mistress's spangles and bracelets, the smell of her ointments, that captivated him first.

To what use, saith Lucian, are pins, pots, glasses, ointments, irons, combs, bodkins, setting-sticks? why bestow they all their patrimonies and husbands' yearly revenues on such fooleries? Why, asks Seneca, use they dragons, wasps, snakes, for chains, enamelled jewels on their necks, ears? They had more need some of them be tied in Bedlam with iron chains, have a whip for a fan, and hair-cloths next to their skins, and instead of wrought smocks, have their cheeks stigmatized with a hot iron, I say, some of our Jezebels, instead of painting, if they were well served. But why is all this labour, all this cost, preparation, riding, running, far-fetched and dear-bought stuff? Because forsooth they would be fair and fine, and where nature is defective, supply it by art, saith Castiglione; and to that purpose they anoint and paint their faces, to make Helen of Hecuba, a misshapen dwarf, into a Europa. To this intent they crush in their feet and bodies, hurt and crucify themselves, sometimes in lax clothes, an hundred yards I think in a gown, a sleeve; and sometimes again so close to show their naked shape. Now long tails and trains, and then short, up, down, high, low, thick, thin, etc.; now little or no bands, then as big as cartwheels; now loose bodies, then great fardingales and closegirt, etc. Why is all this, but with the whore in the Proverbs, to intoxicate some or other? One therefore calls it the trap of lust, and sure token, as an ivy-bush is to a tavern.

O Glycere, in that you paint so much,
Your hair is so bedeckt in order such,
With rings on fingers, bracelets in your ear,
Although no prophet, tell I can, I fear.

To be admired, to be gazed on, to circumvent some novice; as many times they do, that instead of a lady he loves a cap and a feather, instead of a maid that should have a natural colour, a plump and juicy body (as Chaerea describes his mistress in Terence), a painted face, a ruff-band, fair and fine linen, a coronet, a flower, a wrought waistcoat he dotes on, or a pied petticoat, a pure dye instead of a proper woman. For generally, as with rich-furred conies, their cases are far better than their bodies, and like the bark of a cinnamon tree which is dearer than the whole bulk, their outward accoutrements are far more precious than their inward endowments. 'Tis too commonly so:

With gold and jewels all is covered,
And with a strange tire we are won
(While she's the least part of herself),
And with such baubles quite undone.

(OVID)

Why do they keep in so long together, a whole winter sometimes, and will not be seen but by torch- or candlelight, and come abroad with all the preparation may be, when they have no business, but only to show themselves?

For what is beauty if it be not seen,
Or what is't to be seen if not admir'd,
And though admir'd, unless in love desir'd?

(DANIEL)

Why do they go with such counterfeit gait, which Philo Judaeus reprehends them for, and use (I say it again) such gestures, apish, ridiculous, indecent attires, sybaritical tricks, etc., use those sweet perfumes, powders, and ointments in public, flock to hear sermons so frequent? is it for devotion? or rather, as Basil tells them, to meet their sweethearts, and see fashions; for, as he saith, commonly they come so provided to that place, with such curious compliments, with such gestures and tires, as if they should go to a dancing-school, a stage-play, or bawdy-house, fitter than a church.

> *When such a she-priest comes her mass to say,*
> *Twenty to one they all forget to pray.*
>
> (DRAYTON)

They make those holy temples, consecrated to godly martyrs and religious uses, the shops of impudence, dens of whores and thieves, and little better than brothel-houses. When we shall see these things daily done, their husbands bankrupts, if not cornutos, their wives light housewives, daughters dishonest, and hear of such dissolute acts, as daily we do, how should we think otherwise? what is their end, but to deceive and inveigle young men? As tow takes fire, such enticing objects produce their effect, how can it be altered? When Venus stood before Anchises (as Homer feigns in one of his hymns) in her costly robes he was instantly taken:

> *When Venus stood before Anchises first,*
> *He was amaz'd to see her in her tires;*
> *For she had on a hood as red as fire,*
> *And glittering chains, and ivy-twisted spires,*
> *About her tender neck were costly brooches,*
> *And necklaces of gold, enamell'd ouches.*

So when Medea came in presence of Jason first, attended by her nymphs and ladies, as she is described by Apollonius

> *A lustre followed them like flaming fire,*
> *And from their golden borders came such beams,*
> *Which in his eyes provok'd sweet desire.*

Such a relation we have in Plutarch, when the queens came and offered themselves to Antony, with divers presents, and enticing ornaments, Asiatic allurements, with such wonderful joy and festivity, they did so inveigle the Romans, that no man could contain himself, all was turned to delight and pleasure. The women transformed themselves to Bacchus shapes, the men-children to satyrs and Pans; but Antony himself was quite besotted with Cleopatra's sweet speeches, philters, beauty, pleasing tires: for when she sailed along the River Cydnus, with such incredible pomp in a gilded ship, herself dressed like Venus, her maids like the Graces, her pages like so many Cupids, Antony was amazed, and rapt beyond himself.

Heliodorus brings in Damaeneta, stepmother to Cnemon, whom she saw in his scarfs, rings, robes, and coronet, quite mad for the love of him. It was Judith's pantofles that ravished the eyes of Holofernes. And Cardan is not ashamed to confess that, seeing his wife the first time all in white, he did admire and instantly love her. If these outward ornaments were not of such force, why doth Naomi give Ruth counsel how to please Boaz? And Judith, seeking to captivate Holofernes, washed and anointed herself with sweet ointments, dressed her hair, and put on costly attires.

The riot in this kind hath been excessive in times past; no man almost came broad, but curled and anointed: one spent as much as two funerals at once; and with his grey hairs perfumed with roses and Assyrian nard. What strange things doth Suetonius relate in this matter of Caligula's riot! And Pliny. Read more in Dioscorides, Ulmus, Arnoldus, Rondoletius, for it is now an art, as it was of old (so Seneca records). Women are bad and men worse, no difference at all between their and our times. Good manners (as Seneca complains) are extinct with wantonness, in tricking up themselves men go beyond women, they wear harlot's colours, and do not walk, but jet and dance, mannish woman, womanish man, more like players, butterflies, baboons, apes, antics, than men. So ridiculous, moreover, we are in our attires, and for cost so excessive, that, as Jerome said of old, 'tis an ordinary thing to put a thousand oaks and an hundred oxen into a suit of apparel, to wear a whole manor on his back. What with shoe-ties, hangers, points, caps and feathers, scarfs, bands, cuffs, etc., in a short space their whole patrimonies are consumed.

Heliogabalus is taxed by Lampridius, and admired in his age, for wearing jewels in his shoes, a common thing in our times, not for emperors and princes, but almost for serving-men and tailors; all the flowers, stars, constellations, gold, and precious stones do condescend to set out their shoes. To repress the luxury of those Roman matrons, there was the Law Valerian and Oppian, and a Cato to contradict; but no laws will serve to repress the pride and insolency of our days, the prodigious riot in this kind. Lucullus' wardrobe is put down by our ordinary citizens; and a cobbler's wife in Venice, a courtesan in Florence, is no whit inferior to a queen, if our geographers say true: and why is all this? Why do they glory in their jewels (as Bossus saith) or exult and triumph in the beauty of clothes? why is all this cost? to incite men the sooner to burning lust. They pretend decency and ornament; but let them take heed, lest while they set out their bodies they do not damn their souls; 'tis Bernard's counsel: shine in jewels, stink in conditions, have purple robes, and a torn conscience.

Let them take heed of Isaiah's prophecy, that their slippers and attires be not taken from them, their sweet balls, bracelets, ear-rings, veils, wimples, crisping-pins, glasses, fine linen, hoods, lawns, and sweet savours, they become not bald, burnt, and stink upon a sudden. And let maids beware, as Cyprian adviseth, lest, while they wander too closely abroad, they loose not their virginities, and, like Egyptian temples, seem fair without, but prove rotten carcasses within. How much better were it for them to follow that good counsel of Tertullian! to have their eyes painted with chastity, the Word of God inserted into their ears, Christ's yoke tied to the hair, to subject themselves to their husbands. If they would do so, they should be comely enough, clothe themselves with the silk of sanctity, damask of devotion, purple of piety and chastity, and so painted, they shall have God Himself to be a suitor. Let whores and queans prank up themselves, let them paint their faces with minium and ceruse, they are but fuels of lust, and signs of a corrupt soul: if ye be good, honest, virtuous, and religious matrons, let sobriety, modesty, and chastity be your honour, and God Himself your love and desire. A woman smells best, saith Plantus, when she hath no perfume at all; no crown, chain, or jewel (Guevara adds) is such an ornament to a virgin or virtuous woman as chastity is: more credit in a wise man's eye and judgement they get by their plainness, and seem fairer than they that are set out with baubles, as a butcher's meat is with pricks, puffed up, and adorned like so many jays with variety of colours.

It is reported of Cornelia, that virtuous Roman lady, great Scipio's daughter, Titus Sempronius' wife, and the mother of the Gracchi, that being by chance in company with a companion, a strange gentlewoman (some light housewife belike, that was dressed like a May-lady, and, as most of our gentlewomen are) was more solicitous of her head-tire than of her health, that spent her time betwixt a comb and a glass, and had rather be fair than honest, as Cato said, and have the commonwealth turned topsy-turvy than her tires marred; and she did naught but brag of her fine robes and jewels, and provoked the Roman matron to show hers: Cornelia kept her in talk till her children came from school; 'And these,' said she, 'are my jewels,' and so deluded and put off a proud, vain, phantastical housewife. How much better were it for our matrons to do as she did, to go civilly and decently, to use gold as it is gold, and for that use it serves, and when they need it, than to consume it in riot, beggar their husbands, prostitute themselves, inveigle others, and peradventure damn their own souls! How much more would it be for their honour and credit! Thus doing, as Jerome said of Blaesilla, Furius did not so triumph over the Gauls, Papirius of the Samnites, Scipio of Numantia, as she did by her temperance; always soberly attired, etc., they should insult and domineer over lust, folly, vainglory, all such inordinate, furious, and unruly passions.

But I am over-tedious, I confess, and while I stand gaping after fine clothes, there is another great allurement (in the world's eye at least) which had like to have stolen out of sight, and that is money; Love's arrows come from her dowry, money makes the match; 'tis like sauce to their meat, a good dowry with a wife. Many men, if they do hear but of a great portion, a rich heir, are more mad than if they had all the beauteous ornaments and those good parts art and nature can afford; they care not for honesty, bringing up, birth, beauty, person, but for money.

> *Our dogs and horses still from the best breed*
> *We carefully seek, and well may they speed:*
> *But for our wives, so they prove wealthy,*
> *Fair or foul, we care not what they be.*

(THEOGNIS)

If she be rich, then she is fair, fine, absolute, and perfect, then they burn like fire, they love her dearly, like pig and pie, and are ready to hang themselves if they may not have her.

Nothing so familiar in these days as for a young man to marry an old wife, as they say, for a piece of good: an ass laden with gold; and though she may be an old crone, and have never a tooth in her head, neither good conditions nor good face, a natural fool, but only rich, she shall have twenty young gallants to be suitors in an instant. As she said in Suetonius, 'tis not for her sake, but for her lands or money; and an excellent match it were (as he added) if she were away. So, on the other side, many a young lovely maid will cast away herself upon an old, doting, decrepit dizzard, that is rheumatic and gouty, hath some twenty diseases, perhaps but one eye, one leg, never a nose, no hair on his head, wit in his brains, nor honesty, if he have land or money, she will have him before all other suitors. If he be rich, he is the man, a fine man, and a proper man, she will go to Jacaktres or Tidore with him; Gelasimus de Monte Aureo, Sir Giles Goosecap, Sir Amorous La-Foole, shall have her. And as Philematium in Aristaenetus told Eumusus, hang him that hath no money, 'tis to no purpose to talk of marriage without means, trouble me not with such notions; let others do as they will, I'll be sure to have one shall maintain me fine and brave. Most are of her mind; for his conditions, she shall inquire after them another time, or when all is done, the match made, and everybody gone home. Lucian's Lycia was a proper young maid, and had many fine gentlemen to her suitors: Ethecles, a senator's son, Melissus, a merchant, etc.; but she forsook them all for one Passius, a base, hirsute, bald-pated knave; but why was it? His father lately died and left him sole heir of his goods and lands.

This is not among your dust-worms alone, poor snakes that will prostitute their souls for money, but with this bait you may catch our most potent, puissant, and illustrious princes. That proud upstart domineering Bishop of Ely, in the time of Richard the First, viceroy in his absence, as Nubrigensis relates it, to fortify himself and maintain his greatness, married his poor kinswomen which came forth of Normandy by droves, to the chiefest nobles of the land, and they were glad to accept of such matches, fair or foul, for themselves, their sons, nephews, etc. Who would not have done as much for money and preferment? as mine author adds. Vortigern, King of Britain, married Rowena the daughter of Hengist the Saxon prince, his mortal enemy; but wherefore? she had Kent for her dowry. Iagello, the great Duke of Lithuania, 1386, was mightily enamoured on Hedenga, insomuch that he turned Christian from a Pagan, and was baptized himself by the name of Uladislaus, and all his subjects for her sake; but why was it? she was daughter and heir of Poland, and his desire was to have both kingdoms incorporated into one. Charles the Great was an earnest suitor to Irene the Empress, but, saith Zonaras, to annex the empire of the East to that of the West.

Yet what is the event of all such matches, that are so made for money, goods, by deceit, or for burning lust, what follows? they are almost mad at first, but 'tis a mere flash; as chaff and straw soon fired, burn vehemently for a while, yet out in a moment, so are all such matches made by those allurements of burning lust; where there is no respect of honesty, parentage, virtue, religion, education, and the like, they are extinguished in an instant, and instead of love comes hate; for joy, repentance, and desperation itself. Franciscus Barbarus hath a story of one Philip of Padua that fell in love with a common whore, and was now ready to run mad for her; his father, having no more sons, let him enjoy her; but after a few days, the young man began to loathe, could not so much as endure the sight of her, and from one madness fell into another. Such event commonly have all these lovers; and he that so marries, or for such respects, let them look for no better success than Menelaus had with Helen, Vulcan with Venus, Theseus with Phaedra, Minos with Pasiphae, and Claudius with Messalina: shame, sorrow, misery, melancholy, discontent.

XI

Importunity and Opportunity of Time,
Place, Conference, Discourse, Singing,
Dancing, Music, Amorous Tales, Objects,
Kissing, Familiarity, Tokens, Presents,
Bribes, Promises, Protestations, Tears, etc.

ALL THESE ALLUREMENTS hitherto are afar off, and at a distance; I will come nearer to those other degrees of love, which are conference, kissing, dalliance, discourse, singing, dancing, amorous tales, objects, presents, etc., which as so many sirens steal away the hearts of men and women. For, as Tatius observes, it is no sufficient trial of a maid's affection by her eyes alone, but you must say something that shall be more available, and use such other forcible engines; therefore take her by the hand, wring her fingers hard, and sigh withal; if she accept this in good part, and seem not to be much averse, then call her mistress, take her about the neck and kiss her, etc.

But this cannot be done except they first get opportunity of living or coming together, ingress, egress, and regress; letters and commendations may do much, outward gestures and actions; but when they come to live near one another, in the same street, village, or together in a house, love is kindled on a sudden. Many a serving-man by reason of this opportunity and importunity inveigles his master's daughter, many a gallant loves a dowdy, many a gentleman runs upon his wife's maids, many ladies dote upon their serving-men, as the queen in Ariosto did upon the dwarf, many matches are so made in haste, and they are compelled as it were by necessity so to love, which, had they been free, come in company of others, seen that variety which many places afford, or compared them to a third, would never have looked one upon another. Or had not that opportunity of discourse and familiarity been offered, they would have loathed and contemned those whom, for want of better choice and other objects, they are fatally driven on, and by reason of their hot blood, idle life, full diet, etc., are forced to dote upon them that come next. And many times those which at the first sight cannot fancy or affect each other, but are harsh and ready to disagree, offended with each other's carriage, like Benedick and Beatrice in the comedy [Shakespeare's *Much Ado*], and in whom they find many faults, by this living together in a house, conference, kissing, colling, and such-like allurements, begin at last to dote insensibly one upon another.

It was the greatest motive that Potiphar's wife had to dote upon Joseph, and Clitiphon upon Leucippe his uncle's daughter, because the plague being at Byzance, it was his fortune for a time to sojourn with her, to sit next her at the table, as he telleth the tale himself in Tatius (which, though it be but a fiction, is grounded upon good observation, and doth well express the passions of lovers), he had opportunity to take her by the hand, and after a while to kiss, and handle her paps, etc., which made him almost mad.

Ismenias the orator makes the like confession in Eustathius, when he came first to Sosthenes' house, and sat at table with Cratisthenes his friend. Ismene, Sosthenes' daughter, waiting on them with her breasts open, arms half bare, after the Greek fashion in those times, as Daphne was when she fled from Phoebus (which moved him much), was ever ready to give attendance on him, to fill him drink, her eyes were never off him, those speaking eyes, courting eyes, enchanting eyes; but she was still smiling on him, and when they were risen, that she had gotten a little opportunity, she came and drank to him, and withal trod upon his toes, and would come and go, and when she could not speak for the company, she would wring his hand, and blush when she met him: and by this means first she overcame him; she would kiss the cup and drink to him, and smile and drink where he drank on that side of the cup, by which mutual compressions, kissings, wringing of hands, treading of feet, etc., 'I sipt and sipt, and sipt so long, till at length I was drunk in love upon a sudden.' Philochorus, in Aristaenetus, met a fair maid by chance, a mere stranger to him; he looked back at her, she looked back at him again, and smiled withal. It was the sole cause of his farther acquaintance, and love that undid him.

This opportunity of time and place, with their circumstances, are so forcible motives, that it is unpossible almost for two young folks equal in years to live together and not be in love, especially in great houses, princes' courts, where they are idle, fare well, live at ease, and cannot tell otherwise how to spend their time: there, saith Ovid, Hippolytus will be as lewd as Priapus. Achilles was sent by his mother Thetis to the island of Scyros in the Aegean Sea (where Lycomedes then reigned) in his nonage to be brought up, to avoid that hard destiny of the oracle (he should be slain at the siege of Troy): and for that cause was nurtured in the women's apartment, among the king's children in a woman's habit; but see the event: he compressed Deidamia, the king's fair daughter, and had a fine son, called Pyrrhus, by her.

Peter Abelard the philosopher, as he tells the tale himself, being set by Fulbert her uncle to teach Heloise his lovely niece, and to that purpose sojourned in his house, and had committed a tender lamb to a hungry wolf (I use his own words); he soon got her good will, there was more kissing than philosophizing, and he read more of love than any other lecture; such pretty feats can opportunity plea. But when, as I say, youth, wine, and night shall concur, 'tis a wonder they be not all plunged over head and ears in love; for youth is a very combustible matter, naphtha itself, the fuel of love's fire, and most apt to kindle it. If there be seven servants in an ordinary house, you shall have three couple in some good liking at least, and among idle persons how should it be otherwise? 'Living at Rome,' saith Aretine's Lucretia, 'in the flower of my fortunes, rich, fair, young, and so well brought up, my conversation, age, beauty, fortune, made all the world admire and love me.'

Night alone, that one occasion, is enough to set all on fire, and they are so cunning in great houses that they make their best advantage of it. Many a gentlewoman, that is guilty to herself of her imperfections, paintings, impostures, will not willingly be seen by day, but as Castiglione noteth, in the night; she hateth the day like a dormouse, and above all things loves torches and candlelight, and if she must come abroad in the day, she covets, as in a mercer's shop, a very obfuscate and obscure light. And good reason she hath for it: blemishes are not seen at night, and many an amorous gull is fetched over by that means. Gomesius gives instance in a Florentine gentleman, that was so deceived with a wife; she was so radiantly set with rings and jewels, lawns, scarfs, laces, gold, spangles, and gaudy devices, that the young man took her to be a goddess (for he never saw her but by torchlight); but after the wedding solemnities, when he viewed her the next morning without her tires, and in a clear day, she was so deformed, lean, yellow, rivelled, etc., such a beastly creature in his eyes, that he could not endure to look upon her.

Such matches are frequently made in Italy, where they have no other opportunity to woo but when they go to church, or, as in Turkey, see them at a distance, they must interchange few or no words till such time they come to be married, and then, as Sardus and Bohemus relate of those old Lacedaemonians, the bride is brought into the chamber, with her hair girt about her, the bridegroom comes in and unties the knot, and must not see her at all by daylight, till such time as he is made a father by her. In those hotter countries these are ordinary practices at this day; but in our northern parts, among Germans, Danes, French, and Britons, the continent of Scandia and the rest, we assume more liberty in such cases: we allow them, as Bohemus saith, to kiss coming and going, to talk merrily, sport, play, sing, and dance, so that it be modestly done, go to the alehouse and taverns together.

And 'tis not amiss, though Chrysostom, Cyprian, Jerome, and some other of the Fathers speak bitterly against it; but that is the abuse which is commonly seen at some drunken matches, dissolute meetings, or great unruly feasts. A young, pickitivated, trim-bearded fellow, saith Jerome, will come with a company of compliments, and hold you up by the arm as you go, and wringing your fingers, will so be enticed, or entice: one drinks to you, another embraceth, a third kisseth, and all this while the fiddler plays or sings a lascivious song; a fourth singles you out to dance; one speaks by becks and signs, and that which he dares not say, signifies by passions; among so many and so great provocations of pleasure, lust conquers the most hard and crabbed minds, and scarce can a man live honest among feastings and sports, or at such great meetings. For, as he goes on, she walks along, and with the ruffling of her clothes makes men look at her, her shoes creak, her paps tied up, her waist pulled in to make her look small, she is strait-girded, her hairs hang loose about her ears, her upper garment sometimes falls, and sometimes tarries, to show her naked shoulders, and as if she would not be seen, she covers that in all haste which voluntarily she showed. And not at feasts, plays, pageants, and such assemblies, but as Chrysostom objects, these tricks are put in practice at service-time in churches, and at the communion itself.

If such dumb-shows, signs, and more obscure significations of love can so move, what shall they do that have full liberty to sing, dance, kiss, coll, to use all manner of discourse and dalliance? What shall he do that is beleaguered of all sides?

> *After whom so many rosy maids inquire,*
> *Whom dainty dames and loving wights desire,*
> *In every place, still, and at all times sue,*
> *Whom gods and gentle goddesses do woo.*
>
> (JOVIANUS PONTANUS)

How shall he contain?

The very tone of some of their voices, a pretty pleasing speech, an affected tone they use, is able of itself to captivate a young man, but when a good wit shall concur, art and eloquence, fascinating speech, pleasant discourse, sweet gestures, the Sirens themselves cannot so enchant. P. Jovius commends his Italian countrywomen to have an excellent faculty in this kind, above all other nations, and among them the Florentine ladies: some prefer Roman and Venetian courtesans, they have such pleasing tongues, and such elegancy of speech, that they are able to overcome a saint, many please with their voice rather than with their looks. Often a pleasing voice wins fame, saith Petronius in his fragment of pure impurities, I mean his *Satyricon*, she sang so sweetly that she charmed the air, and thou wouldst have thought thou hadst heard a consort of Sirens.

'O good God, when Lais speaks, how sweet it is!' Philocaus exclaims in Aristaenetus. To hear a fair young gentlewoman play upon the virginals, lute, viol, and sing to it, which, as Gellius observes, are the chief delight of lovers, must needs be a great enticement. Parthenis was so taken. 'O sister Harpedona (she laments) I am undone, how sweetly he sings! I'll speak a bold word, he is the properest man that ever I saw in my life: O how sweetly he sings, I die for his sake, O that he would love me again!' If thou didst but hear her sing, saith

Lucian, thou wouldst forget father and mother, forsake all thy friends, and follow her. Helena is highly commended by Theocritus the poet for her sweet voice and music, none could play so well as she; and Daphnis in the same Idyll:

> *How sweet a face hath Daphne, how lovely a voice!*
> *Honey itself is not so pleasant in my choice.*

A sweet voice and music are powerful enticers. Those Samian singing wenches, Aristonica, Oenanthe, and Agathoclea, insulted over kings themselves, as Plutarch contends. Argus had an hundred eyes, all so charmed by one silly pipe that he lost his head. Clitiphon complains in Tatius of Leucippe's sweet tunes; he heard her play by chance upon the lute, and sing a pretty song to it in commendations of a rose, out of old Anacreon belike:

> *Rose the fairest of all flowers,*
> *Rose delight of higher powers,*
> *Rose the joy of mortal men,*
> *Rose the pleasure of fine women,*
> *Rose the Graces' ornament,*
> *Rose Dione's sweet content.*

To this effect the lovely virgin, with a melodious air upon her golden-wired harp or lute, I know not well whether, played and sang, and that transported him beyond himself, and that ravished his heart. It was Jason's discourse as much as his beauty, or any other of his good parts, which delighted Medea so much. It was Cleopatra's sweet voice and pleasant speech which inveigled Antony, above the rest of her enticements. As bulls' horns are bound with ropes so are men's hearts with pleasant words. 'Her words burn as fire.' Roxalana bewitched

Solyman the Magnificent, and Shore's wife by this engine overcame Edward the Fourth. The Wife of Bath in Chaucer confesseth all this out of her experience:

> *Some folk desire us for riches,*
> *Some for shape, some for fairness,*
> *Some for that she can sing or dance,*
> *Some for gentleness, or for dalliance.*

Peter Aretine's Lucretia telleth as much and more of herself: 'I counterfeited honesty, as if I had been more than a vestal virgin, I looked like a wife, I was so demure and chaste, I did add such gestures, tunes, speeches, signs, and motions upon all occasions, that my spectators and auditors were stupefied, enchanted, fastened all to their places, like so many stocks and stones.'

Many silly gentlewomen are fetched over in like sort by a company of gulls and swaggering companions, that frequently belie nobleman's favours, rhyming Corybantiasmi, thrasonian Rhodomantes or Bombomachides, that have nothing in them but a few players' ends and compliments, vain braggadocians, impudent intruders, that can discourse at table of knights' and lords' combats, like Lucian's Leontichus, of other men's travels, brave adventures, and such common trivial news, ride, dance, sing old ballet tunes, and wear their clothes in fashion, with a good grace; a fine sweet gentleman, a proper man, who could not love him? She will have him though all her friends say no, though she beg with him.

Some again are incensed by reading amorous toys, Amadis de Gaul, Palmerin de Oliva, the Knight of the Sun, etc., or hearing such tales of lovers, descriptions of their persons, lascivious discourses, such as Astyanassa, Helena's waiting-woman, by the report of Suidas, writ of old, of various positions, and after her Philaenis and Elephantis, or those light tracts of Aristides Milesius (mentioned by Plutarch) and found by the Persians in Crassus' army among the spoils, Aretine's dialogues, with ditties, love-songs, etc., must needs set them on fire, with suchlike pictures as those of Aretine, or wanton objects of what kind soever; no stronger engine than to hear or read of love-toys, fables, and discourses (one saith), and many by this means are quite mad.

At Abdera in Thrace (*Andromeda*, one of Euripides' tragedies, being played), the spectators were so much moved with the object, and those pathetical love-speeches of Perseus (among the rest, 'O Cupid, prince of gods and men,' etc.), that every man almost, a good while after, spake pure iambics, and raved still on Perseus' speech, 'O Cupid, prince of gods and men.' As carmen, boys, and prentices, when a new song is published with us, go singing that new tune still in the streets, they continually acted that tragical part of Perseus, and in every man's mouth was 'O Cupid,' in every street, 'O Cupid,' in every house almost, 'O Cupid, prince of gods and men,' pronouncing still like stage-players, 'O Cupid'; they were so possessed all with that rapture, and thought of that pathetical love-speech, they could not a long time after forget, or drive it out of their minds, but 'O Cupid, prince of gods and men,' was ever in their mouths.

This belike made Aristotle forbid young men to see comedies, or to hear amorous tales. Let not young folk meddle at all with such matters. And this made the Romans, as Vitruvius relates, put Venus' temple in the suburbs to avoid all occasions and objects. For what will not such an object do? Ismenias, as he walked in Sosthenes' garden, being now in love, when he saw so many lascivious pictures, Thetis' Marriage, and I know not what, was almost beside himself. And to say truth, with a lascivious object who is not moved, to see others dally, kiss, dance? And much more when he shall come to be an actor himself.

To kiss and be kissed, which, among other lascivious provocations, is as a burden in a song, and a most forcible battery, as infectious,

Xenophon thinks, as the poison of a spider; a great allurement, a fire itself, the prologue of burning lust (as Apuleius adds), lust itself, which Venus hath imbued with the quintessence of her own nectar, a strong assault, that conquers captains, and those all-commanding forces, you may conquer with the sword, but are conquered by a kiss.

Aretine's Lucretia, when she would in kindness overcome a suitor of hers and have her desire of him, took him about the neck, and kissed him again and again, and to that, which she could not otherwise effect, she made him so speedily and willingly condescend. And 'tis a continual assault, always fresh, and ready to begin as at first, is never finished, always new, and hath a fiery touch. 'Only touch her, and immediately your members will glow' [Petronius]. Especially when they shall be lasciviously given, as he feelingly said, 'when Fotis kissed him hard, with arms intertwined, and twisted lips'. The soul and all is moved: kissing again and again, as their lips joined their souls commingled. They breathe out their souls and spirits together with their kisses, saith Baldassare Castiglione, change hearts and spirits, and mingle affections as they do kisses, and it is rather a connexion of the mind than of the body. And although these kisses be delightsome and pleasant, ambrosial kisses, such as Ganymede gave Jupiter, sweeter than nectar, balsam, honey, love-dropping kisses; for

> *The gilliflower, the rose is not so sweet,*
> *As sugared kisses be when lovers meet:*

yet they leave an irksome impression, like that of aloes or gall:

> *At first ambrose itself was not sweeter,*
> *At last black hellebore was not so bitter.*
>
> (CATULLUS)

They are deceitful kisses:

> *Why dost within thine arms me lap,*
> *And with false kisses me entrap.*
>
> (BUCHANAN)

They are destructive, and the more the worse: they are the bane of these miserable lovers.

There be honest kisses, I deny not, friendly kisses, modest kisses, vestal-virgin kisses, officious and ceremonial kisses, etc. Kissing and embracing are proper gifts of nature to a man; but these are too lascivious kisses, 'with her arms right about my neck', etc., too continuate and too violent, they cling like ivy, close as an oyster, bill as doves, meretricious kisses, biting of lips, and more besides (saith Lucian), with open mouths so close they scarce withdraw, biting as they kiss, with caressing of breasts, etc., such kisses as she gave to Giton, innumerable kisses, etc. More than kisses, or too homely kisses: as those that Apuleius spake of, having enjoyed seven kinds of love, etc., with such other obscenities that vain lovers use, which are abominable and pernicious. If, as Peter de Ledesmo holds, every kiss a man gives his wife after marriage be a mortal sin, or that of Jerome, he who loves his wife too passionately is an adulterer; or that of Thomas, touching and kissing is mortal sin; or that of Durand, married couples should abstain throughout the whole period when the nuptial act is forbidden, what shall become of all such immodest kisses and obscene actions, the forerunners of brutish lust, if not lust itself? What shall become of them that often abuse their own wives? But what have I to do with this?

That which I aim at is to show you the progress of this burning lust: to epitomize therefore all this which I have hitherto said, with a familiar example out of that elegant Musaeus, observe but with me those amorous proceedings of Leander and Hero. They began first to look one on another with a lascivious look:

> *With becks and nods he first began*
> *To try the wench's mind,*
> *With becks and nods and smiles again*
> *An answer he did find.*
> *And in the dark he took her by the hand,*
> *And wrung it hard, and sighed greviously,*
> *And kiss'd her too, and woo'd her as he might,*
> *With Pity me, sweetheart, or else I die,*
> *And with such words and gestures as there past,*
> *He won his mistress' favour at the last.*

The same proceeding is elegantly described by Apollonius in his Argonautics, between Jason and Medea, by Eustathius in the ten books of the loves of Ismenias and Ismene, Achilles Tatius between his Clitiphon and Leucippe, Chaucer's neat poem of Troilus and Creseid; and in that notable tale in Petronius of a soldier and a gentlewoman of Ephesus, that was so famous all over Asia for her chastity, and that mourned for her husband: the soldier wooed her with such rhetoric as lovers use to do; at last, he got her good will, not only to satisfy his lust, but to hang her dead husband's body on the cross which he watched, instead of the thief's that was newly stolen away while he wooed her in her cabin. These are tales, you will say, but they have most significant morals, and do well express those ordinary proceedings of doting lovers.

Many such allurements there are, nods, jests, winks, smiles, wrestlings, tokens, favours, symbols, letters, valentines, etc. For which cause belike, Godefridus would not have women learn to write. Many

such provocations are used when they come in presence, they will
and will not.

> *My mistress with an apple woos me,*
> *And hastily to covert goes*
> *To hide herself, but would be seen*
> *With all her heart before, God knows.*
>
> (VIRGIL)

Hero so tripped away from Leander as one displeased,

> *Yet as she went full often look'd behind,*
> *And many poor excuses did she find*
> *To linger by the way.*
>
> (MARLOWE)

but if he chance to overtake her she is most averse, nice, and coy,

> *She seems not won, but won she is at length,*
> *In such wars women use but half their strength.*

Sometimes they lie open and are most tractable and coming, apt,
yielding, and willing to embrace, to take a green gown, with that
shepherdess in Theocritus, to let their coats, etc., to play and dally,
at such seasons, and to some, as they spy their advantage; and then
coy, close again, so nice, so surly, so demure, you had much better
tame a colt, catch or ride a wild horse, than get her favour or win
her love, not a look, not a smile, not a kiss for a kingdom.

Aretine's Lucretia was an excellent artisan in this kind, as she tells
her own tale: 'Though I was by nature and art most beautiful and
fair, yet by these tricks I seemed to be far more amiable than I was,

for that which men earnestly seek and cannot attain, draws on their affection with a most furious desire. I had a suitor loved me dearly [said she], and the more he gave me, the more eagerly he wooed me, the more I seemed to neglect, to scorn him, and, which I commonly gave others, I would not let him see me, converse with me, no, not have a kiss. To gull him the more and fetch him over (for him only I aimed at), I personated mine own servant to bring in a present from a Spanish count, while he was in my company, as if he had been the count's servant, which he did excellently well perform: "The Count, my lord and master, hath sent your ladyship a small present, and part of his hunting, a piece of venison, a pheasant, a few partridges, etc. [all which she bought with her own money], commends his love and service to you, desiring you to accept of it in good part, and he means very shortly to come and see you."' Withal she showed him rings, gloves, scarfs, coronets which others had sent her, when there was no such matter, but only to circumvent him. 'By these means [as she concludes] I made the poor gentleman so mad, that he was ready to spend himself and venture his dearest blood for my sake.'

Philinna, in Lucian, practised all this long before, as it shall appear unto you by her discourse; for when Diphilus her sweetheart came to see her (as his daily custom was), she frowned upon him, would not vouchsafe him her company, but kissed Lamprias, his corrival, at the same time before his face; but why was it? To make him (as she telleth her mother that chid her for it) more jealous; to whetten his love, to come with a greater appetite, and to know that her favour was not so easy to be had. Many other tricks she used besides this (as she there confesseth), for she would fall out with, and anger him of set purpose, pick quarrels upon no occasion, because she would be reconciled to him again. As the old saying is, the falling out of lovers the renewing is of love; and according to that of Aristaenetus, love is increased by injuries, as the sunbeams are more gracious after a cloud.

And surely this aphorism is most true; for as Ampelis informs Chrysis in the said Lucian, if a lover be not jealous, angry, waspish, apt to fall out, sigh and swear, he is no true lover. To kiss and coll, hang about her neck, protest, swear, and wish are but ordinary symptoms, earliest signs of a love; but if he be jealous, angry, apt to mistake, etc., you may well hope, sweet sister, he is thine own; yet if you let him alone, humour him, please him, etc., and that he perceive once he hath you sure, without any corrival, his love will languish, and he will not care so much for you. 'Hitherto [saith she] can I speak out of experience: Demophantus, a rich fellow, was a suitor of mine; I seemed to neglect him, and gave better entertainment to Callides the painter before his face; at first he went away all in a chafe, cursing and swearing, but at last he came submitting himself, vowing and protesting he loved me most dearly, I should have all he had, and that he would kill himself for my sake. Therefore I advise thee, dear sister Chrysis, and all maids, not to use your suitors over-kindly; 'twill make them proud and insolent; but now and then reject them, estrange thyself, shut him out of doors once or twice, let him dance attendance; follow my counsel, and by this means you shall make him mad, come off roundly, stand to any conditions, and do whatsoever you will have him.'

These are the ordinary practises; yet, in the said Lucian, Melissa methinks had a trick beyond all this; for when her suitor came coldly on, to stir him up, she writ one of his corrival's names and her own in a paper, 'Melissa loves Hermotimus, and he her,' causing it to be stuck upon a post for all gazers to behold, and lost it in the way where he used to walk; which when the silly novice perceived, instantly apprehended it was so, came raving, etc.; 'and so, when I was in despair of his love, four months after I recovered him again'. Eugenia drew Timocles for her valentine, and wore his name a long time after in her bosom; Camaena singled out Pamphilus to dance, at Myson's wedding (some say), for there she saw him first; Felicianus overtook Caelia by the highway side, offered his service, thence came further acquaintance, and thence came love. But who can repeat half their devices? what Aretine experienced, what conceited Lucian, or wanton Aristaenetus? They will deny and take, stiffly refuse, and yet earnestly seek the same, repel to make them come with more eagerness, fly from if you follow, but if averse, as a shadow they will follow you again, with a regaining retreat, a gentle reluctancy, a smiling threat, a pretty pleasant peevishness they will put you off, and have a thousand such several enticements. For as Petronius saith,

> *'Tis not enough, though she be fair of hue,*
> *For her to use this vulgar compliment:*
> *But pretty toys and jests, and saws and smiles,*
> *As far beyond what beauty can attempt.*

For this cause, belike Philostratus, in his Images, makes divers loves, some young, some of one age, some of another, some winged, some of one sex, some of another, some with torches, some with golden apples, some with darts, gins, snares, and other engines in their hands, as Propertius hath prettily painted them out, and which some interpret, divers enticements, or divers affections of lovers, which if not alone, yet jointly may batter and overcome the strongest constitutions.

It is reported of Decius and Valerianus, those two notorious persecutors of the Church, that when they could enforce a young Christian by no means (as Jerome records) to sacrifice to their idols, by no torments or promises, they took another course to tempt him: they put him into a fair garden, and set a young courtesan to dally with him; she took him about the neck and kissed him, and that which is not to be named, and all those enticements which might be used, that whom torments could not, love might batter and beleaguer. But such was his constancy, she could not overcome, and when this last engine would take no place they left him to his own ways.

At Berkeley in Gloucestershire there was in times past a nunnery (saith Gualterus Mapes, an old historiographer, that lived 400 years since), of which there was a noble and a fair lady abbess: Godwin, that subtle Earl of Kent, travelling that way (seeking not her but hers), leaves a nephew of his, a proper young gallant (as if he had been sick), with her, till he came back again, and gives the young man charge so long to counterfeit till he had deflowered the abbess, and as many besides of the nuns as he could, and leaves him withal rings, jewels, girdles, and such toys to give them still, when they came to visit him. The young man, willing to undergo such a business, played his part so well, that in short space he got up most of their bellies, and when he had done, told his lord how he had sped; his lord made instantly to the court, tells the king how such a nunnery was become a bawdy-house, procures a visitation, gets them to be turned out, and begs the lands to his own use. This story I do therefore repeat, that you may see of what force these enticements are, if they be opportunely used, and how hard it is even for the most averse and sanctified souls to resist such allurements.

John Major, in the life of John the Monk, that lived in the days of Theodosius, commends the hermit to have been a man of singular continency, and of a most austere life; but one night by chance the devil came to his cell in the habit of a young market wench that had lost her way, and desired for God's sake some lodging with him. The old man let her in, and after some common conference of her mishap, she began to inveigle him with lascivious talk and jests, to play with his beard, to kiss him, and do worse, till at last she overcame him. As he went to address himself to that business, she vanished on a sudden, and the devils in the air laughed him to scorn. Whether this be a true story, or a tale, I will not much contend; it serves to illustrate this which I have said.

Yet were it so, that these of which I have hitherto spoken, and such-like enticing baits, be not sufficient, there be many others which will of themselves intend this passion of burning lust, among which dancing is none the least; and it is an engine of such force, I may not omit it. Petrarch calls it the spur of lust, a circle of which the devil himself is the centre. Many women that use it have come dishonest home, most indifferent, none better. Another terms it the companion of all filthy delights and enticements, and 'tis not easily told what inconveniences come by it, what scurrile talk, obscene actions, and many times such monstrous gestures, such lascivious motions, such wanton tunes, meretricious kisses, homely embracings that it will make the spectators mad.

When that epitomizer of Trogus had to the full described and set out King Ptolemy's riot as a chief engine and instrument of his overthrow, he adds fiddling and dancing: the king was not a spectator only, but a principal actor himself. A thing nevertheless frequently used, and part of a gentlewoman's bringing up, to sing, dance, and play on the lute, or some such instrument, before she can say her paternoster or Ten Commandments. 'Tis the next way, their parents think, to get them husbands; they are compelled to learn, and by that means from tender years their thoughts are wanton; 'tis a great allurement as it is often used, and many are undone by it. Thais, in Lucian, inveigled Lamprias in a dance. Herodias so far pleased Herod that she made him swear to give her what she would ask, John Baptist's head in a platter. Robert Duke of Normandy, riding by Falaise, spied Arletta, a fair maid, as she danced on a green, and was so much enamoured with the object that he must needs lie with her that night, of whom he begat William the Conqueror; by the same token she tore her smock down, saying, etc. Owen Tudor won Queen Catherine's affection in a dance, falling by chance with his head in her lap.

Who cannot parallel these stories out of his experience? Speucippus, a noble gallant in that Greek Aristaenetus, seeing Panareta, a fair young gentlewoman dancing by accident, was so far in love with her that for a long time after he could think of nothing but Panareta; he came raving home full of Panareta: 'Who would not admire her, who would not love her, that should but see her dance as I did? O admirable, O divine Panareta! I have seen old and new Rome, many fair cities, many proper women, but never any like to Panareta, they are dross, dowdies all to Panareta! O how she danced, how she tripped, how she turned, with what a grace! happy is that man that shall enjoy her. O most incomparable, only, Panareta!'

When Xenophon had discoursed of love, and used all the engines that might be devised to move Socrates, among the rest, to stir him the more, he shuts up all with a pleasant interlude or dance of Dionysus and Ariadne. First Ariadne dressed like a bride came in and took her place; by and by Dionysus entered, dancing to the music. The spectators did all admire the young man's carriage; and Ariadne herself was so much affected with the sight that she could scarce sit. After a while Dionysus, beholding Ariadne, and incensed with love, bowing to her knees, embraced her first, and kissed her with a grace; she embraced him again, and kissed him with like affection, etc., as the dance required; but they that stood by and saw this, did much applaud and commend them both for it. And when Dionysus rose up, he raised her up with him, and many pretty gestures, embraces, kisses, and love compliments passed between them: which when they saw fair Bacchus and beautiful Ariadne so sweetly and so unfeignedly kissing each other, so really embracing, they swore they loved indeed, and were so inflamed with the object that they began to rouse up themselves, as if they would have flown.

At the last, when they saw them still so willingly embracing, and now ready to go to the bride-chamber, they were so ravished with it, that they that were unmarried swore they would forthwith marry, and those that were married called instantly for their horses, and galloped home to their wives. What greater motive can there be than this burning lust? what so violent an oppugner? Not without good cause therefore so many general councils condemn it, so many Fathers abhor it, so many grave men speak against it. 'Use not the company of a woman,' saith Siracides [Ecclesiasticus], 'that is a singer or a dancer; neither hear, lest thou be taken in her craftiness.' Haedus holds, lust in theatres is not seen, but learned. Gregory Nazianzen, that eloquent divine (as he relates the story himself), when a noble friend of his solemnly invited him, with other bishops, to his daughter Olympia's wedding, refused to come: for it is absurd to see an old gouty bishop sit among dancers; he held it unfit to be a spectator, much less an actor. Tully writes, he is not a sober man that danceth; for some such reason (belike) Domitian forbade the Roman senators to dance, and for that fact removed many of them from the senate.

But these, you will say, are lascivious and pagan dances, 'tis the abuse that causeth such inconvenience, and I do not well therefore to condemn, speak against, or innocently to accuse the best and pleasantest thing (so Lucian calls it) that belongs to mortal men. You misinterpret, I condemn it not; I hold it notwithstanding an honest disport, a lawful recreation, if it be opportune, moderately and soberly used: I am of Plutarch's mind, that which respects pleasure alone, honest recreation, or bodily exercise, ought not to be rejected, and contemned. I subscribe to Lucian, 'tis an elegant thing, which cheereth up the mind, exerciseth the body, delights the spectators, which teacheth many comely gestures, equally affecting the ears, eyes, and soul itself. Sallust discommends singing and dancing in

Sempronia, not that she did sing or dance, but that she did it in excess, 'tis the abuse of it; and Gregory's refusal doth not simply condemn it, but in some folks. Many will not allow men and women to dance together, because it is a provocation to lust; they may as well, with Lycurgus and Mahomet, cut down all vines, forbid the drinking of wine, for that it makes some men drunk.

I say of this, as of all other honest recreations, they are like fire, good and bad, and I see no such inconvenience but that they may so dance, if it be done at due times, and by fit persons: and conclude with Wolfongus Hider, and most of our modern divines: if seemly, staid, and modest, and in view of good men and honest matrons, at proper hours, it should be approved. 'There is a time to mourn, a time to dance' (Eccles, iii, 4). Let them take their pleasures then, and as he [Apuleius] said of old, young men and maids flourishing in their age, fair and lovely to behold, well attired, and of comely carriage, dancing a Greek galliard, and as their dance required, kept their time, now turning, now tracing, now apart, now together, now a courtesy, then a caper, etc., and it was a pleasant sight to see those pretty knots and swimming figures. The sun and moon (some say) dance about the earth, the three upper planets about the sun as their centre, now stationary, now direct, now retrograde, now in apogee, now in perigee, now swift, then slow, occidental, oriental, they turn round, jump and trace, Venus and Mercury about the sun with those thirty-three Maculae or Borbonian planets, dance round the harping sun, saith Fromundus. Four Medicean stars dance about Jupiter, two Austrian about Saturn, etc., and all (belike) to the music of the spheres. Our greatest counsellors, and staid senators, at some times dance, as David before the ark (2 Sam. vi, 14), Miriam (Exod. xv, 20), Judith (xv, 13) (though the devil hence perhaps hath brought in those bawdy bacchanals), and well may they do it.

The greatest soldiers, as Quintilianus, Aemilius Probus, Caelius Rhodiginus, have proved at large, still use it in Greece, Rome, and the most worthy senators sing and dance. Lucian, Macrobius, Libanius, Plutarch, Julius Pollux, Athenaeus, have written just tracts in commendation of it. In this our age it is in much request in those countries, as in all civil commonwealth, as Alexander ab Alexandro hath proved at large, among the barbarians themselves none so precious; all the world allows it.

Plato, in his Commonwealth, will have dancing-schools to be maintained, that young folks might meet, be acquainted, see one another, and be seen; nay more, he would have them dance naked, and scoffs at them that laugh at it. But Eusebius and Theodoret worthily lash him for it; and well they might: for as one saith, the very sight of naked parts causeth enormous, exceeding concupiscences, and stirs up both men and women to burning lust. There is a mean in all things; this is my censure in brief: dancing is a pleasant recreation of body and mind, if sober and modest (such as our Christian dances are), if tempestively used; a furious motive to burning lust, if, as by pagans heretofore, unchastely abused. But I proceed.

If these allurements do not take place, for Simierus, that great master of dalliance, shall not behave himself better, the more effectually to move others and satisfy their lust, they will swear and lie, promise, protest, forge, counterfeit, brag, bribe, flatter, and dissemble of all sides. 'Twas Lucretia's counsel in Aretine, if you would profit from your lovers, promise, invent, swear, forswear, boast, cheat, lie; and they put it well in practice, as Apollo to Daphne:

> *Delphos, Claros, and Tenedos serve me,*
> *And Jupiter is known my sire to be.*

(OVID)

The poorest swains will do as much; I have a thousand sheep, good store of cattle, and they are all at her command: house, land, goods, are at her service, as he is himself.

Dinomachus, a senator's son in Lucain, in love with a wench inferior to him in birth and fortunes, the sooner to accomplish his desire, wept unto her, and swore he loved her with all his heart and her alone, and that as soon as ever his father died (a very rich man and almost decrepit) he would make her his wife. The maid by chance made her mother acquainted with the business, who being an old fox, well experienced in such matters, told her daughter, how ready to yield to his desire, that he meant nothing less; 'for dost thou think he will ever care for thee, being a poor wench, that may have his choice of all the beauties in the city, one noble by birth, with so many talents, as young, better qualified, and fairer than thyself? Daughter, believe him not.' The maid was abashed, and so the matter broke off.

When Jupiter wooed Juno first (Lilius Giraldus relates it out of an old comment on Theocritus), the better to effect his suit, he turned himself into a cuckoo, and spying her one day walking alone, separated from the other goddesses, caused a tempest suddenly to arise, for fear of which she fled to shelter; Jupiter to avoid the storm likewise flew into her lap, whom Juno for pity covered in her apron. But he turned himself forthwith into his own shape, began to embrace and offer violence unto her, but she by no means would yield, till he vowed and swore to marry her, and then she gave consent. This fact was done at Thornax Hill, which ever after was called Cuckoo Hill, and in perpetual remembrance there was a temple erected to Juno Teleia in the same place. So powerful are fair promises, vows, oaths, and protestations.

It is an ordinary thing too in this case to belie their age, which widows usually do, that mean to marry again, and bachelors too sometimes, approaching forty, to say they are younger than they are. Charmides in the said Lucian loved Philematium, an old maid of forty-five years; she swore to him she was but thirty-two next December. But to dissemble in this kind is familiar of all sides, and often it takes. 'Tis soon done, no such great mastery, and nothing so frequent as to belie their estates, to prefer their suits, and to advance themselves. Many men, to fetch over a young woman, widows, or whom they love, will not stick to crack, forge, and feign, anything comes next, bid his boy fetch his cloak, rapier, gloves, jewels, etc., in such a chest, scarlet-golden-tissue breeches, etc., when there is no such matter; or make any scruple to give out, as he did in Petronius, that he was master of a ship, kept so many servants; and to personate their part the better, take upon them to be gentlemen of good houses, well descended and allied, hire apparel at brokers', some scavenger or pricklouse tailors to attend upon them for the time, swear they have great possessions, bribe, lie, cog, and foist how dearly they love, how bravely they will maintain her, like any lady, countess, duchess, or queen; they shall have gowns, tires, jewels, coaches, and caroches, choice diet,

> *The heads of parrots, tongues of nightingales,*
> *The brains of peacocks, and of ostriches,*
> *Their bath shall be the juice of gilliflowers,*
> *Spirit of roses and of violets,*
> *The milk of unicorns, etc.,*

as old Volpone courted Celia in the [Jonson's] comedy, whenas they are no such men, not worth a groat, but mere sharkers, to make a fortune, to get their desire, or else pretend love to spend their idle hours, to be more welcome, and for better entertainment. The conclusion is, they mean nothing less.

> *Oaths, vows, promises, are much protested;*
> *But when their mind and lust is satisfied,*
> *Oaths, vows, promises, are quite neglected.*
>
> (CATULLUS)

Though he solemnly swear by the genius of Caesar, by Venus' shrine, Hymen's deity, by Jupiter and all the other gods, give no credit to his words. For when lovers swear, Venus laughs, Jupiter himself smiles, and pardons it withal; as grave Plato gives out, of all perjury, that alone for love matters is forgiven by the gods.

If promises, lies, oaths, and protestations will not avail, they fall to bribes, tokens, gifts, and such-like feats. Love is chiefly won by gold: as Jupiter corrupted Danae with a golden shower and Liber Ariadne with a lovely crown (which was afterwards translated into the heavens, and there for ever shines), they will rain chequins, florins, crowns, angels, all manner of coins and stamps in her lap. And so must he certainly do that will speed, make many feasts, banquets, invitations, send her some present or other every foot. He must be very bountiful and liberal, seek and sue, not to her only, but to all her followers, friends, familiars, fiddlers, panders, parasites, and house-hold servants; he must insinuate himself, and surely will, to all, of all sorts, messengers, porters, carriers; no man must be unrewarded or unrespected.

'I had a suitor [saith Aretine's Lucretia] that when he came to my house, flung gold and silver about, as if it had been chaff. Another suitor I had was a very choleric fellow; but I so handled him, that for all his fuming, I brought him upon his knees. If there had been an excellent bit in the market, any novelty, fish, fruit, or fowl, muscadel, or malmsey, or a cup of neat wine in all the city, it was presented presently to me, though never so dear, hard to come by, yet I had it: the poor fellow was so fond at last, that I think if I would

I might have had one of his eyes out of his head. A third suitor was a merchant of Rome, and his manner of wooing was with exquisite music, costly banquets, poems, etc. I held him off till at length he protested, promised, and swore that in exchange for my virginity I should have all he had, house, goods, and lands, neither was there ever any conjuror, I think, to charm his spirits that used such attention or mighty words, as he did exquisite phrases, or general of any army so many stratagems to win a city, as he did tricks and devices to get the love of me.'

Thus men are active and passive, and women not far behind them in this kind:

> *For half so boldly can there no man*
> *Swear and lyen as a woman can.*
>
> (CHAUCER)

They will crack, counterfeit, and collogue as well as the best with handkerchiefs and wrought nightcaps, purses, posies, and such toys: as he justly complained:

> *Why dost thou send me violets, my dear?*
> *To make me burn more violent, I fear,*
> *With violets too violent thou art,*
> *To violate and wound my gentle heart.*
>
> (JOVIANUS PONTANUS)

When nothing else will serve, the last refuge is in their tears. 'Twixt tears and sighs I write this (I take love to witness), saith Chelidonia to Philonius. Those burning torches are now turned to floods of tears. Aretine's Lucretia, when her sweetheart came to town, wept in his bosom, that he might be persuaded those tears were shed for joy of his return. Quartilla in Petronius, when naught would move, fell a-weeping, and, as Baldassare Castiglione paints them out, to these crocodile's tears they will add sobs, fiery sighs, and sorrowful countenance, pale colour, leanness, and if you do but stir abroad, these fiends are ready to meet you at every turn, with such a sluttish neglected habit, dejected look, as if they were now ready to die for your sake; and how, saith he, shall a young novice, thus beset, escape? But, believe them not. The sea is more constant than woman's faith. Thou thinkest, peradventure, because of her vows, tears, smiles, and protestations, she is solely thine, thou hast her heart, hand, and affection, whenas indeed there is no such matter, as the Spanish bawl said, she will have one sweetheart in bed, another in the gate, a third sighing at home, a fourth, etc. Every young man she sees and likes hath as much interest, and shall as soon enjoy as thyself.

On the other side, which I have said, men are as false, let them swear, protest, and lie; they saying to you what they have said to a thousand more. They love some of them those eleven thousand virgins at once, and make them believe, each particular, he is besotted on her; or love one till they see another, and then her alone; like Milo's wife in Apuleius, who as she sees a handsome youth, is fascinated by him and seduces him. 'Tis their common compliment in that case, they care not what they swear, say, or do. One while they slight them, care not for them, rail downright and scoff at them, and then again they will run mad, hang themselves, stab and kill, if they may not enjoy them. Henceforth, therefore, let not maids believe them. These tricks and counterfeit passions are more familiar with women; 'this day will end either my misery or my life, pity a lover,' quoth Phaedra to Hippolytus. Ioessa, in Lucian, told Pythias, a young man, to move him the more, that if he would not have her, she was resolved to make away herself. 'There is a Nemesis, and it cannot choose but grieve and trouble thee to hear that I have either strangled or drowned myself for thy sake.'

Nothing so common to this sex as oaths, vows, and protestations, and as I have already said, tears, which they have at command; for they can so weep that one would think their very hearts were dissolved within them, and would come out in tears; their eyes are like rocks, which still drop water; saith Aristaenetus, they wipe away their tears like sweat, weep with one eye, laugh with the other; or as children weep and cry, they can both together.

> *Care not for women's tears, I counsel thee,*
> *They teach their eyes as much to weep as see.*

(OVID)

And as much pity is to be taken of a woman's weeping as of a goose going barefoot. When Venus lost her son Cupid, she sent a crier about, to bid everyone that met him take heed.

> *Take heed of Cupid's tears, if cautelous,*
> *And of his smiles and kisses, I thee tell,*
> *If that he offer't, for they be noxious,*
> *And very poison in his lips doth dwell.*

(MOSCHUS)

A thousand years, as Castiglione conceives, will scarce serve to reckon up those allurements and guiles that men and women use to deceive one another with.

XII

Bawds, Philters, Causes.

WHEN ALL OTHER engines fail, that they can proceed no farther of themselves, their last refuge is to fly to bawds, panders, magical philters, and receipts; rather than fail, to the devil himself. And by those indirect means many a man is overcome, and precipitated into this malady, if he take not good heed. For these bawds first, they are everywhere so common and so many, that, as he said of old Croton, all here either inveigle or be inveigled, we may say of most of our cities, there be so many professed, cunning bawds in them. Besides, bawdry is become an art, or a liberal science, as Lucian calls it; and there be such tricks and subtilities, so many nurses, old women, panders, letter-carriers, beggars, physicians, friars, confessors, employed about it, that as Plantus saith, three hundred verses would not suffice to tell the tale of their debaucheries.

Such occult notes, stenography, polygraphy, or magnetical telling of their minds, which Cabeus the Jesuit, by the way, counts fabulous and false; cunning conveyances in this kind, that neither Juno's jealousy, nor Danae's custody, nor Argo's vigilancy can keep them safe. 'Tis the last and common refuge to use an assistant, such as that Catanean Philippa was to Joan Queen of Naples, a bawd's help, an old woman in the business, as Myrrha did when she doted on Cinyras, and could not compass her desire, the old jade her nurse was ready at a pinch, 'fear it not, if it be possible to be done, I will effect it': as Caelestina said, let him or her be never so honest, watched, and reserved, 'tis hard but one of these old women will get access: and scarce shall you find, as Augustine observes, in a nunnery a maid alone; if she cannot have egress, before her window you shall have an old woman or some prating gossip tell her some tales of this clerk and that monk, describing or commending some young gentleman or other unto her. 'As I was walking in the street [saith a good fellow in Petronius] to see the town served one evening, I spied an old woman in a corner selling cabbages and roots' (as our hucksters do plums, apples, and such-like fruits); 'Mother [quoth I], can you tell where I can dwell? She, being well pleased with my foolish urbanity, replied, And why, sir, should I not tell? With that she rose up and went before me; I took her for a wise woman. And by and by she led me into a by-lane, and told me there I should dwell; I replied again, I knew not the house; but I perceived on a sudden, by the naked queans, that I was now come into a bawdy-house, and then too late I began to curse the treachery of this old jade.'

Such tricks you shall have in many places, and among the rest it is ordinary in Venice, and in the island of Zante, for a man to be bawd to his own wife. No sooner shall you land or come on shore, but, as Plautus the comical poet hath it:

> *The courtesans within the place are wont*
> *To send their slaves and girls down to the harbour,*
> *Whenever any strange ship comes to port;*
> *They ask the vessel's name, and where it comes from,*
> *Then swoop upon the officers and crew.*

These white devils have their panders, bawds, and factors in every place, to seek about and bring in customers, to tempt and waylay novices and silly travellers. And when they have them once within their clutches, as Aegidius Maserius in his comment upon Valerius Flaccus describes them, with promises and pleasant discourse, with gifts, tokens, and taking their opportunities, they lay nets which Lucretia cannot avoid, and baits that Hippolytus himself would swallow; they make such strong assaults and batteries that the Goddess of Virginity cannot withstand them: give gifts and bribes to move Penelope and with threats able to terrify Susanna. How many Proserpinas with those catchpoles doth Pluto take! These are the sleepy rods with which their souls touched descend to hell; this the glue or lime with which the wings of the mind once taken cannot fly away; the devil's ministers to allure, entice, etc. Many young men and maids, without all question, are inveigled by these Eumenides and their associates.

But these are trivial and well known. The most sly, dangerous, and cunning bawds are your knavish physicians, empirics, mass-priests, monks, Jesuits, and friars. Though it be against Hippocrates' oath, some of them will give a dram, promise to restore maidenheads and do it without danger, make an abort if need be, keep down their paps, hinder conception, procure lust, make them able with satyrions, and now and then step in themselves. No monastery so close, house so private, or prison so well kept, but these honest men are admitted to censure and ask questions, to feel their pulse beat at their bedside, and all under pretence of giving physic. Now as for monks, confessors, and friars, as he [Aeneas Sylvius] said,

> *That Stygian Pluto dares not tempt or do,*
> *What an old hag or monk will undergo;*

either for himself to satisfy his own lust, for another, if he be hired thereto, or both at once, having such excellent means. For under colour of visitation, auricular confession, comfort, and penance, they have free egress and regress, and corrupt God knows how many. They can use trades, some of them, practise physic, use exorcisms, etc.

> *That there was wont to walken was an elf,*
> *There walketh now the limiter himself,*
> *In every bush and under every tree,*
> *There needs no other incubus but he.*

(CHAUCER)

In the mountains betwixt Dauphiné and Savoy, the friars persuaded the goodwives to counterfeit themselves possessed, that their husbands might give them free access, and were so familiar in those days with some of them, that, as one observes, wenches could not sleep in their beds for necromantic friars: and the good abbess in Boccaccio may in some sort witness, that rising betimes, mistook and put on the friar's breeches instead of her veil or hat.

You have heard the story, I presume, of Paulina, a chaste matron in Hegesippus, whom one of Isis' priests did prostitute to Mundus, a young knight, and made her believe it was their god Anubis. Many such pranks are played by our Jesuits, sometimes in their own habits, sometimes in others, like soldiers, courtiers, citizens, scholars, gallants, and women themselves. Proteus-like, in all forms and disguises, they go abroad in the night, to inescate [entice] and beguile young women, or to have their pleasure of other men's wives; and, if we may believe some relations, they have wardrobes of several suits in their colleges for that purpose. Howsoever, in public they pretend much zeal, seem to be very holy men, and bitterly preach against adultery, fornication, there are no verier bawds or whoremasters in a country. But I spare these men for the present.

The last battering engines are philters, amulets, spells, charms, images, and such unlawful means: if they cannot prevail of themselves by the help of bawds, panders, and their adherents, they will fly for succour to the devil himself. I know there be those that deny the devil can do any such thing (Crato and many divines), there is no other fascination than that which comes by the eyes, of which I have formerly spoken; and if you desire to be better informed, read Camerarius. It was given out of old that a Thessalian wench had bewitched King Philip to dote upon her, and by philters enforced his love; but when Olympias, the queen, saw the maid of an excellent beauty, well brought up and qualified, these, quoth she, were the philters which inveigled King Philip; those the true charms, as Henry to Rosamund [in Drayton]:

One accent from thy lips the blood more warms,
Than all their philters, exorcisms, and charms.

With this alone, Lucretia brags, in Aretine, she could do more than all philosophers, astrologers, alchemists, necromancers, witches, and the rest of the crew. 'As for herbs and philters, I could never skill of them; the sole philter that ever I used was kissing and embracing, by which alone I made men rave like beasts stupefied, and compelled them to worship me like an idol.' In our times it is a common thing, saith Erastus, for witches to take upon them the making of these philters, to force men and women to love and hate whom they will, to cause tempests, diseases, etc., by charms, spells, character, knots. St Jerome proves that they can do it; as in Hilarion's life, he hath a story of a young man that with a philter made a maid mad for the love of him, which maid was after cured by Hilarion.

Plutarch records of Lucullus, that he died of a philter; and that Cleopatra used philters to inveigle Antony, among other allurements. Eusebius reports as much of Lucretius the poet. Panormitan hath a story of one Stephen, a Neapolitan knight, that by a philter was forced to run mad for love. But of all others, that which Petrarch relates of Charles the Great is most memorable. He foolishly doted upon a woman of mean favour and condition, many years together, wholly delighting in her company, to the great grief and indignation of his friends and followers. When she was dead he did embrace her corpse, as Apollo did the bay-tree for his Daphne, and caused her coffin (richly embalmed and decked with jewels) to be carried about with him, over which he still lamented. At last a venerable bishop that followed his court, prayed earnestly to God (commiserating his lord and master's case) to know the true cause of this mad passion, and whence it proceeded; it was revealed to him, in fine, that the cause of the emperor's mad love lay under the dead woman's tongue. The bishop went hastily to the carcass, and took a small ring thence; upon the removal the emperor abhorred the corpse, and, instead of it, fell as furiously in love with the bishop, he would not suffer him to be out of his presence; which when the bishop perceived, he flung the ring into the midst of a great lake, where the king then was. From that hour the emperor neglected all his other houses, dwelt at Ache, built a fair house in the midst of the marsh, to his infinite expense, and a temple by it, where after he was buried, and in which city all his posterity ever since used to be crowned.

Marcus the heretic is accused by Irenaeus to have inveigled a young maid by this means; and some writers speak hardly of the Lady Katherine Cobham that by the same art she circumvented Humphrey Duke of Gloucester to be her husband. Sicinius Aemilianus summoned Apuleius to come before Claudius Maximus, proconsul of Africa, that he, being a poor fellow, had bewitched by philters Pudentilla, an ancient rich matron, to love him, and, being worth so many thousand sesterces, to be his wife.

Agrippa attributes much in this kind to philters, amulets, images. Leo Afer saith, 'tis an ordinary practice at Fez in Africa, where are many magicians to bring lovers together in bed: as skilful all out as that Hyperborean magician, of whom Cleodemus, in Lucian, tells so many fine feats performed in this kind. But Erastus, Wierus, and others are against it; they grant indeed such things may be done, but (as Wierus discourseth) not by charms, incantations, philters, but the devil himself; he contends as much; so doth Freitagius, Andreas Cisalpinus; and so much Sigismundus Scheretzius proves at large. 'Unchaste women by the help of these witches, the devil's kitchen-maids, have their loves brought to them in the night, and carried back again by a phantasm flying in the air in the likeness of a goat. I have heard [saith he] divers confess that they have been so carried on a goat's back to their sweethearts, many miles in a night.'

Others are of opinion that these feats, which most suppose to be done by charms and philters, are merely effected by natural causes, as by man's blood chemically prepared, which much avails, saith Ernestus Burgravius, to cause love or hatred (so huntsmen make their dogs love them, and farmers their pullen); 'tis an excellent philter, as he holds, but not fit to be made common: and so be mandrake roots, mandrake apples, precious stones, dead men's clothes, candles, a certain hair in a wolf's tail, etc., of which Rhasis, Dioscorides, Porta, Wecker, Rubeus, Mizaldus, Albertus, treat: a swallow's heart, dust of a dove's heart, viper's tongues, asses' brains, cauls of new-born infants, the rope by which a man has been hanged, a stone from an eagle's nest, etc. See more in Sckenkius, which are as forcible and of as much virtue as that fountain Salmacis in Vitruvius, Ovid, Strabo, that made all such mad for love that drank of it, or that hot bath at Aix in Germany, wherein Cupid once dipt his arrows, which ever since hath a peculiar virtue to make them lovers all that wash in it. These above-named remedies have haply as much power as that bath of Aix, or Venus' enchanted girdle, in which, saith Natalis Comes, love-toys and dalliance, pleasantness, sweetness, persuasions, subtili-ties, gentle speeches, and all witchcraft to enforce love, was contained.

XIII

Symptoms or Signs of Love-Melancholy,
in Body, Mind, good, bad, etc.

SYMPTOMS ARE either of body or mind; of body, paleness, leanness, dryness, etc. All lovers are pale, this hue becomes love, as the poet [Ovid] describes lovers; love causeth leanness. Avicenna makes hollow eyes, dryness, symptoms of this disease, to go smiling to themselves, or acting as if they saw or heard some delectable object. Valleriola, Laurentius, Aelianus Montaltus, Langius deliver as much, the body bloodless and pale, a lean body, hollow eyes; lean, pale, 'like one who has trodden bare foot upon a snake', hollow-eyed, their eyes are hidden in their heads, they pine away, and look ill with waking, cares, sighs, with groans, griefs, sadness, dullness, want of appetite, etc.

A reason of all this Jason Pratensis gives, because of the distraction of the spirits the liver doth not perform his part, nor turns the aliment into blood as it ought, and for that cause the members are weak for want of sustenance, they are lean and pine as the herbs of my garden do this month of May for want of rain. The green-sickness therefore often happeneth to young women, a cachexia or an evil habit to men, besides their ordinary sighs, complaints, and lamentations, which are too frequent. As drops from a still, doth Cupid's fire provoke tears from a true lover's eyes:

> *The mighty Mars did oft for Venus shriek,*
> *Privily moistening his horrid cheek*
> *With womanish tears;*

(SPENSER)

with many such-like passions.

When Chariclea was enamoured of Theagenes, as Heliodorus sets her out, she was half distracted, and spake she knew not what, sighed to herself, lay much awake, and was lean upon a sudden: and when she was besotted on her son-in-law she had ugly paleness, hollow eyes, restless thoughts, short wind, etc. Euryalus, in an epistle sent to Lucretia his mistress, complains among other grievances, 'Thou hast taken my stomach and my sleep from me.' So Chaucer describes it aright:

> *His sleep, his meat, his drink, is him bereft,*
> *That lean he wax, and dry as is a shaft,*
> *His eyes hollow and grisly to behold,*
> *His hew falwe and pale as ashen cold,*
> *And solitary he was and ever alone,*
> *And waking all the night, making his moan.*

Theocritus makes a fair maid of Delphi, in love with a young man of Minda, confess as much:

> *No sooner seen I had, than mad I was,*
> *My beauty fail'd, and I no more did care*
> *For any pomp, I knew not where I was,*
> *But sick I was, and evil I did fare;*
> *I lay upon my bed ten days and nights,*
> *A skeleton I was in all men's sights.*

All these passions are well expressed by that heroical poet [Virgil] in the person of Dido:

> *Unhappy Dido could not sleep at all,*
> *But lies awake, and takes no rest:*

> *And up she gets again, whilst care and grief,*
> *And raging love torment her breast.*

Accius Sannazarius in the same manner feigns his Lycoris torment-
ing herself for want of sleep, sighing, sobbing, and lamenting; and
Eustathius his Ismenias much troubled, and panting at heart, at the
sight of his mistress, he could not sleep, his bed was thorns. All make
leanness, want of appetite, want of sleep ordinary symptoms, and
by that means they are brought often so low, so much altered and
changed, that as he [Terence] jested in the comedy, one can scarce
know them to be the same men.

Many such symptoms there are of the body to discern lovers by.
'Can a man,' saith Solomon (Prov. vi, 27), 'carry fire in his bosom and
not burn?' it will hardly be hid; though they do all they can to hide
it, it must out. 'Twas Antiphanes the comedian's observation of old,
love and drunkenness cannot be concealed; words, looks, gestures, all
will betray them; but two of the most notable signs are observed by
the pulse and countenance. When Antiochus, the son of Selecus, was
sick for Stratonice, his mother-in-law, and would not confess his grief,
or the cause of his disease, Erasistratus the physician found him by
his pulse and countenance to be in love with her, because that when
she came in presence, or was named, his pulse varied, and he blushed
besides. In this very sort was the love of Charicles, the son of Polycles,
discovered by Panacius the physician, as you may read the story at
large in Aristaenetus. By the same signs Galen brags that he found
out Justa, Boethius the consul's wife, to dote on Pylades the player,
because at his name still she both altered pulse and countenance, as
Poliarchus did at the name of Argenis.

Franciscus Valesius denies there is any such pulse of love, or that
love may be so discerned; but Avicenna confirms this of Galen out of
his experience; and Gordonius; 'Their pulse,' he saith, 'is inordinate

and swift, if she go by whom he loves'; Langius; Nevisanus; Valescus de Taranta; Guianerius. Valleriola sets down this for a symptom: difference of pulse, neglect of business, want of sleep, often sighs, blushings when there is any speech of their mistress, are manifest signs. But among the rest, Josephus Struthius, that Polonian, in the fifth book of his Doctrine of Pulses, holds that this and all other passions of the mind may be discovered by the pulse. And if you will know, saith he, whether the men suspected be such or such, touch their arteries, etc. And in his fourth book, fourteenth chapter, he speaks of this particular pulse, 'Love makes an unequal pulse,' etc.; he gives instance of a gentlewoman, a patient of his, whom by this means he found to be much enamoured, and with whom: he named many persons, but at the last when his name came whom he suspected, her pulse began to vary and to beat swifter, and so, by often feeling her pulse, he perceived what the matter was. Apollonius, poetically setting down the meeting of Jason and Medea, makes them both to blush at one another's sight, and at the first they were not able to speak.

Phaedria trembled at the sight of Thais, others sweat, blow short, their legs shake, are troubled with palpitation of heart upon the like occasion; saith Aristaenetus, their heart is at their mouth, leaps, these burn and freeze (for love is fire, ice, hot, cold, itch, fever, frenzy, pleurisy, what not), they look pale, red, and commonly blush at their first congress, and sometimes through violent agitation of spirits bleed at nose, or when she is talked of; which very sign Eustathius makes an argument of Ismene's affection, that when she met her sweetheart by chance, she changed her countenance to a maiden-blush.

'Tis a common thing among lovers, as Arnulphus, that merry conceited bishop, hath well expressed in a facetious epigram of his:

> *Their faces answer, and by blushing say,*
> *How both affected are, they do betray.*

But the best conjectures are taken from such symptoms as appear when they are both present; all their speeches, amorous glances, actions, lascivious gestures will bewray them; they cannot contain themselves, but that they will be still kissing. Stratocles, the physician, upon his wedding-day, when he was at dinner, could not eat his meat for kissing the bride, etc. First a word, and then a kiss, then some other compliment, and then a kiss, then an idle question, then a kiss, and when he had pumped his wits dry, can say no more, kissing and colling are never out of season, 'tis never at an end, another kiss, and then another, another, and another, etc.: 'Come, kiss me, Corinna!' 'Ten thousand kisses, a hundred thousand, a thousand thousand, as many thousand thousand as there are drops in the Sicilian Gulf, as many as stars in the heavens, will I impress without ceasing on those glowing cheeks, those pouting lips, those speaking eyes of thine, O lovely Neaera.' Or as Catullus to Lesbia:

> *First gave an hundred,*
> *Then a thousand, then another*
> *Hundred, then unto the other*
> *Add a thousand, and so more,*
> *Till you equal with the store*
> *All the grass, etc.*

So Venus did by her Adonis, the Moon with Endymion, they are still dallying and calling, as so many doves, and that with alacrity and courage:

> *Hungrily they embrace, mingle their spittle,*
> *And breathe each other's breath, teeth against lips,*

bending back the head and pressing mouth so closely that scarce could lips be separated, as Lamprias in Lucian kissed Thais; Philippus her in Aristaenetus, 'mad with passion, he fastened his lips on mine in such frenzy that he could scarce free them, bruising my mouth'; Aretine's Lucretia by a suitor of hers was so saluted, and 'tis their ordinary fashion: With bitten lips, mouth hard on mouth.

They cannot, I say, contain themselves, they will be still not only joining hands, kissing, but embracing, treading on their toes, etc., diving into their bosoms, and that lasciviously, as Philostratus confesseth to his mistress; and Lamprias in Lucian, feeling their paps, and that scarce honestly sometimes: as the old man in the comedy well observed of his son, 'Did not I see thee put thy hand into her bosom? Go to!' with many such love tricks. Juno in Lucian, complains to Jupiter of Ixion, he looked so attentively on her, and sometimes would sigh and weep in her company: 'And when I drank by chance, and gave Ganymede the cup, he would desire to drink still in the very cup that I drank of, and in the same place where I drank, and would kiss the cup, and then look steadily on me, and sometimes sigh, and then again smile.' If it be so they cannot come near to dally, have not that opportunity, familiarity, or acquaintance to confer and talk together; yet, if they be in presence, their eye will bewray them: as the common saying is, 'Where I look I like, and where I like I love'; but they will lose themselves in her looks.

They cannot look off whom they love, they will deflower her with their eyes, be still gazing staring, stealing faces, smiling, glancing at her, as Apollo on Leuconthoe, the Moon on her Endymion, when she stood still in Caria, and at Latmos caused her chariot to be stayed. They must all stand and admire, or, if she go by, look after her as long as they can see her; she is the charioteer, as Anacreon calls her, they cannot go by her door or window but, as an adamant, she draws their eyes to it; though she be not there present, they must needs glance that way, and look back to it. Aristaenetus of Euxitheus, Lucian, in his Images, of himself, and Tatius of Clitiphon say as much, he never turned his eyes away from her, and many lovers confess, when they came in their mistress' presence, they could not hold off their eyes, but looked wistly and steadfastly on her, with much eagerness and greediness, as if they would look through, or should never have enough sight of her. So she will do by him, drink to him with her eyes, nay, drink him up, devour him, swallow him, as Martial's Mamurra is remembered to have done.

There is a pleasant story to this purpose in Vertomannus. The Sultan of Sana's wife in Arabia, because Vertomannus was fair and white, could not look off him, from sunrising to sunsetting; she could not desist; she made him one day come into her chamber, for two hours' space she still gazed on him. A young man in Lucian fell in love with Venus' picture; he came every morning to her temple, and there continued all day long from sunrising to sunset, unwilling to go home at night, sitting over against the goddess' picture, he did continually look upon her, and mutter to himself I know not what. If so be they cannot see them whom they love, they will still be walking and waiting about their mistress' doors, taking all opportunity to see them; as in Longus Sophista, Daphnis and Chloe, two lovers, were still hovering at one another's gates, he sought all occasions to be in her company, to hunt in summer, and catch birds in the frost about her father's house in the winter, that she might see him, and he her. 'A king's palace was not so diligently attended,' saith Aretine's Lucretia, 'as my house was when I lay in Rome; the porch and street was ever full of some, walking or riding on set purpose to see me; their eye still upon my window; as they passed by, they could not choose but look back to my house when they were past, and sometimes hem or cough, or take some impertinent occasion to speak aloud, that I might look out and observe them.'

'Tis so in other places, 'tis common to every lover, 'tis all his felicity to be with her, to talk with her; he is never well but in her company, and will walk seven or eight times a day through the street where she dwells, and make sleeveless errands to see her; plotting still where, when, and how to visit her, and when he is gone, he thinks every minute an hour, every hour as long as a day, ten days a whole year, till he sees her again. And if thou be in love, thou wilt say so too, farewell, sweetheart, farewell, my dear Argenis, once more farewell, farewell. And though he is to meet her by compact, and that very shortly, perchance tomorrow, yet loth to depart, he'll take his leave again and again, and then come back again, look after, and shake his hand, wave his hat afar off. Now gone, he thinks it long till he see her again, and she him, the clocks are surely set back, the hour's past. She looks out at window still to see whether he come, and by report Phyllis went nine times to the seaside that day, to see if her Demophoon were approaching, and Troilus to the city gates, to look for his Creseid. She is ill at ease, and sick till she sees him again, peevish in the meantime, discontent, heavy, sad; and why comes he not? where is he? why breaks he promise? why tarries he so long? sure he is not well; sure he hath some mischance; sure he forgets himself and me; with infinite such. And then, confident again up she gets, out she looks, listens and inquires, hearkens, kens; every man afar off is sure he, every stirring in the street, now he is there, that's he, etc., the longest day that ever was, so she raves, restless, and impatient.

For love brooks no delays: the time's quickly gone that's spent in her company, the miles short, the way pleasant; all weather is good while he goes to her house, heat or cold; though his teeth chatter in his head, he moves not; wet or dry, 'tis all one; wet to the skin, he feels it not, cares not at least for it, but will easily endure it and much more, because it is done with alacrity, and for his mistress' sweet sake; let the burden be never so heavy, love makes it light. Jacob served seven years for Rachel, and it was quickly gone because he loved her. None so merry if he may haply enjoy her company, he is in heaven for a time; and if he may not, depected in an instant, solitary, silent, he departs weeping, lamenting, sighing, complaining.

But the symptoms of the mind in lovers are almost infinite, and so diverse that no art can comprehend them; though they be merry sometimes, and rapt beyond themselves for joy, yet most part, love is a plague, a torture, an hell, a bitter-sweet passion at last. 'Tis a sweet bitterness, a delightful pain, a cheerful torment, like a summer fly or sphinx's wings, or a rainbow of all colours, fair, foul, and full of variation, though most part irksome and bad. For, in a word, the Spanish Inquisition is not comparable to it; a torment and execution it is, as he calls it in the poet, an unquenchable fire, and what not? From it, saith Augustine, arise biting cares, perturbations, passions, sorrows, fears, suspicions, discontents, contentions, discords, wars, treacheries, enmities, flattery, cozening, riot, impudence, cruelty, knavery, etc.

Grief, quarrels, tears, care, bitterness, and even worse than these, these be the companions of lovers, and the ordinary symptoms, as the poet repeats them.

> *In love these vices are: suspicions,*
> *Peace, war, and impudence, detractions,*
> *Dreams, cares, and errors, terrors and affrights,*
> *Immodest pranks, devices, sleights and flights,*
> *Heart-burnings, wants, neglects, desire of wrong,*
> *Loss continual, expense, and hurt among.*
>
> (TERENCE)

Every poet is full of such catologues of love-symptoms; but fear and sorrow may justly challenge the chief place. Though Hercules de Saxonia will exclude fear from love-melancholy, yet I am otherwise persuaded. 'Tis full of fear, anxiety, doubt, care, peevishness, suspicion; it turns a man into a woman, which made Hesiod belike put Fear and Paleness as Venus' daughters because fear and love are still linked together. Moreover, they are apt to mistake, amplify, too credulous sometimes, too full of hope and confidence, and then again very jealous, unapt to believe or entertain any good news. The comical poet [Terence] hath prettily painted out this passage among the rest in a dialogue betwixt Micio and Aeschines, a gentle father and a lovesick son. 'M. Be of good cheer, my son, thou shalt have her to wife. Ae. Ah, father, do you mock me now? M. I mock thee, why? Ae. That which I so earnestly desire, I more suspect and fear. M. Get you home, and send for her to be your wife. Ae. What now, a wife? now, father, etc.'

These doubts, anxieties, suspicions are the least part of their torments; they break many times from passions to actions, speak fair, and flatter, now most obsequious and willing, by and by they are averse, wrangle, fight, swear, quarrel, laugh, weep; and he that doth not so by fits, Lucian holds, is not throughly touched with this loadstone of love. So their actions and passions are intermixed, but of all other passions, sorrow hath the greatest share; love to many is bitterness itself; Plato calls it, a bitter potion, an agony, a plague.

> *O take away this plague, this mischief from me,*
> *Which, as a numbness over all my body,*
> *Expels my joys, and makes my soul so heavy.*
>
> (CATULLUS)

Phaedria [in Terence] had a true touch of this, when he cried out:

> *O Thais, would thou hadst of these my pains a part,*
> *Or, as it doth me now, so it would make thee smart.*

So had that young man, when she roared again for discontent:

I am vext and toss'd, and rack'd on love's wheel:
Where not, I am; but where am, do not feel.

(PLAUTUS)

The Moon, in Lucian, made her moan to Venus, that she was almost dead for love, and after a long tale, she broke off abruptly and wept: 'O Venus, thou knowest my poor heart.' Charmides, in Lucian, was so impatient that he sobbed and sighed, and tore his hair, and said he would hang himself: 'I am undone, O sister Tryphaena, I cannot endure these love pangs; what shall I do?' O ye Gods, free me from these cares and miseries! out of the anguish of his soul, Theocles prays. Shall I say, most part of a lover's life is full of agony, anxiety, fear, and grief, complaints, sighs, suspicions, and cares (heigh-ho, my heart is woe), full of silence and irksome solitariness?

Frequenting shady bowers in discontent,
To the air his fruitless clamours he will vent,

except at such times that he hath lucid intervals, pleasant gales, or sudden alterations, as if his mistress smile upon him, give him a good look, a kiss, or that some comfortable message be brought him, his service is accepted, etc.

He is then too confident and rapt beyond himself, as if he had heard the nightingale in the spring before the cuckoo, or as Callisto was at Meliboea's presence. Who ever saw so glorious a sight, what man ever enjoyed such delight? More content cannot be given of the gods, wished, had, or hoped of any mortal man. There is no happiness in the world comparable to his, no comment, no joy to this, no life to love, he is in paradise.

Who lives so happy as myself? what bliss
In this our life may be compared to this?

(CATULLUS)

He will not change fortune in that case with a prince: the Persian kings are not so jovial as he is. O happy day! so Chaerea exclaims when he came from Pamphila, his sweetheart, well pleased: he could find in his heart to be killed instantly, lest, if he lives longer, some sorrow or sickness should contaminate his joys. A little after, he was so merrily set upon the same occasion that he could not contain himself. 'Is't possible (O my countrymen) for any living to be so happy as myself? No, sure, it cannot be, for the gods have showed all their power, all their goodness in me.' Yet by and by, when this young gallant was crossed in his wench, he laments, and cries, and roars downright: 'I am undone, the Virgin's gone, and I am gone, she's gone, she's gone, and what shall I do? where shall I seek her, where shall I find her, whom shall I ask? what way, what course shall I take? what will become of me?' He was weary of his life, sick, mad, and desperate.

'Tis not Chaerea's case this alone, but his, and his, and every lover's in the like state. If he hear ill news, have bad success in his suit, she frown upon him, or that his mistress in his presence respect another more (as Haedus observes), prefer another suitor, speak more familiarly to him, or use more kindly than himself, if by nod, smile, message she discloseth herself to another, he is instantly tormented, none so dejected as he is, utterly undone, a castaway, a dead man, the scorn of fortune, a monster of fortune, worse than naught, the loss of a kingdom had been less.

Aretine's Lucretia made very good proof of this, as she relates it herself. 'For when I made some of my suitors believe I would betake myself to a nunnery, they took on as if they had lost father and mother, because they were for ever after to want my company.' All other labour was light; but this might not be endured, for I cannot be without thy company, mournful Amyntas, painful Amyntas, careful Amyntas; better a metropolitan city were sacked, a royal army overcome, an invincible armada sunk, and twenty thousand kings should perish, than her little finger ache, so zealous are they, and so tender of her good. 'They would all turn friars for my sake,' as she follows it, 'in hope by that means to meet or see me again, as my confessors, at stood-ball or at barley-break.' And so afterwards, when an importunate suitor came, 'If I had bid my maid say that I was not at leisure, not within, busy, could not speak with him, he was instantly astonished, and stood like a pillar of marble; another went swearing, chafing, cursing, foaming, etc.' The voice of a mandrake had been sweeter music; 'but he to whom I gave entertainment was in the Elysian Fields, ravished for joy, quite beyond himself'. 'Tis the general humour of all lovers, she is their stern, pole-star, and guide.

As a tulipant to the sun (which our herbalists call narcissus), when it shines, is a glorious flower exposing itself; but when the sun sets, or a tempest comes, it hides itself, pines away, and hath no pleasure left (which Carolus Gonzaga, Duke of Mantua, in a cause not unlike, sometimes used for an impress), do all inamorates to their mistress; she is their sun, their prime mover, or animating soul; this one hath elegantly expressed by a windmill, still moved by the wind, which otherwise hath no motion of itself. He is wholly animated from her breath, his soul lives in her body, she keeps the keys of his life: his fortune ebbs and flows with her favour, a gracious or bad aspect turns him up or down. Howsoever his present state be pleasing or displeasing, 'tis continuate so long as he loves, he can do nothing, think of nothing but her; desire hath no rest, she is his cynosure, his morning and evening star, his goddess, his mistress, his life, his soul, his everything; dreaming, waking, she is always in his mouth; his heart, his eyes, ears, and all his thoughts are full of her. His Laura, his Victorina, his Columbina, Flavia, Flaminia, Caelia, Delia, or Isabella (call her how you will), she is the sole object of his senses, the substance of his soul, he magnifies her above measure, full of her, can breathe nothing but her. I adore Meliboea saith lovesick Callisto, I believe in Meliboea, I honour, admire, and love my Meliboea; his soul was soused, imparadised, imprisoned in his lady. When Thais took her leave of Phaedria, 'Sweetheart [she said] will you command me any further service?' He readily replied, and gave this in charge:

> *Dost ask (my dear) what service I will have?*
> *To love me day and night is all I crave,*
> *To dream on me, to expect, think on me,*
> *Depend and hope, still covet me to see,*
> *Delight thyself in me, be wholly mine,*
> *For know, my love, that I am wholly thine.*

But all this needed not, you will say; if she affect once, she will be his, settle her love on him, on him alone. Though parted, seeing and hearing him, she can, she must think and dream of naught else but him, continually of him, as did Virgil's Orpheus on his Eurydice:

> *On thee, sweet wife, was all my song.*
> *Morn, evening, and all along.*

And Dido upon her Aeneas:

> *And ever and anon she thinks upon the man*
> *That was so fine, so fair, so blithe, so debonair*

Clitiphon, in the first book of Achilles Tatius, complaineth how that his mistress Leucippe tormented him much more in the night than in the day. For all day long he had some object or other to distract his senses, but in the night all ran upon her. All night long he lay awake, and could think of nothing else but her, he could not get her out of his mind; towards morning, sleep took a little pity on him, he slumbered awhile, but all his dreams were of her.

> *In the dark night I speak, embrace, and find*
> *That fading joys deceive my careful mind.*

The same complaint Euryalus makes to his Lucretia: 'Day and night I think of thee, I wish for thee, I talk of thee, call on thee, look for thee, hope for thee, delight myself in thee, day and night I love thee. Morning, evening, all is alike with me, I have restless thoughts. Still I think on thee. The soul is not where it lives but where it loves. I live and breathe in thee, I wish for thee. O happy day that shall restore thee to my sight!' In the meantime he raves on her; her sweet face, eyes, actions, gestures, hands, feet, speech, length, breadth, height, depth, and the rest of her dimensions, are so surveyed, measured, and taken by that astrolabe of phantasy, and that so violently sometimes, with such earnestness and eagerness, such continuance, so strong an imagination, that at length he thinks he sees her indeed; he talks with her, he embraceth her, Ixion-like, a cloud for Juno, as he said, 'I see and meditate of naught but Leucippe.' Be she present or absent, all is one: that impression of her beauty is still fixed in her mind; as he that is bitten with a mad dog thinks all he sees dogs, dogs in his meat, dogs in his dish, dogs in his drink, his mistress is in his eyes, ears, heart, in all his senses. Valleriola had a merchant, his patient, in the same predicament; and Ulricus Molitor, out of Augustine, hath a story of one that through vehemency of his love passion still thought he saw his mistress present with him; she talked with him, still embracing him.

Now if this passion of love can produce such effects if it be pleas-
antly intended, what bitter torments shall it breed when it is with fear
and continual sorrow, suspicion, care, agony, as commonly it is, still
accompanied! what an intolerable pain must it be!

> *Mount Gargarus hath not so many stems*
> *As lover's breast hath grievous wounds,*
> *And linked cares, which love compounds.*

When the King of Babylon would have punished a courtier of his for
loving of a young lady of the royal blood and far above his fortunes,
Apollonius in presence by all means persuaded to let him alone; for to
love and not enjoy was a most unspeakable torment, no tyrant could
invent the like punishment; as a gnat at a candle, in a short space he
would consume himself. For love is a perpetual flux, mental anguish,
a warfare, a grievous wound is love still, and a lover's heart is Cupid's
quiver, a consuming fire, an inextinguishable fire. As Aetna rageth,
so doth love, and more than Aetna of any material fire. Vulcan's
flames are but smoke to this. For fire, saith Xenophon, burns them
alone that stand near it, or touch it; but this fire of love burneth and
scorcheth afar off, and is more hot and vehement than any material
fire; 'tis a fire in a fire, the quintessence of fire. For when Nero burnt
Rome, as Callisto urgeth, he fired houses, consumed men's bodies
and goods; but this fire devours the soul itself, and one soul is worth
an hundred thousand bodies. No water can quench this wild-fire.

> *A fire he took into his breast,*
> *Which water could not quench,*
> *Nor herb, nor art, nor magic spells*
> *Could quell, nor any drench,*

(MAUTUAN)

except it be tears and sighs, for so they may chance find a little ease.

> *So thy white neck, Neaera, my poor soul*
> *Doth scorch, thy cheeks, thy wanton eyes that roll:*
> *Were it not for my dropping tears that hinder,*
> *I should be quite burnt up forthwith to cinder.*
>
> (MARULLUS)

This fire strikes like lightning, which made those old Grecians paint Cupid in many of their temples with Jupiter's thunderbolts in his hands; for it wounds, and cannot be perceived how, whence it came, where it pierced: and can hardly be discerned at first.

> *A gentle wound, an easy fire it was,*
> *And sly at first, and secretly did pass.*
>
> (VIRGIL)

But by and by it began to rage and burn amain:

> *This fiery vapour rageth in the veins,*
> *And scorcheth entrails, as when fire burns*
> *A house, it nimbly runs along the beams,*
> *And at the last the whole it overturns.*
>
> (SENECA)

Abraham Hoffemannus relates out of Plato how that Empedocles the philosopher was present at the cutting up of one that died for love, his heart was combust, his liver smoky, his lungs dried up, insomuch that he verily believed his soul was either sod or roasted through the vehemency of love's fire. Which belike made a modern writer of amorous emblems express love's fury by a pot hanging over the fire, and Cupid blowing the coals. As the heat consumes the water, so doth love dry up his radical moisture. Another compares love to a melting torch, which stood too near the fire.

> *The nearer he unto his mistress is,*
> *The nearer he unto his ruin is.*

So that to say truth, as Castiglione describes it, the beginning, middle, end of love is naught else but sorrow, vexation, agony, torment, irksomeness, wearisomeness; so that to be squalid, ugly, miserable, solitary, discontent, dejected, to wish for death, to complain, rave, and to be peevish, are the certain signs and ordinary actions of a lovesick person. This continual pain and torture makes them forget themselves, if they be far gone with it, in doubt, despair of obtaining, or eagerly bent, to neglect all ordinary business.

Lovesick Dido left her work undone, so did Phaedra: Faustus, in Mantuan, took no pleasure in anything he did.

> *Nor work were pleasant, my senses were inert,*
> *In my love-sick condition neither rest*
> *My mind lay imbecile, I had no love,*
> *As erst, for song.*

And 'tis the humour of them all to be careless of their persons and their estates, as the shepherd in Theocritus, their beards flag, and they have no more care of pranking themselves, or of any business; they care not, as they say, which end goes forward.

> *Forgetting flocks of sheep and country farms,*
> *The silly shepherd always mourns and burns.*

Lovesick Chaerea, when he came from Pamphila's house and had not so good welcome as he did expect, was all amort, Parmeno meets him: 'Why art thou so sad, man? whence com'st, how dost?' but he sadly replies, 'I have so forgotten myself, I neither know where I am, nor whence I come, nor whether I will, what I do.' P. 'How so?' Ch. 'I am still in love.' He that erst had his thoughts free (as Philostratus Lemnius, in an epistle of his, describes this fiery passion), and spent his time like an hard student, in those delightsome philosophical precepts, he that with the sun and moon wandered all over the world, with stars themselves ranged about, and left no secret or small mystery in Nature unsearched, since he was enamoured can do nothing now but think and meditate of love-matters, day and night composeth himself how to please his mistress; all his study, endeavour, is to approve himself to his mistress, to win his mistress' favour, to compass his desire, to be counted her servant. When Peter Abelard, that great scholar of his age, to whom alone was known whatever is knowable, was now in love with Heloise, he had no mind to visit or frequent schools and scholars any more, all his mind was on his new mistress.

Now to this end and purpose, if there be any hope of obtaining his suit, to prosecute his cause, he will spend himself, goods, fortunes for her, and though he lose and alienate all his friends, be threatened, be cast off, and disinherited; for, as the poet saith, Who can lay down the law to love; though he be utterly undone by it, disgraced, go a-begging, yet for her sweet sake, to enjoy her, he will willingly beg, hazard all he hath, goods, lands, shame, scandal, fame, and life itself.

> *Till she or death do make me mute.*
> *I'll never rest or cease my suit*
>
> (PLAUTUS)

Parthenis in Aristaenetus was fully resolved to do as much: 'I may have better matches, I confess, but farewell shame, farewell honour, farewell honesty, farewell friends, and fortunes, etc. O Harpedona, keep my counsel, I will leave all for his sweet sake, I will have him, say no more, against all the world, I am resolved, I will have him.' Gobryas the captain, when he had espied Rhodanthe, the fair captive maid, fell upon his knees before Mystylus the general, with tears, vows, and all the rhetoric he could, by the scars he had formerly received, the good service he had done, or whatsoever else was dear unto him, besought his governor he might have the captive virgin to be his wife, as a reward of his worth and service; and moreover, he would forgive him the money which was owing, and all reckonings besides due unto him: 'I ask no more, no part of booty, no portion, but Rhodanthe to be my wife.' And whenas he could not compass her by fair means, he fell to treachery, force, and villainy, and set his life at stake at last to accomplish his desire. 'Tis a common humour this, a general passion of all lovers to be so affected, and which Aemilia told Aretine, a courtier in Castiglione's discourse: 'Surely, Aretine, if thou werst not so indeed, thou didst not love; ingenuously confess, for if thou hadst been throughly enamoured, thou wouldst have desired nothing more than to please thy mistress. For that is the law of love, to will and nill the same.'

Undoubtedly this may be pronounced of them all, they are very slaves, melancholy drudges for the time, madmen, fools, dizzards, beside themselves, and as blind as beetles. Their dotage is most eminent, as Seneca holds, Jupiter himself cannot love and be wise both together; the very best of them, if once they be overtaken with this passion, the most staid, discreet, grave, generous, and wise, otherwise able to govern themselves, in this commit many absurdities, many indecorums, unbefitting their gravity and persons. Samson, David, Solomon, Hercules, Socrates, etc., are justly taxed of indiscretion in this point; the middle sort are betwixt hawk and buzzard, and although they do perceive and acknowledge their own dotage, weakness, fury, yet they cannot withstand it; as well may witness those expostulations and confessions of Dido in Virgil: 'She began to speak, but stopped with word half uttered.' Phaedra in Seneca: 'Reason is overborne and swayed by passion, the God of Love reigns in her soul.' Myrrha in Ovid:

> *She sees and knows her fault, and doth resist,*
> *Against her filthy lust she doth contend,*
> *And 'Whither go I, what am I about?'*
> *And 'God forbid!' yet doth it in the end.*

Again:

> *With raging lust she burns, and now recalls*
> *Her vow, and then despairs, and when 'tis past,*
> *Her former thoughts she'll prosecute in haste,*
> *And what to do she knows not at the last.*

She will and will not, abhors; and yet as Medea did, doth it:

> *Reason pulls one way, burning lust another,*
> *She sees and knows what's good, but she doth neither.*
>
> (OVID)

The major part of lovers are carried headlong like so many brute beasts; reason counsels one way, thy friends, fortunes, shame, disgrace, danger, and an ocean of cares that will certainly follow; yet this furious lust precipitates, counterpoiseth, weighs down on the other; though it be their utter undoing, perpetual infamy, loss, yet they will do it, and become at last void of sense; degenerate into dogs, hogs, asses, brutes; as Jupiter into a bull, Apuleius an ass, Lycaon a wolf, Tereus a lapwing, Callisto a bear, Elpenor and Gryllus into swine by Circe. For what else may we think those ingenious poets to have shadowed in their witty fictions and poems, but that a man once given over to his lust (as Fulgentius interprets that of Apuleius, Alciat of Tereus) is no better than a beast.

> *I was a king, my crown my witness is,*
> *But by my filthiness am come to this.*
>
> (ALCIATI)

Their blindness is all out as great, as manifest as their weakness and dotage, or rather an inseparable companion, an ordinary sign of it. Love is blind, as the saying is, Cupid's blind, and so are all his followers. 'Who loves a frog, thinks it as fair as Diana.' Every lover admires his mistress, though she be very deformed of herself, ill-favoured, wrinkled, pimpled, pale, red, yellow, tanned, tallow-faced, have a swollen juggler's platter face, or a thin, lean, chitty face, have clouds in her face, be crooked, dry, bald, goggle-eyed, blear-eyed, or with staring eyes, she looks like a squis'd cat, hold her head still awry, heavy, dull, hollow-eyed, black or yellow about the eyes, or squint-eyed, sparrow-mouthed, Persian hook-nosed, have a sharp fox-nose, a red nose, China flat, great nose, snub and flat nose, a nose like a promontory, gubber-tushed, rotten teeth, black, uneven, brown teeth, beetle-browed, a witch's beard, her breath stink all over the room, her nose drop winter and summer, with a Bavarian poke under her chin, a sharp chin, lave-eared, with a long crane's neck, which stands awry too, with hanging breasts, her dugs like two double jugs, or else no dugs, in that other extreme, bloody-fallen fingers, she have filthy, long unpared nails, scabbed hands or wrists, a tanned skin, a rotten carcass, crooked back, she stoops, is lame, splay-footed, as slender in the middle as a cow in the waist, gouty legs, and ankles hang over her shoes, her feet stink, she breeds lice, a mere changeling, a very monster, an oaf imperfect, her whole complexion savours, an harsh voice, incondite gesture, vile gait, a vast virago, or an ugly tit, a slug, a fat fustilugs, a truss, a long lean rawbone, a skeleton, a sneaker, suppose her unseen charms are better, and to thy judgement looks like a merd in a lanthorn, whom thou couldst not fancy for a world, but hatest, loathest, and wouldest have spit in her face, or blow thy nose in her bosom, a cure for love to another man, a dowdy, a slut, a scold, a nasty, rank, rammy, filthy, beastly quean, dishonest per-adventure, obscene, base, beggarly, rude, foolish, untaught, peevish, Irus' daughter, Thersites' sister, Grobian's scholar; if he love her once, he admires her for all this, he takes no notice of any such errors or imperfections of body or mind, he had rather have her than any woman in the world.

If he were a king, she alone should be his queen, his empress. O that he had but the wealth and treasure of both the Indies to endow her with, a carrack of diamonds, a chain of pearl, a carcanet of jewels (a pair of calf-skin gloves of fourpence a pair were fitter), or some such toy, to send her for a token, she should have it with all his heart; he would spend myriads of crowns for her sake. Venus herself, Panthea, Cleopatra, Tarquin's Tanaquil, Herod's Mariamne, or Mary of Burgundy, if she were alive, would not match her. Her beauty surpasseth Helen's, let Paris himself be judge, renowned Helen comes short, that Rhodopeian Phyllis, Larissaean Coronis, Babylonian Thisbe, Polyxena, Laura, Lesbia, etc., your counterfeit ladies were never so fair as she is.

> *Whate'er is pretty, pleasant, facet, well,*
> *Whate'er Pandora had, she doth excel.*

Diana was not to be compared to her, nor Juno, nor Minerva, nor any goddess. Thetis' feet were as bright as silver, the ankles of Hebe clearer than crystal, the arms of Aurora as ruddy as the rose, Juno's breasts as white as snow, Minerva wise, Venus fair; but what of this? Dainty, come thou to me. She is all in all: Caelia is Venus laughing, Juno walking, Minerva speaking. 'Fairest of fair, that fairness doth excel.'

Euemerus, in Aristaenetus, so far admireth his mistress' good parts that he makes proclamation of them, and challengeth all comers in her behalf. Who ever saw the beauties of the East, or of the West, let them come from all quarters, all, and tell truth, if ever they saw such an excellent feature as this is. A good fellow in Petronius cries out, no tongue can tell his lady's fine feature, or express it.

> *No tongue can her perfections tell,*
> *In whose each part all tongues may dwell.*
>
> (SIDNEY)

Most of your lovers are of his humour and opinion. She is second to none, a rare creature, a phoenix, the sole commandress of his thoughts, queen of his desires, his only delight: as Triton now feelingly sings, that lovesick sea-god:

> *Fair Leucothoe, black Melaene please me well,*
> *But Galatea doth by odds the rest excel.*
>
> (CALAGNINUS)

All the gracious elogies, metaphors, hyperbolical comparisons of the best things in the world, the most glorious names; whatsoever, I say, is pleasant, amiable, sweet, grateful, and delicious, are too little for her.

His Phoebe is so fair, she is so bright,
She dims the sun's lustre, and the moon's light.

Stars, sun, moons, metals, sweet-smelling flowers, odours, perfumes, colours, gold, silver, ivory, pearls, precious stones, snow, painted birds, doves, honey, sugar, spice, cannot express her, so soft, so tender, so radiant, sweet, so fair is she.

Fine Lydia, my mistress, white and fair,
The milk, the lily do not thee come near;
The rose so white, the rose so red to see,
And Indian ivory comes short of thee.

(PETRONIUS)

Such a description our English Homer [Chaucer] makes of a fair lady:

That Emilia that fairer was to seen,
Than is the lily upon his stalk green:
And fresher than the May with flowers new,
For with the rose colour strove her hue,
I no't which was the fairer of hem two.

In this very phrase Polyphemus courts Galatea:

Whiter Galatea than the white withy-wind,
Fresher than a field, higher than a tree,
Brighter than glass, more wanton than a kid,
Softer than swan's down, or aught that may be.

(OVID)

So she admires him again, in that conceited dialogue of Lucian, which John Secundus, an elegant Dutch modern poet, hath translated into verse. When Doris and those other sea-nymphs upbraided her with her ugly misshapen lover Polyphemus, she replies, they speak out of envy and malice,

> *Plainly 'tis envy prompts you, since he*
> *Doth not love you as he loves me.*

Say what they could, he was a proper man. And as Heloise writ to her sweetheart Peter Abelard, she had rather be his vassal, his quean, than the world's empress or queen; she would not change her love for Jupiter himself.

To thy thinking she is a most loathsome creature; and as when a country fellow discommended once that exquisite picture of Helen, made by Zeuxis, for he saw no such beauty in it, Nichomachus, a lovesick spectator, replied, 'Take mine eyes, and thou wilt think she is a goddess, dote on her forthwith, count all her vice virtues, her imperfections infirmities, absolute and perfect. If she be flat-nosed, she is lovely; if hook-nosed, kingly; if dwarfish and little, pretty; if tall, proper and man-like, our brave British Boadicea; if crooked, wise; if monstrous, comely; her defects are no defects at all, she hath no deformities. Though she be nasty, fulsome, as Sistratus' bitch, or Parmeno's sow; thou hadst as lieve have a snake in thy bosom, a toad in thy dish, and callest her witch, devil, hag, with all the filthy names thou canst invent; he admires her on the other side, she is his idol, lady, mistress, little Venus, queen, the quintessence of beauty, an angel, a star, a goddess.'

> *Thou art my Vesta, thou my goddess art,*
> *Thy hallowed temple only is my heart.*

(DRAYTON)

The fragrancy of a thousand courtesans is in her face: 'tis not Venus'
picture that, nor the Spanish Infanta's, as you suppose (good sir), no
princess, or king's daughter; no, no, but his divine mistress forsooth,
his dainty Dulcinea, his dear Antiphila, to whose service he is wholly
consecrate, whom he alone adores,

> *To whom conferr'd a peacock's undecent,*
> *A squirrel's harsh, a phoenix too frequent,*
>
> (MARTIAL)

All the Graces, veneries, elegancies, pleasures, attend her. He prefers
her before a myriad of court ladies.

> *He that commends Phyllis or Neaera,*
> *Or Amaryllis, or Galatea,*
> *Tityrus of Meliboea, by your leave,*
> *Let him be mute, his love the praises have.*
>
> (ARIOSTO)

Nay, before all the gods and goddesses themselves. So Quintus Catulus
admired his squint-eyed friend Roscius:

> *By your leave, gentle gods, this I'll say true,*
> *There's none of you that have so fair a hue.*
>
> (CICERO)

All the bombast epithets, pathetical adjuncts, incomparably fair, curiously neat, divine, sweet, dainty, delicious, etc., pretty diminutives,
little heart, little kiss, etc., pleasant names may be invented, bird,
mouse, lamb, puss, pigeon, pigsney, kid, honey, love, dove, chicken,
etc., he puts on her: My honest, my sweetest, my heart, my kiss, my

darling, my life, my light, my jewel, my glory, my sweet Margaret, my sole delight and darling. And as Rhodomant courted Isabella:

> *By all kind words and gestures that he might,*
> *He calls her his dear heart, his sole beloved,*
> *His joyful comfort, and his sweet delight,*
> *His mistress, and his goddess, and such names,*
> *As loving knights apply to lovely dames.*

(ARIOSTO)

Every cloth she wears, every fashion pleaseth him above measure; her hand, those fingers, those hands are hers! pretty foot, pretty coronets, her sweet carriage, sweet voice, tone, O that pretty tone, her divine and lovely looks, her every thing, lovely, sweet, amiable, and pretty, pretty, pretty! Her very name (let it be what it will) is a most pretty, pleasing name; I believe now there is some secret power and virtue in names; every action, sight, habit, gesture he admires, whether she play, sing, or dance, in what tires soever she goeth, how excellent it was! how well it became her! never the like seen or heard. A thousand dresses she hath, and all become her. Let her wear what she will, do what she will, say what she will, he applauds and admires everything she wears, saith or doth.

> *Whate'er she doth, or whither e'er she go,*
> *A sweet and pleasing grace attends forsooth;*
> *Or loose, or bind her hair, or comb it up,*
> *She's to be honoured in what she doth.*

(TIBULLUS)

Let her be dressed or undressed, all is one, she is excellent still, beautiful, fair, and lovely to behold. Women do as much by men; nay more, far wonder, weaker, and that by many parasangs. 'Come to me, my dear Lysias [saith Musarium in Aristaenetus], come quickly, sweetheart, all other men are satyrs, mere clowns, blockheads to thee, nobody to thee; thy looks, words, gestures, actions, etc., are incomparably beyond all others.' Venus was never so much besotted on her Adonis, Phaedra so delighted in Hippolytus, Ariadne in Theseus, Thisbe in her Pyramus, as she is enamoured on her Mopsus.

> *Be thou the marigold, and I will be the sun,*
> *Be thou the friar, and I will be the nun.*

I could repeat centuries of such. Now tell me what greater dotage or blindness can there be than this in both sexes? and yet their slavery is more eminent, a greater sign of their folly than the rest.

They are commonly slaves, captives, voluntary servants, as Castiglione terms him, a lover is his mistress' servant, her drudge, prisoner, bondman, what not? He composeth himself wholly to her affections to please her, and, as Aemilia said, makes himself her lackey. All his cares, actions, all his thoughts, are subordinate to her will and commandment; her most devote, obsequious, affectionate servant and vassal. For love (as Cyrus in Xenophon well observed) is a mere tyranny, worse than any disease, and they that are troubled with it desire to be free and cannot, but are harder bound than if they were in iron chains. What greater captivity or slavery can there be (as Tully expostulates) than to be in love? Is he a free man over whom a woman domineers, to whom she prescribes laws, commands, forbids what she will herself? that dares deny nothing she demands? she asks, he gives; she calls, he comes; she threatens, he fears; I account this man a very drudge. And as he follows it, 'Is this no small servitude for an enamorate to be every hour combing his head, stiffening his beard, perfuming his hair, washing his face with sweet waters, painting, curling, and not to come abroad but sprucely crowned, decked, and apparelled?'

Yet these are but toys in respect, to go to the barber, baths, theatres, etc., he must attend upon her wherever she goes, run along the streets by her doors and windows to see her, take all opportunities, sleeveless errands, disguises, counterfeit shapes, and as many forms as Jupiter himself ever took; and come every day to her house (as he will surely do if he be truly enamoured) and offer her service, and follow her up and down from room to room, as Lucretia's suitors did, he cannot contain himself but he will do it, he must and will be where she is, sit next her, still talking with her. 'If I did but let my glove fall by chance [as the said Aretine's Lucretia brags], I had one of my suitors, nay, two or three at once, ready to stoop and take it up, and kiss it, and with a low congee deliver it unto me; if I would walk, another was ready to sustain me by the arm; a third to provide fruits, pears, plums, cherries, or whatsoever I would eat or drink.'

All this and much more he doth in her presence, and when he comes home, as Troilus on his Creseid, 'tis all his meditation to recount with himself his actions, words, gestures, what entertainment he had, how kindly she used him in such a place, how she smiled, how she graced him, and that infinitely pleased him; and then he breaks out, 'O sweet Areusa, O my dearest Antiphila, O most divine looks, O lovely graces!' and thereupon instantly he makes an epigram, or a sonnet to five or seven tunes, in her commendation, or else he ruminates how she rejected his service, denied him a kiss, disgraced him, etc., and that as effectually torments him. And these are his exercises betwixt comb and glass, madrigals, elegies, etc., these his cogitations till he sees her again. But all this is easy and gentle, and the least part of his labour and bondage; no hunter will take such pains for his game, fowler for his sport, or soldier to sack a city, as he will for his mistress' favour.

I will be your companion, naught shall fright me,
Nor rugged rocks, nor tusk of savage boar,

as Phaedra to Hippolytus.

No danger shall affright, for if that be true the poets feign, Love is the son of Mars and Venus; as he hath delights, pleasures, elegancies from his mother, so hath he hardness, valour, and boldness from his father. And 'tis true that Bernard hath: nothing so boisterous, nothing so tender as love. If once therefore enamoured, he will go, run, ride many a mile to meet her, day and night, in a very dark night, endure scorching heat, cold, wait in frost and snow, rain, tempests, till his teeth chatter in his head, those northern winds and showers cannot cool or quench his flames of love. The stormy night will not deter him, he will, take my word, he will sustain hunger, thirst, penetrate all, overcome all, love will find out a way, through thick and thin he will to her, he will swim through an ocean, ride post over the Alps, Apennines, or Pyrenean hills, though it rain daggers with their points downward, light or dark, all is one; for her sweet sake he will undertake Hercules' twelve labours, endure, hazard, etc., he feels it not.

'What shall I say,' saith Haedus, 'of their great dangers they undergo, single combats they undertake, how they will venture their lives, creep in at windows, gutters, climb over walls to come to their sweethearts [anointing the doors and hinges with oil, because they should not creak, tread soft, swim, wade, watch, etc.], and if they be surprised, leap out at windows, cast themselves headlong down, bruising or breaking their legs or arms, and sometimes losing life itself,' as Callisto did for his lovely Meliboea. Hear some of their own confessions, protestations, complaints, proffers, expostulations, wishes, brutish attempts, labours in this kind. Hercules served Omphale, put on an apron, took a distaff and spun; Thraso the soldier was so submissive to Thais that he was resolved to do whatever she enjoined.

Philostratus, in an epistle to his mistress: 'I am ready to die, sweetheart, if it be thy will; allay his thirst whom thy star hath scorched and undone; the fountains and rivers deny no man drink that comes; the fountain doth not say, Thou shalt not drink; nor the apple, Thou shalt not eat; nor the fair meadow, Walk not in me; but thou alone wilt not let me come near thee or see thee; contemned and despised, I die for grief.' Polyaenus, when his mistress Circe did but frown upon him in Petronius, drew his sword, and bade her kill, stab, or whip him to death, he would strip himself naked, and not resist. Another will take a journey to Japan; a third (if she say it) will not speak a word for a twelvemonth's space, her command shall be most inviolably kept; a fourth will take Hercules' club from him, and with that centurion in the Spanish Caelestina, will kill ten men for his mistress Areusa, for a word of her mouth, he will cut bucklers in two like pippins, and flap down men like flies.

Galeatus of Mantua did a little more; for when he was almost mad for love of a fair maid in the city, she, to try him, belike, what he would do for her sake, bade him in jest leap into the River Po if he loved her; he forthwith did leap headlong off the bridge and was drowned. Another at Ficinum in like passion, when his mistress by chance (thinking no harm, I dare swear) bade him go hang, the next night at her doors hanged himself. 'Money [saith Xenophon] is a very acceptable and welcome guest, yet I had rather give it my dear Cleinias than take it of others, I had rather serve him than command others, I had rather be his drudge than take my ease, undergo any danger for his sake than live in security. For I had rather see Cleinias than all the world besides, and had rather want the sight of all other things than him alone; I am angry with the night and sleep that I may not see him, and thank the light and sun because they show me my Cleinias; I will run into the fire for his sake, and if you did but see him, I know that you likewise would run with me.' So Philostratus to his mistress: 'Command me what you will, I will do it; bid me go to sea, I am gone in an instant; take so many stripes, I am ready; run through the fire, and lay down my life and soul at thy feet, 'tis done.' So did Aeolus to Juno:

> *O queen, it is thy pains to enjoin me still,*
> *And I am bound to execute thy will.*

And Phaedra to Hippolytus:

> *O call me sister, call me servant, choose,*
> *Or rather servant, I am thine to use.*
> *It shall not grieve me to the snowy hills,*
> *Or frozen Pindus' tops forthwith to climb,*
> *Or run through fire, or through an army,*
> *Say but the word, for I am always thine.*

(SENECA)

Callicratides, in Lucian, breaks out into this passionate speech: 'O God of Heaven, grant me this life for ever to sit over against my mistress, and to hear her sweet voice, to go in and out with her, to have every other business common with her; I would labour when she labours, sail when she sails; he that hates her should hate me; and if a tyrant kill her, he should kill me; if she should die, I would not live, and one grave should hold us both.' Abrocomas in Aristaenetus makes the like petition for his Delphis. 'Gladly I'd live with thee, or gladly die.' 'Tis the same strain which Theagenes used to his Chariclea: 'So that I may but enjoy thy love, let me die presently'; Leander to his Hero, when he besought the sea waves to let him go quietly to his love, and kill him coming back. 'Tis the common humour of them all, to contemn death, to wish for death, to confront death in this case; caring neither for wild beasts nor fire nor precipice nor sea nor sword nor noose, 'tis their desire (saith Tyrius) to die. 'He fears not death, nay he desires to run upon the very swords' (Seneca).

Though a thousand dragons or devils kept the gates, Cerberus himself, Sciron and Procrustes lay in wait, and the way as dangerous, as inaccessible as hell, through fiery flames and over burning coulters, he will adventure for all this. And as Peter Abelard lost his testicles for his Heloise, he will (I say) not venture an incision, but life itself. For how many gallants offered to lose their lives for a night's lodging with Cleopatra in those days! And in the hour or moment of death, 'tis their sole comfort to remember their dear mistress, as Zerbino slain in France, and Brandimart in Barbary; as Arcite did his Emily:

> When he felt death,
> Dusked been his eyen, and faded in his breath,
> But on his lady yet casteth he his eye,
> His last word was, Mercy Emely,
> His spirit chang'd, and out went there,
> Whither I cannot tell, ne where.
>
> (CHAUCER)

When Captain Gobrias by an unlucky accident had received his death's wound, 'Miserable man that I am!' (instead of other devotions), he cries out, 'shall I die before I see Rhodanthe my sweetheart?' So love triumphs, contemns, insults over death itself.

Thirteen proper young men lost their lives for that fair Hippodamia's sake, the daughter of Oenomaus, King of Elis: when that hard condition was proposed of death or victory, they made no account of it, but courageously for love died, till Pelops at last won her by a sleight. As many gallants desperately adventured their dearest blood for Atalanta, the daughter of Schoeneus, in hope of marriage, all vanquished and overcame, till Hippomenes by a few golden apples happily obtained his suit. Perseus of old fought with a sea-monster for Andromeda's sake; and our St George freed the king's daughter of Sabea (the Golden Legend is mine author) that was exposed to a dragon, by a terrible combat. Our knights errant, and the Sir Lancelots of these days, I hope will adventure as much for ladies' favours, as the Squire of Dames, Knight of the Sun, Sir Bevis of Southampton, or that renowned peer,

> *Orlando, who long time had loved dear*
> *Angelica the fair, and for her sake*
> *About the world in nations far and near,*
> *Did high attempts perform and undertake.*
>
> (ARIOSTO)

He is a very dastard, a coward, a block, and a beast, that will not do as much, but they will sure, they will; for it is an ordinary thing for these inamoratos of our time to say and do more, to stab their arms, carouse in blood, or as that Thessalian Thero, that bit off his own thumb, to make his corrival do as much. 'Tis frequent with them to challenge the field for their lady and mistress' sake, to run a tilt,

> *That either bears (so furiously they meet)*
> *The other down under the horses' feet,*
>
> (SPENSER)

and then up and to it again,

> *And with their axes both so sorely pour,*
> *That neither plate nor mail sustain'd the stour,*

> *But rivall'd wreak like rotten wood asunder,*
> *And fire did flash like lightning after thunder;*

and in her quarrel, to fight so long till their head-piece, bucklers be all broken, and swords hacked like so many saws, for they must not see her abused in any sort, 'tis blasphemy to speak against her, a dishonour without all good respect to name her.

'Tis common with these creatures, to drink healths upon their bare knees, though it were a mile to the bottom (no matter of what mixture), off it comes. If she bid them they will go barefoot to Jerusalem, to the Great Cham's court, to the East Indies, to fetch her a bird to wear in her hat: and with Drake and Cavendish sail round about the world for her sweet sake, in the teeth of the wind; serve twice seven years as Jacob did for Rachel; do as much as Gismunda, the daughter of Tancredus, Prince of Salerna, did for Guiscardus, her true love, eat his heart when he died; or as Artemisia drank her husband's bones beaten to powder, and so bury him in herself, and endure more torments than Theseus or Paris. With such sacrifices as these (as Aristaenetus holds) Venus is well pleased. Generally they undertake any pain, any labour, any toil, for their mistress' sake, love and admire a servant, not to her alone, but to all her friends and followers, they hug and embrace them for her sake; her dog, picture, and everything she wears, they adore it as a relique. If any man come from her, they feast him, reward him, will not be out of his company, do him all offices, still remembering, still talking of her: 'For though the object of your love is absent, her image is present, and her sweet name still ringing in your ears' (Lucretius).

The very carrier that comes from him to her is a most welcome guest; and if he bring a letter, she will read it twenty times over, and as Lucretia did by Euryalus, kiss the letter a thousand times together,

and then read it; and as Chelidonia by Philonius, after many sweet
kisses, put the letter in her bosom,

> *And kiss again, and often look thereon,*
> *And stay the messenger that would be gone,*
>
> (ARISTAENETUS)

and ask many pretty questions, over and over again, as how he looked,
what he did, and what he said? In a word,

> *He strives to please his mistress, and her maid,*
> *Her servants, and her dog, and's well apaid.*
>
> (PLAUTUS)

If he get any remnant of hers, a busk-point, a feather of her fan, a
shoe-tie, a lace, a ring, a bracelet of hair, 'some token snatched from
her shoulders but half-resisting finger', he wears it for a favour on his
arm, in his hat, finger, or next his heart. Her picture he adores twice a
day, and for two hours together will not look off it; as Laodamia did by
Protesilaus, when he went to war, sit at home with his picture before
her; a garter or a bracelet of hers is more precious than any saint's
relique, he lays it up in his casket (O blessed relique!), and every day
will kiss it; if in her presence, his eye is never off her, and drink he will
where she drank, if it be possible, in that very place, etc. If absent,
he will walk in the walk, sit under that tree where she did use to sit,
in that bower, in that very seat, and kiss the very door, many years
after sometimes; though she be far distant and dwell many miles off,
he loves yet to walk that way still, to have his chamber-window look
that way, to walk by that river's side, which (though far away) runs
by the house where she dwells; he loves the wind blows to that coast:

> *O happy western winds that blow that way,*
> *For you shall see my love's fair face today.*
>
> (BUCHANAN)

He will send a message to her by the wind: 'Ye Alpine breezes from the placid mountains, this message bear to my beloved.'

He desires to confer with some of her acquaintance, for his heart is still with her, to talk of her, admiring and commending her, lamenting, moaning, wishing himself anything for her sake, to have opportunity to see her, O that he might but enjoy her presence! So did Philostratus to his mistress, 'O happy ground on which she treads! and happy were I if she would tread upon me. I think her countenance would make the rivers stand, and when she comes abroad, birds will sing and come about her.'

> *The fields will laugh, the pleasant valleys burn,*
> *And all the grass will into flowers turn.*
> *All the air will breathe ambrosia.*

'When she is in the meadow she is fairer than any flower, for that lasts but for a day; the river is pleasing, but it vanisheth on a sudden, but thy flower doth not fade, thy stream is greater than the sea. If I look upon the heaven, methinks I see the sun fallen down to shine below, and thee to shine in his place, whom I desire. If I look upon the night, methinks I see two more glorious stars, Hesperus and thyself. A little after he thus courts his mistress: If thou goest forth of the city, the protecting gods that keep the town will run after to gaze upon thee: if thou sail upon the seas, as so many small boats they will follow thee: what river would not run into the sea?'

Another, he sighs and sobs, swears he hath a heart bruised to powder, dissolved and melted within him, or quite gone from him, to his mistress' bosom belike; he is in an oven, a salamander in the fire, so scorched with love's heat; he wisheth himself a saddle for her to sit on, a posy for her to smell to, and it would not grieve him to be hanged, if he might be strangled in her garters; he would willingly die tomorrow, so that she might kill him with her own hands. Ovid would be a flea, a gnat, a ring; Catullus, a sparrow; Anacreon, a glass, a gown, a chain, anything:

> *But I a looking-glass would be,*
> *Still to be lookt upon by thee,*
> *Or I, my love, would be thy gown,*
> *By thee to be worn up and down;*
> *Or a pure well full to the brims,*
> *That I might wash thy purer limbs:*
> *Or, I'd be precious balm to 'noint,*
> *With choicest care each choicest joint;*
> *Or, if I might, I would be fain*
> *About thy neck thy happy chain,*
> *Or would it were my blessed hap*
> *To be the lawn o'er thy fair pap,*
> *Or would I were thy shoe to be*
> *Daily trod upon by thee.*

O thrice happy man that shall enjoy her! as they that saw Hero in Musaeus, and Salmacis to Hermaphroditus.

The same passion made her break out in the comedy, happy are his bed-fellows; and as she said of Cyrus, blessed is that woman that shall be his wife, nay thrice happy she that shall enjoy him but a night. Such a night's lodging is worth Jupiter's sceptre. O what a blissful night would it be, how soft, how sweet a bed! She will adventure all her estate for such a night, for a nectarean, a balsam kiss alone.

'Happy is he who sees thee, happier still he who hears thee, a god who enjoys thee.'

The Sultan of Sana's wife in Arabia, when she had seen Vertomannus, that comely traveller, lamented to herself in this manner: 'O God, thou hast made this man whiter than the sun, but me, mine husband, and all my children black; I would to God he were my husband, or that I had such a son'; she fell a-weeping, and so impatient for love at last, that (as Potiphar's wife did by Joseph) she would have had him gone in with her, she sent away Gazella, Tegeia, Galzerana, her waiting-maids, loaded him with fair promises and gifts, and wooed him with all the rhetoric she could: 'grant this last favour to your hapless lover'. But when he gave no consent, she would have gone with him, and left all, to be his page, his servant, or his lackey, so that she might enjoy him, threatening, moreover, to kill herself, etc. Men will do as much and more for women, spend goods, lands, lives, fortunes; kings will leave their crowns, as King John for Matilda the nun at Dunmow.

> *But kings in this yet privileg'd may be,*
> *I'll be a monk so I may live with thee.*
>
> (DRAYTON)

The very gods will endure any shame, be a spectacle as Mars and Venus were to all the rest; so did Lucian's Mercury wish, and peradventure so dost thou. They will adventure their lives with alacrity: 'I will not fear to die for her, nay more, I will die twice, nay, twenty times for her.' If she die, there's no remedy, they must die with her, they cannot help it. A lover in Calcagninus wrote this on his darling's tomb:

> *Quincia my dear is dead, but not alone,*
> *For I am dead, and with her I am gone:*

> *Sweet smiles, mirth, graces, all with her do rest,*
> *And my soul too, for 'tis not in my breast.*

How many doting lovers upon the like occasion might say the same! But these are toys in respect, they will hazard their very souls for their mistress' sake.

> *One said, To heaven would I not desire at all to go,*
> *If that at mine own house I had such a fine wife as Hero.*

Venus forsook heaven for Adonis' sake. Old January in Chaucer, thought when he had his fair May he should never go to heaven, he should live so merrily here on earth; had I such a mistress, he protests,

> *I would not envy their prosperity,*
> *The gods should envy my felicity.*

Another as earnestly desires to behold his sweetheart, he will adventure and leave all this, and more than this, to see her alone.

> *If all my mischiefs were recompensed,*
> *And God would give me what I requested,*
> *I would my mistress' presence only seek,*
> *Which doth mine heart in prison captive keep.*
>
> (PETRARCH)

But who can reckon upon the dotage, madness, servitude and blindness, the foolish phantasms and vanities of lovers, their torments, wishes, idle attempts?

Yet for all this, among so many irksome, absurd, troublesome symptoms, inconveniences, phantastical fits and passions which are usually incident to such persons, there be some good and graceful qualities in lovers, which this affection causeth. As it makes wise men fools, so many times it makes fools become wise; it makes base fellows become generous, cowards courageous, as Cardan notes out of Plutarch; covetous, liberal and magnificent; clowns, civil; cruel, gentle; wicked, profane persons to become religious; slovens, neat; churls, merciful; and dumb dogs, eloquent; your lazy drones, quick and nimble. Love subdues savage breasts; that fierce, cruel, and rude Cyclops Polyphemus sighed and shed many a salt tear for Galatea's sake.

No passion causeth greater alterations, or more vehement of joy or discontent. Plutarch saith that the soul of a man in love is full of perfumes and sweet odours, and all manner of pleasing tones and tunes, insomuch that it is hard to say (as he adds) whether love do mortal men more harm than good. It adds spirits and makes them, otherwise soft and silly, generous and courageous; 'love made him bold'. Ariadne's love made Theseus so adventurous, and Medea's beauty Jason so victorious; 'love drives fear from the heart'. Plato is of opinion that the love of Venus made Mars so valorous: A young man will be much abashed to commit any foul offence that shall come to the hearing or sight of his mistress. As he that desired of his enemy, now dying, to lay him with his face upward, lest his sweetheart should say he was a coward. And if it were possible to have an army consist of lovers, such as love, or are beloved, they would be extraordinary valiant and wise in their government, modesty would detain them from doing amiss, emulation incite them to do that which is good and honest, and a few of them would overcome a great company of others. There is no man so pusillanimous, so very a dastard, whom love would not incense, make of a divine temper and an heroical spirit. As he said in like case, though the heavens fall, etc. Nothing can terrify, nothing can dismay them; but as Sir Blandamour and

Paridell, those two brave fairy knights [in Spenser's *Faerie Queene*] fought for the love of fair Florimell in presence:

> *And drawing both their swords with rage anew,*
> *Like two mad mastives each other slew,*
> *And shields did share, and mails did rash, and helms did hew:*
> *So furiously each other did assail,*
> *As if their souls at once they would have rent*
> *Out of their breasts, that streams of blood did trail*
> *Adown, as if their springs of life were spent,*
> *That all the ground with purple blood was sprent,*
> *And all their armour stain'd with bloody gore;*
> *Yet scarcely once to breathe would they relent.*
> *So mortal was their malice and so sore,*
> *That both resolved (than yield) to die before.*

Every base swain in love will dare to do as much for his dear mistress' sake. He will fight and fetch that famous buckler of Argos, to do her service, adventure at all, undertake any enterprise. And as Serranus the Spaniard, then Governor of Sluys, made answer to Marquess Spinola, if the enemy brought 50,000 devils against him he would keep it. The Nine Worthies, Oliver and Roland, and forty dozen of peers are all in him, he is all mettle, armour of proof, more than a man, and in this case improved beyond himself. For as Agatho contends, a true lover is wise, just, temperate, and valiant.

I doubt not, therefore, but if a man had such an army of lovers (as Castiglione supposeth) he might soon conquer all the world, except by chance he met with such another army of inamoratos to oppose it. For so perhaps they might fight as that fatal dog and fatal hare in the heavens, course one another round, and never make an end. Castiglione thinks Ferdinand King of Spain would never have conquered Granada, had not Queen Isabel and her ladies been present at the siege. It cannot be expressed what courage the Spaniard knights took when the ladies were present; a few Spaniards overcame a multitude of Moors. They will undergo any danger whatsoever, as Sir Walter Manny in Edward the Third's time, stuck full of ladies' favours, fought like a dragon. For as Plato holds, only lovers will die for their friends, and in their mistress' quarrel. And for that cause he would have women follow the camp, to be spectators and encouragers of noble actions: upon such an occasion, the Squire of Dames himself, Sir Lancelot or Sir Tristram, Caesar or Alexander, shall not be more resolute or go beyond them.

Not courage only doth love add, but as I said, subtility, wit, and many pretty devices. Jupiter, in love with Leda, and not knowing how to compass his desire, turned himself into a swan, and got Venus to pursue him in the likeness of an eagle; which she doing, for shelter he fled to Leda's lap. Leda embraced him, and so fell fast asleep, by which means Jupiter had his will. Infinite such tricks love can devise, such fine feats in abundance, with wisdom and wariness—all manner of civility, decency, compliment and good behaviour, polite graces and merry conceits.

Boccaccio hath a pleasant tale to this purpose, which he borrowed from the Greeks, and which Beroaldus hath turned into Latin, Bebelius in verse, of Cymon and Iphigenia. This Cymon was a fool, a proper man of person, and the governor of Cyprus's song, but a very ass, insomuch that his father, being ashamed of him, sent him to a farmhouse he had in the country, to be brought up; where by chance, as his manner was, walking alone, he espied a gallant young gentlewoman, named Iphigenia, a burgomaster's daughter of Cyprus, with her maid, by a brookside in a little thicket, fast asleep in her smock, where she had newly bathed herself. When Cymon saw her, he stood leaning on his staff, gaping on her immovable, and in a maze;

at last he fell so far in love with the glorious object that he began to rouse himself up, to bethink what he was, would needs follow her to the city, and for her sake began to be civil, to learn to sing and dance, to play on instruments, and got all those gentlemanlike qualities and compliments in a short space, which his friends were most glad of. In brief, he became, from an idiot and a clown, to be one of the most complete gentlemen in Cyprus, did many valorous exploits, and all for the love of Mistress Iphigenia.

In a word, I may say thus much of them all, let them be never so clownish, rude and horrid, Grobians and sluts, if once they be in love they will be most neat and spruce; they will follow the fashion, begin to trick up, and to have a good opinion of themselves, for Venus is the mother of the graces; a ship is not so long a-rigging as a young gentlewoman a-trimming up herself against her sweetheart comes. A painter's shop, a flowery meadow, no so gracious aspect in nature's storehouse as a young maid, or a Venetian bride, that looks for a husband, or a young man that is her suitor; composed looks, composed gait, clothes, gestures, actions, all composed; all the graces, elegancies in the world are in her face. Their best robes, ribbons, chains, jewels, lawns, linens, laces, spangles, must come on, they are beyond all measure coy, nice, and too curious on a sudden: 'tis all their study, all their business, how to wear their clothes neat, to be polite and terse, and to set out themselves. No sooner doth a young man see his sweetheart coming, but he smugs up himself, pulls up his cloak now fallen about his shoulders, ties his garters, points, sets his band, cuffs, slicks his hair, twires his beard, etc.

When Mercury was to come before his mistress,

> *He put his cloak in order, that the lace,*
> *And hem, and gold-work, all might have his grace.*

(OVID)

Salmacis would not be seen of Hermaphroditus, till she had spruced up herself first.

> *Nor did she come, although 'twas her desire,*
> *Till she compos'd herself, and trimm'd her tire,*
> *And set her looks to make him to admire.*

> (OVID)

Venus had so ordered the matter, that when her son Aeneas was to appear before Queen Dido he was like a god, for she was the tire-woman herself, to set him out with all natural and artificial impostures, as mother Mamaea did her son Heliogabalus, new chosen emperor, when he was to be seen of the people first. When the hirsute cyclopical Polyphemus courted Galatea:

> *And then he did begin to prank himself,*
> *To plait and comb his head, and beard to shave,*
> *And look his face i' th' water as a glass,*
> *And to compose himself for to be brave.*

> (OVID)

He was upon a sudden now spruce, and keen as a new-ground hatchet. He now began to have a good opinion of his own features and good parts, now to be a gallant.

> *Come now, my Galatea, scorn me not,*
> *Nor my poor presents; for but yesterday*
> *I saw myself i' th' water, and methought*
> *Full fair I was; then scorn me not, I say.*

> (OVID)

'Tis the common humour of all suitors to trick up themselves, to be prodigal in apparel, pure lotus, neat, combed and curled, with powdered hairs, with a long lovelock, a flower in his ear, perfumed gloves, rings, scarfs, feathers, points, etc., as if he were a prince's Ganymede, with every day new suits, as the fashion varies; going as if he trod upon eggs; and, as Heinsius writ to Primerius, If once he be besotten on a wench, he must lie awake anights, renounce his book, sigh and lament, now and then weep for his hard hap, and mark above all things what hats, bands, doublets, breeches, are in fashion, how to cut his beard and wear his locks, to turn up his mushatos and curl his head, prune his pickitivant, or if he wear it abroad, that the east side be correspondent to the west: he may be scoffed at otherwise, as Julian, that apostate emperor, was for wearing a long hirsute goatish beard, fit to make ropes with, as in his Misopogon, or that apologetical oration he made at Antioch to excuse himself, he doth ironically confess it hindered his kissing, but he did not much esteem it, as it seems by the sequel, I am not, he said, much concerned about kisses, yet [to follow mine author] it may much concern a young lover, he must be more respectful in this behalf, he must be in league with an excellent tailor, barber, have neat shoe-ties, points, garters, speak in print, walk in print, eat and drink in print, and that which is all in all, he must be mad in print.

Among other good qualities an amorous fellow is endowed with, he must learn to sing and dance, play upon some instrument or other, as without all doubt he will, if he truly touched with this loadstone of love. For as Erasmus hath it, love will make them musicians, and to compose ditties, madrigals, elegies, love-sonnets, and sing them to several pretty tunes, to get all good qualities may be had. Jupiter perceived Mercury to be in love with Philologia, because he learned languages, polite speech (for Suadela [Persuasion] herself was Venus' daughter, as some write), arts and sciences, all to ingratiate himself and please his mistress. 'Tis their chiefest study to sing, dance; and without question, so many gentlemen and gentlewomen would not be so well qualified in this kind, if love did not incite them. Who, saith Castiglione, would learn to play, or give his mind to music, learn to dance, or make so many rhymes, love-songs, as most do, but for women's sake, because they hope by that means to purchase their good wills and win their favour.

We see this daily verified in your women and wives, they that being maids took so much pains to sing, play, and dance, with such cost and charge to their parents to get those graceful qualities, now being married will scarce touch an instrument, they care not for it. Constantine makes Cupid himself to be a great dancer; by the same token as he was capering among the gods, he flung down a bowl of nectar, which, distilling upon the white rose, ever since made it red: and Callistratus, by the help of Daedalus, about Cupid's statue made a many of young wenches still a-dancing, to signify belike that Cupid was much affected with it, as without all doubt he was. For at his and Psyche's wedding, the gods being present to grace the feast, Ganymede filled nectar in abundance (as Apuleius describes it), Vulcan was the cook, the Hours made all fine with roses and flowers, Apollo played on the harp, the Muses sang to it, but his mother Venus danced to his and their sweet content. Witty Lucian in that pathetical love-passage or pleasant description of Jupiter's stealing of Europa and swimming from Phoenicia to Crete, makes the sea calm, the winds hush, Neptune and Amphitrite riding in their chariot to break the waves before them, the tritons dancing round about, with every one a torch, the sea-nymphs half naked, keeping time on dolphins' back, and singing *Hymenaeus* the nuptial song, Cupid nimbly tripping on the top of the waters, and Venus herself coming after in a shell, strewing roses and flowers on their heads. Praxiteles, in all his pictures of Love, feigns Cupid ever smiling, and looking upon dancers; and in Saint

Mark's garden in Rome (whose work I know not) one of the most delicious pieces is a many of satyrs dancing about a wench asleep.

So that dancing still is, as it were, a necessary appendix to love matters. Young lasses are never better pleased than whenas upon an holiday, after evensong, they may meet their sweethearts, and dance about a maypole, or in a town-green under a shady elm. Nothing so familiar in France as for citizens' wives and maids to dance a round in the streets, and often too, for want of better instruments, to make good music of their own voices, and dance after it. Yea many times this love will make old men and women, that have more toes than teeth, dance, 'John come kiss me now,' mask and mum; for Comus and Hymen love masks and all such merriments above measure; will allow men to put on women's apparel in some cases, and promiscuously to dance, young and old, rich and poor, generous and base, of all sorts.

Paulus Jovius taxeth Augustine Niphus the philosopher, for that being an old man, and a public professor, a father of many children, he was mad for the love of a young maid (that which many of his friends were ashamed to see), an old gouty fellow, yet would dance after fiddlers. Many laughed him to scorn for it, but this omnipotent love would have it so.

> *Love hasty with his purple staff did make*
> *Me follow and the dance to undertake.*

> (ANACREON)

And 'tis no news this, no indecorum; for why? a good reason may be given of it. Cupid and death met both in an inn; and being merrily disposed, they did exchange some arrows from either quiver; ever since young men die, and oftentimes old men dote. And who can then withstand it? If once we be in love, young or old, though our teeth shake in our heads like virginal jacks, or stand parallel asunder like the arches of a bridge, there is no remedy, we must dance trenchmore for a need, over tables, chairs, and stools, etc.

Plutarch doth in some sort excuse it, and telleth us, moreover, in what sense love teacheth music, how love makes them that had no skill before learn to sing and dance; he concludes, 'tis only that power and prerogative love hath over us. Love (as he holds) will make a silent man speak, a modest man most officious; dull, quick; slow, nimble; and that which is most to be admired, a hard, base, untractable churl, as fire doth iron in a smith's forge, free, facile, gentle, and easy to be entreated. Nay, 'twill make him prodigal in the other extreme, and give an hundred sesterces for a night's lodging, as they did of old to Lais of Corinth, or two thousand drachmas for a single night, as Mundus to Paulina, spend all his fortunes (as too many do in like case) to obtain his suit. For which cause many compare love to wine, which makes men jovial and merry, frolic and sad, whine, sing, dance, and what not.

But above all the other symptoms of lovers, this is not lightly to be overpassed, that likely of what condition soever, if once they be in love, they turn to their ability, rhymers, ballet-makers, and poets. For, as Plutarch saith, They will be witnesses and trumpeters of their paramours' good parts, bedecking them with verses and commendatory songs, as we do statues with gold, that they may be remembered and admired of all. Ancient men will dote in this kind sometimes as well as the rest; the heat of love will thaw their frozen affections, dissolve the ice of age, and so far enable them, though they be sixty years of age above the girdle, to be scarce thirty beneath. Jovianus Pontanus makes an old fool rhyme, and turn poetaster to please his mistress.

> *Sweet Marian, do not mine age disdain,*
> *For thou canst make an old man young again.*

They will be still singing amorous songs and ditties (if young especially), and cannot abstain, though it be when they go to, or should be at church.

We have a pretty story to this purpose in Westmonasteriensis, an old writer of ours (if you will believe it). *An. Dom.* 1012, at Colewiz in Saxony, on Christmas Eve a company of young men and maids, while the priest was at mass in the church, were singing catches and love-songs in the churchyard; he sent to them to make less noise, but they sung on still; and if you will, you shall have the very song itself:

> *A fellow rid by the greenwood side,*
> *And fair Meswinde was his bride,*
> *Why stand we so, and do not go?*

This they sung, he chafed, till at length, impatient as he was, he prayed to St Magnus, patron of the church, they might all there sing and dance till that time twelvemonth, and so they did, without meat and drink, wearisomeness or giving over, till at year's end they ceased singing, and were absolved by Herebertus, Archbishop of Cologne.

They will in all places be doing thus, young folks especially, reading love stories, talking of this or that young man, such a fair maid, singing, telling or hearing lascivious tales, scurrile tunes; such objects are their sole delight, their continual meditation, and as Guastavinius adds, abundance of seed comes from thoughts of love-making and voluptuous memories of it, etc., and earnest longing comes hence, itching body, itching mind, amorous conceits, tickling thoughts, sweet and pleasant hopes; hence it is, they can think, discourse willingly, or speak almost of no other subject. 'Tis their only desire, if it may be done by art, to see their husband's picture in a glass, they'll give anything to know when they shall be married, how many husbands they shall have, by crommyomantia, a kind of divination with onions laid on the altar on Christmas Eve, or by fasting on St Agnes' Eve or Night, to know who shall be their first husband, or by alphitomantia, by beans in a cake, etc., to burn the same.

This love is the cause of all good conceits, neatness, exornations, plays, elegancies, delights, pleasant expressions, sweet motions and gestures, joys, comforts, exultancies, and all the sweetness of our life. What would life be worth, or what pleasure would there be, without golden Aphrodite? 'Let me live no longer than I may love,' saith a mad merry fellow in Minnermus. This love is that salt that seasoneth our harsh and dull labours, and gives a pleasant relish to our other unsavoury proceedings; when love goes, darkness enters, sluggishness, old age, disease, etc.

All our feasts almost, masques, mummings, banquets, merry meetings, weddings, pleasing songs, fine tunes, poems, love stories, plays, comedies, Atellanes [farces], jigs, Fescennines, elegies, odes, etc., proceed hence. Danaus, the son of Belus, at his daughter's wedding at Argos, instituted the first plays (some say) that ever were heard of. Symbols, emblems, impresses, devices, if we shall believe Jovius, Contiles, Paradine, Camillus de Camillis, may be ascribed to it. Most of our arts and sciences; painting among the rest was first invented, saith Patricius, for love's sake. For when the daughter of Deburiades the Sicyonian was to take leave of her sweetheart now going to wars, to comfort herself in his absence, she took his picture with coal upon a wall, as the candle gave the shadow, which her father admiring perfected afterwards, and it was the first picture by report that ever was made. And long after, Sicyon for painting, carving, statuary, music, and philosophy, was preferred before all the cities in Greece.

Apollo was the first inventor of physic, divination, oracles; Minerva found out weaving, Vulcan curious ironwork, Mercury letters; but who prompted all this into their heads? Love. They loved such things, or some party, for whose sake they were undertaken at first. 'Tis true, Vulcan made a most admirable brooch or necklace, which long after Axion and Temenus, Phegeus' sons, for the singular worth of it, consecrated to Apollo at Delphi, but Pharyllus the tyrant stole it away, and presented it to Ariston's wife, on whom he miserably doted (Parthenius tells the story out of Phylarchus); but why did Vulcan make this excellent ouch? To give Hermione, Cadmus' wife, whom he dearly loved.

All our tilts and tournaments, Orders of the Garter, Golden Fleece, etc., owe their beginnings to love, and many of our histories. By this means, saith Jovius, they would express their loving minds to their mistress, and to the beholders. 'Tis the sole subject almost of poetry, all our invention tends to it, all our songs, and therefore Hesiod makes the Muses and Graces still follow Cupid, and, as Plutarch holds, Menander and the rest of the poets were Love's priests; whatever those old Anacreons, all our Greek and Latin epigrammatists, love writers, Antony Diogenes the most ancient, whose epitome we find in Photius' Bibliotheca, Longus Sophista, Eustathius, Achilles, Tatius, Aristaenetus, Heliodorus, Plato, Plutarch, Lucian, Parthenius, Theodorus Prodromus, Ovid, Cataullus, Tibullus, etc., our new Ariostos, Boiardos, authors of Arcadia, Urania, Faerie Queene, etc., Marullus, Lotichius, Angerianus, Stroza, Secundus, Capellanus, etc., with the rest of those facete modern poets, have written in this kind, are but as so many symptoms of love.

Their whole books are a synopsis or breviary of love, the portuous of love, legends of lovers' lives and deaths, and of their memorable adventures; nay more, it is due to love that they are read and admired; as Nevisanus the lawyer holds, there never was any excellent poet that invented good fables, or made laudable verses, which was not in love himself; had he not taken a quill from Cupid's wings, he could never have written so amorously as he did.

> *Wanton Propertius and witty Gallus,*
> *Subtile Tibullus, and learned Catullus,*
> *It was Cynthia, Lesbia, Lycoris,*
> *That made you poets all: and if Alexis,*
> *Or Corinna chance my paramour to be,*
> *Virgil and Ovid shall not despise me.*
>
> (MARTIAL)

Petrarch's Laura made him so famous, Astrophel's Stella, and Jovianus Pontanus' mistress was the cause of his Roses, Violets and Lilies, flatteries, elegancies, etc. Why are Italians at this day generally so good poets and painters? Because every man of any fashion among them hath his mistress. The very rustics and hog-rubbers, Menalcas and Corydon, stinking of horse dung, those fulsome knaves, if once they taste of this love-liquor, are inspired in an instant. Instead of those accurate emblems, curious impresses, gaudy masques, tilts, tournaments, etc., they have their wakes, Whitsun-ales, shepherds' feasts, meetings on holidays, country dances, roundelays, writing their names on trees, true-lovers' knots, pretty gifts.

> *With tokens, hearts divided, and half rings,*
> *Shepherds in their loves are as coy as kings.*

Choosing lords, ladies, kings, queens, and valentines, etc., they go by couples:

> *Corydon's Phyllis, Nysa and Mopsus,*
> *With dainty Dousibel and Sir Tophus.*

Instead of odes, epigrams, and elegies, etc., they have their ballads, country tunes, 'O the broom, the bonny, bonny broom,' ditties and songs, 'Bess a Bell, she doth excel'; they must write likewise and indite all in rhyme.

> *Thou honeysuckle of the hawthorn hedge,*
> *Vouchsafe in Cupid's cup my heart to pledge;*
> *My heart's dear blood, sweet Cis, is thy carouse*
> *Worth all the ale in Gammer Gubbin's house.*
> *I say no more, affairs call me away,*
> *My father's horse for provender doth stay.*
> *Be thou the Lady Cressetlight to me,*
> *Sir Trolly Lolly will I prove to thee.*
> *Written in haste, farewell, my cowslip sweet,*
> *Pray let's a' Sunday at the alehouse meet.*
>
> (SAMUEL ROWLANDS)

Your most grim Stoics and severe philosophers will melt away with this passion, and if Athenaeus belie them not, Aristippus, Apollodorus, Antiphanes, etc., have made love-songs and commentaries of their mistresses' praises, orators write epistles, princes give titles, honours, what not? Xerxes gave to Themistocles Lampsacus to find him wine, Magnesia for bread, and Myus for the rest of his diet. The Persian kings allotted whole cities to like use, one whole city served to dress her hair, another her neck, a third her hood. Ahasuerus would have given Esther half his empire, and Herod bid Herodias ask what she would, she should have it. Caligula gave an 100,000 sesterces to his courtesan at first word to buy her pins, and yet when he was solicited by the senate to bestow something to repair the decayed walls of Rome for the commonwealth's good, he would give but 6,000 sesterces at most. Dionysius, that Sicilian tyrant, rejected all his privy councillors, and was so besotted on Myrrha, his favourite and mistress, that he would bestow no office, or in the most weightiest business of the kingdom do aught, without her especial advice, prefer, depose, send, entertain no man, though worthy and well-deserving, but by her consent; and he again whom she commended, howsoever unfit, unworthy, was as highly approved.

Kings and emperors, instead of poems, build cities; Hadrian built Antinoe in Egypt, besides constellations, temples, altars, statues, images, etc., in the honour of his Antinous. Alexander bestowed infinite sums to set out his Hephaestion to all eternity. Socrates professeth himself love's servant, ignorant in all arts and science, a doctor alone in love matters, saith Maximus Tyrius, etc., and this he spake at home and abroad, at public feasts, in the academy, in the Piraeus, the Lyceum, under the plane-tree, etc., the very blood-hound of beauty, as he is styled by others.

But I conclude there is no end of love's symptoms, 'tis a bottomless pit. Love is subject to no dimensions; not to be surveyed by any art or engine: and besides, I am of Haedus' mind, no man can discourse of love matters, or judge of them aright, that hath not made trial in his own person, or, as Aeneas Sylvius adds, hath not a little doted, been mad or love-sick himself. I confess I am but a novice, a contemplator only, 'I am not in love, nor do I know what love may be'; I have not a tincture, for why should I lie, dissemble, or excuse it? yet I am a man, etc., not altogether inexpert in this subject, but not an instructor in love, and what I say is merely reading, the triflings of others, by mine own observation and others' relation.

XIV

Prognostics of Love-Melancholy.

W HAT FIRES, torments, cares, jealousies, suspicions, fears, griefs, anxieties accompany such as are in love, I have sufficiently said; the next question is, what will be the event of such miseries, what they foretell. Some are of opinion that this love cannot be cured ('love cannot be cured by herbs'), it accompanies them to the last, the same passion afflicts both sheep and shepherd, and is so continuate, that by no persuasion almost it may be relieved. 'Bid me not love,' saith Euryalus, 'bid the mountains come down into the plains, bid the rivers run back to their fountains; I can as soon leave to love, as the sun leave his course.'

> *First seas shall want their fish, the mountains shade,*
> *Woods singing-birds, the wind's murmur shall fade,*
> *Than my fair Amaryllis' love allay'd.*
>
> (BUCHANAN)

Bid me not love, bid a deaf man hear, a blind man see, a dumb speak, lame run, counsel can do no good, a sick man cannot relish, no physic can ease me. The art that helps all others helps not him, as Apollo confessed, and Jupiter himself could not be cured.

> *Physic can soon cure every disease,*
> *Excepting love, that can it not appease.*
>
> (PROPERTIUS)

But whether love may be cured or no, and by what means, shall be explained in his place; in the meantime, if it take his course and be not otherwise eased or amended, it breaks out into often outrageous and prodigious events.

As Tatius observes, Love and Bacchus are so violent gods, so furiously rage in our minds, that they make us forget all honesty, shame, and common civility. For such men ordinarily as are throughly possessed with this humour, become senseless, mad, for it is insane love, as the poet calls it, beside themselves, and as I have proved, no better than beasts, irrational, stupid, headstrong, void of fear of God or men, they frequently forswear themselves, spend, steal, commit incests, rapes, adulteries, murders, depopulate towns, cities, countries, to satisfy their lust.

> *A devil 'tis, and mischief such doth work,*
> *As never yet did Pagan, Jew, or Turk.*

> (TOFTE)

The wars of Troy may be a sufficient witness; and as Appian saith of Antony and Cleopatra, Their love brought themselves and all Egypt into extreme and miserable calamities. 'The end of her is as bitter as wormwood, and as sharp as a two-edged sword. Her feet go down to death, her steps lead on to hell' (Prov. v, 4:5). 'She is more bitter than death and the sinner shall be taken by her' (Eccles. vii, 26).

He that runs headlong from the top of a rock is not in so bad a case as he that falls into this gulf of love. For hence, saith Platina, comes repentance, dotage, they lose themselves, their wits, and make shipwreck of their fortunes altogether; madness, to make away themselves and others, violent death. The prognostication is, saith Gordonius, they will either run mad or die. For if this passion continue, saith Aelian Montaltus, it makes the blood hot, thick, and black; and if the inflammation get into the brain, with continual meditation and waking, it so dries it up that madness follows, or else they make away themselves. Now, as Arnoldus adds, it will speedily work these effects if it be not presently helped; they will pine away, run mad, and die upon a sudden; run quickly mad, saith Valescus, if good order be not taken:

> *Oh heavy yoke of love, which whoso bears,*
> *Is quite undone, and that at unawares.*
>
> (CALCAGNINUS)

So she confessed of herself in the poet:

> *I shall be mad before it be perceived,*
> *A hair-breath off scarce am I, now distracted.*
>
> (LUCIAN)

As mad as Orlando for his Angelica, or Hercules for his Hylas:

> *He went he car'd not whither, mad he was,*
> *The cruel god so tortured him, alas!*
>
> (THEOCRITUS)

At the sight of Hero I cannot tell how many ran mad:

> *And whilst he doth conceal his grief,*
> *Madness comes on him like a thief.*
>
> (MUSAEUS)

Go to Bedlam for examples.

It is so well known in every village, how many have either died for love or voluntarily made away themselves, that I need not much labour to prove it; death is the common catastrophe to such persons.

> *Would I were dead, for nought, God knows,*
> *But death can rid me of these woes.*
>
> (ANACREON)

As soon as Euryalus departed from Senes, Lucretia, his paramour, never looked up, no jests could exhilarate her sad mind, no joys comfort her wounded and distressed soul, but a little after she fell sick and died. But this is a gentle end, a natural death, such persons commonly make away themselves: So did Dido: 'But let me die, she said, so let me descend to the shades': Pyramus and Thisbe, Medea, Coresus and Callirhoe, Theagenes the philosopher, and many myriads besides, and so will ever do:

> *Who ever heard a story of more woe,*
> *Than that of Juliet and her Romeo?*
>
> (SHAKESPEARE)

Read Parthenius in Eroticis, and Plutarch's love stories, all tending, almost, to this purpose.

Valleriola hath a lamentable narration of a merchant, his patient, that raving through impatience of love, had he not been watched, would every while have offered violence to himself. Amatus Lusitanus hath such another story, and Felix Plater, a third of a young gentleman that studied physic, and for the love of a doctor's daughter, having no hope to compass his desire, poisoned himself. *Anno* 1615, a barber in Frankfort, because his wench was betrothed to another, cut his own throat. At Neuburg, the same year, a young man, because he could not get her parents' consent, killed his sweetheart, and afterwards himself, desiring this of the magistrate, as he gave up the ghost, that they might be buried in one grave, which Gismunda besought of Tancredus, her father, that she might be in like sort buried with Guiscardus, her lover, that so their bodies might lie together in the grave, as their souls wander about the Elysian Fields.

You have not yet heard the worst, they do not offer violence to themselves in this rage of lust, but unto others, their nearest and dearest friends. Catiline killed his only son for the love of Aurelia Orestilla, because she refused to marry him while his son was alive. Laodice, the sister of Mithridates, poisoned her husband, to give content to a base fellow whom she loved. Alexander, to please Thais, a concubine of his, set Persepolis on fire. Nereus' wife, a widow and lady of Athens, for the love of a Venetian gentleman, betrayed the city; and he for her sake murdered his wife, the daughter of a nobleman in Venice. Constantine Despota made away Catherine his wife, turned his son Michael and his other children out of doors, for the love of a base scrivener's daughter in Thessalonica, with whose beauty he was enamoured. Leucophrye betrayed the city where she dwelt, for her sweetheart's sake, that was in the enemies' camp. Pisidice, the governor's daughter of Methymna, for the love of Achilles, betrayed the whole island to him, her father's enemy. Diognetus did as much in the city where he dwelt, for the love of Polycrite, and Medea for the love of Jason; she taught him how to tame the fire-breathing, brass-feeted bulls, and kill the mighty dragon that kept the golden fleece, and tore her little brother Absyrtus in pieces that her father Æetes might have something to detain him, while she ran away with her beloved Jason, etc.

Such acts and scenes hath this tragi-comedy of love.

XV

Cure of Love-Melancholy, by Labour,
Diet, Physic, Fasting, etc.

ALTHOUGH IT BE controverted by some whether love-melancholy may be cured, because it is so irresistible and violent a passion—for as you know, from Virgil,

> *It is an easy passage down to hell,*
> *But to come back, once there, you cannot well—*

yet without question, if it be taken in time, it may be helped, and by many good remedies amended.

Avicenna sets down seven compendious ways how this malady may be eased, altered, and expelled. Savonarola nine principal observations, Jason Pratensis prescribes eight rules, beside physic, how this passion may be tamed, Laurentius two main precepts, Arnoldus, Valleriola, Montaltus, Hildesheim, Langius, and others inform us otherwise, and yet all tending to the same purpose. The sum of which I will briefly epitomize (for I light my candle from their torches), and enlarge again upon occasion, as shall seem best to me, and that after mine own method.

The first rule to be observed in this stubborn and unbridled passion is exercise and diet. It is an old and well-known sentence, Venus grows cool without bread and wine. As an idle sedentary life, liberal feeding, are great causes of it, so the opposite, labour, slender and

209

sparing diet, with continual business, the best and most ordinary means to prevent it.

> *Take idleness away, and put to flight*
> *Are Cupid's arts, his torches give no light.*
>
> (OVID)

Minerva, Diana, Vesta, and the nine Muses were not enamoured at all, because they never were idle.

> *In vain are all your flatteries,*
> *In vain are all your knaveries,*
> *Delights, deceits, procacities,*
> *Sighs, kisses, and conspiracies,*
> *And whate'er is done by art,*
> *To bewitch a lover's heart.*
>
> (BUCHANAN)

'Tis in vain to set upon those that are busy. 'Tis Savonarola's third rule, occupy oneself with important affairs, and Avicenna's precept ('love yields to business; keep busy and you will be safe'). To be busy still, and, as Guianerius enjoins, about matters of great moment, if it may be. Magninus adds, never to be idle but at the hours of sleep.

> *For if thou dost not ply thy book,*
> *By candle-light to study bent,*
> *Employ'd about some honest thing,*
> *Envy or love shall thee torment.*
>
> (HORACE)

No better physic is than to be always occupied, seriously intent.

Why, dost thou ask, poor folks are often free,
And dainty places still molested be?

(SENECA)

Because poor people fare coarsely, work hard, go woolward and bare. Poverty hath not the means for feeding this passion. Guianerius therefore prescribes his patient to go with hair-cloth next his skin, to go bare-footed, and bare-legged in cold weather, to whip himself now and then, as monks do, but above all, to fast. Not with sweet wine, mutton, and pottage, as many of those tenter-bellies do, howsoever they put on Lenten faces, and whatsoever they pretend, but from all manner of meat.

Fasting is an all-sufficient remedy of itself; for, as Jason Pratensis holds, the bodies of such persons that feed liberally, and live at ease, are full of bad spirits and devils, devilish thoughts; no better physic for such parties than to fast. Hildesheim, to this of hunger, adds often baths, much exercise and sweat, but hunger and fasting he prescribes before the rest. And 'tis indeed our Saviour's oracle, this kind of devil is not cast out but by fasting and prayer, which makes the Fathers so immoderate in commendation of fasting. As hunger, saith Ambrose, is a friend of virginity, so is it an enemy to lasciviousness, but fullness overthrows chastity and fostereth all manner of provocations. If thine horse be too lusty, Jerome adviseth thee to take away some of his provender; by this means those Pauls, Hilaries, Antonies, and famous anchorites subdued the lusts of the flesh; by this means Hilarion made his ass, as he called his own body, leave kicking (so Jerome relates of him in his life), when the devil tempted him to any such foul offence. By this means those Indian Brachmanni kept themselves continent: they lay upon the ground covered with skins, as the redshanks [Highlanders] do on heather, and dieted themselves sparingly on one dish, which Guianerius would have all young men put in practice; and if that will not serve, Gordonius would have them soundly whipped, or, to cool their courage, kept in prison, and there fed with bread and water till they acknowledge their error and become of another mind. If imprisonment and hunger will not take them down, according to the directions of that Theban Crates, time must wear it out; if time will not, the last refuge is an halter. But this, you will say, is comically spoken. Howsoever, fasting by all means must be still used; and as they must refrain from such meats formerly mentioned, which cause venery or provoke lust, so they must use an opposite diet.

Wine must be altogether avoided of the younger sort. So Plato prescribes, and would have the magistrates themselves abstain from it, for example's sake, highly commending the Carthaginians for their temperance in this kind. And 'twas a good edict, a commendable thing, so that it were not done for some sinister respect, as those old Egyptians abstained from wine because some fabulous poets had given out, wine sprang first from the blood of the giants, or out of superstition, as our modern Turks, but for temperance, it being a poison to the mind, stimulant of vice, a plague itself if immoderately taken. Women of old for that cause, in hot countries, were forbid the use of it, as severely punished for drinking of wine as for adultery; and young folks, as Leonicus hath recorded, out of Athenaeus and others, and is still practised in Italy and some other countries of Europe and Asia, as Claudius Minos hath well illustrated in his comment on the 23rd Emblem of Alciat.

So choice is to be made of other diet.

Eringos are not good for to be taken,
And all lascivious meats must be forsaken.

(OVID)

Those opposite meats which ought to be used are cucumbers, melons, purslane, water-lilies, rue, woodbine, ammi, lettuce, which Lemnius so much commends, and Mizaldus to this purpose; vitex, or agnus castus, before the rest, which, saith Magninus, hath a wonderful virtue in it. Those Athenian women, in their solemn feasts called Thesmophories, were to abstain nine days from the company of men, during which time, saith Aelian, they laid a certain herb, named hanea, in their beds, which assuaged those ardent flames of love, and freed them from the torments of that violent passion. See more in Porta, Matthiolus, Crescentius, *lib.* 5, etc., and what every herbalist almost and physician hath written of satyriasis and priapism; Rhasis among the rest.

In some cases again, if they be much dejected and brought low in body, and now ready to despair through anguish, grief, and too sensible a feeling of their misery, a cup of wine and full diet is not amiss, and, as Valescus adviseth, with other honest means the frequent use of Venus, which Langius approves out of Rhasis, and Guianerius seconds it, as a very profitable remedy. Jason Pratensis subscribes to this counsel of the poet, such excretions will at once cure or at least allay the trouble, as it did the raging lust of Ahasuerus, who deflowered virgins every night. And to be drunk too by fits; but this is mad physic, if it be at all to be permitted.

If not, yet some pleasure is to be allowed, as that which Vives speaks of: A lover that hath as it were lost himself through impotency, impatience, must be called home as a traveller, by music, feasting, good wine, if need be to drunkenness itself, which many so much commend for the easing of the mind, all kinds of sports and merriments, to see fair pictures, hangings, buildings, pleasant fields, orchards, gardens, groves, ponds, pools, rivers, fishing, fowling, hawking, hunting, to hear merry tales and pleasant discourse, reading, to use exercise till he sweat, that new spirits may succeed, or by some vehement affection or contrary passion to be diverted till he be fully weaned from anger, suspicion, cares, fears, etc., and habituated into another course. As Sempronius adviseth Callisto his lovesick master, still have a pleasant companion to sing and tell merry tales, songs and facete histories, sweet discourse, etc. And as the melody of music, merriment, singing, dancing, doth augment the passion of some lovers, as Avicenna notes, so it expelleth it in others, and doth very much good. These things must be warily applied, as the parties' symptoms vary, and as they shall stand variously affected.

If there be any need of physic, that the humours be altered, or any new matter aggregated, they must be cured as melancholy men. Carolus à Lorme, among other questions discussed for his degree at Montpelier in France, hath this: Whether lovers and madmen be cured by the same remedies? He affirms it; for love extended is mere madness. Such physic, then, as is prescribed is either inward or outward, as hath been formerly handled in the precedent partition in the cure of melancholy, Consult with Valleriola, Lodovicus Mercatus, Daniel Sennertus, Jacobus Ferrandus the Frenchman, in his tract on erotic love; Forestus, Jason Pratensis, and others for peculiar receipts. Amatus Lusitanus cured a young Jew, that was almost mad for love, with the syrup of hellebore, and such other evacuations and purges which are usually prescribed to black choler; Avicenna confirms as much if need require, and blood-letting above the rest, which makes lovers to come to themselves, and keep in their right minds. 'Tis the same which the School of Salerno, Jason Pratensis, Hildesheim, etc., prescribe, blood-letting to be used as a principal remedy. Those old Scythians had a trick to cure all appetite of burning lust, by letting themselves blood under the ears, and to make both men and women barren, as Sabellicus in his Enneades relates of them. Which Salmuth, Mercurialis, out of Hippocrates and Benzo, say still is in use among the Indians, a reason of which Langius gives.

They make medicines for cooling lust, such as camphor to be applied to the private parts; carried in the breeches it is said to keep the member flaccid. Being thus afflicted a noble virgin was prescribed a thin sheet of perforated lead to bear on her back for twenty-one days; and to dry up her seed her physician ordered that she be frugal in her diet, chewing constantly coriander and lettuce with vinegar; so she was cured. They also, to impede or prevent coitus, use a decoction of willow; frequently taken it helps total abstinence. A topaz, worn in a ring, is recommended, as also the right testicle, brayed, of a wolf, and oil or water of roses, according to Alexander Benedictus, conduces to make venery tedious. Buttermilk, seed of canabis, and camphor are prescribed. Verbena extinguished libidinousness, likewise a frog desiccated and pulverized. Coitus is discouraged by anointing the genitals, belly, and chest with water in which opium Thebaicum is dissolved; camphor is eminently inimical to lust, and dried coriander by hindering erection prevents coition; a mustard drink has the like effect. Verbena in a potion makes erection impossible for six days; dried mint in vinegar for the uterus, juice of henbane or hemlock for the genitals, destroy the appetite for coitus, etc. One recipe is, take lettuce seeds, purslane, coriander, each I drachm, dried mint a half-drachm, white sugar 4 ounces; pulverize fine, mix with water of nenuphar, and make into lozenges; one to be taken on rising. See similar recipes in Hildesheim, Mizaldus, Porta, and others.

XVI

*Withstand the beginnings, avoid occasions,
change his place; fair and foul means,
contrary passions, with inventions: to bring
in another, and discommend the former.*

OTHER GOOD RULES and precepts are enjoined by our physicians, which, if not alone, yet certainly conjoined may do much; the first of which is to withstand the beginning. He that will but resist at first, may easily be a conqueror at the last. Baldassare Castiglione urgeth this prescript above the rest. When he shall chance (saith he) to light upon a woman that hath good behaviour joined with her excellent person, and shall perceive his eyes with a kind of greediness to pull unto them this image of beauty, and carry it to the heart; shall observe himself to be somewhat incensed with this influence, which moveth within; when he shall discern those subtile spirits sparkling in her eyes to administer more fuel to the fire, he must wisely withstand the beginnings, rouse up reason, stupefied almost, fortify his heart by all means, and shut up all those passages by which it may have entrance. 'Tis a precept which all concur upon.

> *Thy quick disease, whilst it is fresh today,*
> *By all means crush, thy feet at first step stay.*

(OVID)

Which cannot speedier be done, than if he confess his grief and passion to some judicious friend (the more he conceals, the greater is his pain), that by his good advice may happily ease him on a sudden; and withal to avoid occasions, or any circumstance that may aggravate his disease, to remove the object by all means; for who can stand by a fire and not burn? 'Leap back ye bolts, and cast her out of doors, for the love of her has drained my very life-blood' (Plautus).

'Tis good therefore to keep quite out of her company, which Jerome so much labours to Paula, to Nepotian; Chrysostom so much inculcates Cyprian, and many other Fathers of the Church, Siracides [Ecclesiasticus] in his ninth chapter, Jason Pratensis, Savonarola, Arnoldus, Valleriola, etc., and every physician that treats of this subject. Not only to avoid, as Gregory Tholosanus exhorts, kissing, dalliance, all speeches, tokens, love-letters, and the like, or as Castiglione, to converse with them, hear them speak or sing, 'thou hadst better hear,' saith Cyprian, 'a serpent hiss,' those amiable smiles, admirable graces, and sweet gestures, which their presence affords ('let them not bow their heads for kisses, nor toy with the nipples of their mistresses') [Lipsius], but all talk, name, mention, or cogitation of them, and of any other women, persons, circumstance, amorous book or tale that may administer any occasion of remembrance. Prosper adviseth young men not to read the Canticles, and some parts of Genesis at other times; but for such as are enamoured they forbid, as before, the name mentioned, etc., especially all sight, they must not so much as come near, or look upon them. It is well to shun all sights that feed love, and to turn the mind away from it.

Gaze not on a maid, saith Siracides [Ecclesiasticus], 'turn away thine eyes from a beautiful woman'. Avert thine eyes, said David, or if thou dost see them, as Ficinus adviseth, let not thine eye be intent on lust, do not intend her more than the rest: for as Propertius holds, love provides its own nourishment, love as a snowball enlargeth itself by sight: but as Jerome to Nepotian, either see all alike, or let all alone; make a league with thine eyes, as Job did, and that is the safest course, let all alone, see none of them.

Nothing sooner revives, or waxeth sore again, as Petrarch holds, than love doth by sight. As pomp renews ambition, the sight of gold covetousness, a beauteous object sets on fire this burning lust. The sight of drink makes one dry, and the sight of meat increaseth appetite. 'Tis dangerous therefore to see. A young gentleman in merriment would needs put on his mistress' clothes, and walk abroad alone, which some of her suitors espying, stole him away for her that he represented. So much can sight enforce. Especially if he have been formerly enamoured, the sight of his mistress strikes him into a new fit, and makes him rave many days after.

> *A sickly man a little thing offends,*
> *As brimstone doth a fire decayed renew,*
> *And make it burn afresh, doth love's dead flames,*
> *If that the former object it review.*

> (OVID)

Or, as the poet compares it to embers in ashes, which the wind blows, a scald head (as the saying is) is soon broken, dry wood quickly kindles, and when they have been formerly wounded with sight, how can they by seeing but be inflamed? Ismenias acknowledgeth as much of himself, when he had been long absent, and almost forgotten his mistress: 'At the first sight of her, as straw in a fire, I burned afresh, and more than ever I did before.' Chariclea was as much moved at the sight of her dear Theagenes, after he had been a great stranger. Myrtila, in Aristaenetus, swore she would never love Pamphilus again, and did moderate her passion so long as he was absent; but the next time he came in presence, she could not contain, she broke her vow, and did profusely embrace him. Hermotinus, a young man (in the said author), is all out as unstaid; he had forgot his mistress quite, and by his friends was well weaned from her love; but seeing her by chance, he raved amain, she did appear as a blazing star or an angel to his sight.

And it is the common passion of all lovers to be overcome in this sort. For that cause belike, Alexander, discerning this inconvenience and danger that comes by seeing, when he heard Darius' wife so much commended for her beauty, would scarce admit her to come in his sight, foreknowing belike that of Plutarch, how full of danger it is to see a proper woman; and though he was intemperate in other things, yet in this he carried himself bravely. And so whenas Araspus, in Xenophon, had so much magnified that divine face of Panthea to Cyrus, by how much she was fairer than ordinary, by so much he was the more unwilling to see her.

Scipio, a young man of twenty-three years of age, and the most beautiful of the Romans, equal in person to that Grecian Cleinias, or Homer's Nireus, at the siege of a city in Spain, whenas a noble and most fair young gentlewoman was brought unto him, and he had heard she was betrothed to a lord, rewarded her, and sent her back to her sweetheart. St. Augustine, as Gregory reports of him, would not live in the house with his own sister. Xenocrates lay with Lais of Corinth all night, and would not touch her. Socrates, though all the city of Athens supposed him to dote upon fair Alcibiades, yet when he had an opportunity to lie alone in the chamber with him, and was wooed by him besides, as the said Alcibiades publicly confessed, he scornfully rejected him. Petrarch, that had so magnified his Laura in several poems, when by the Pope's means she was offered unto him, would not accept her. It is a good happiness to be free from this passion of love, and great discretion it argues in such a man that he can so contain himself; but when thou art once in love, to moderate thyself (as Heliodorus saith) is a singular point of wisdom.

To avoid such nets is no such mastery,
But ta'en, to escape is all the victory.

(LUCRETIUS)

But, forasmuch as few men are free, so discreet lovers, or that can contain themselves and moderate their passions, to curb their senses, as not to see them, not to look lasciviously, not to confer with them, such is the fury of this headstrong passion of raging lust, and their weakness, as he [Haedus] terms it, such a furious desire nature hath inscribed, such unspeakable delight, which neither reason, counsel, poverty, pain, misery, drudgery, throes of childbirth, etc., can deter them from; we must use some speedy means to correct and prevent that, and all other inconveniences which come by conference and the like. The best, readiest, surest way, and which all approve, is change of place, to send them several ways, that they may neither hear of, see, nor have an opportunity to send to one another again, or live together, entirely by themselves, as so many Gilbertines. Go abroad— 'tis Savonarola's fourth rule, and Gordonius' precept, send him to travel. 'Tis that which most run upon, as so many hounds with full cry, poets, divines, philosophers, physicians, all, change his country (Valesius); as a sick man, he must be cured with change of air (Tully). The best remedy is to get thee gone (Jason Pratensis); change air and soil (Laurentius); shun the well-loved shore (Virgil); keep away from the neighbourhood (Ovid); go far from hence; safety lies in flight.

Travelling is an antidote of love. For this purpose, saith Propertius, my parents sent me to Athens; time and patience wear away pain and grief, as fire goes out for want of fuel. Out of sight, out of mind. But so as they tarry out long enough: a whole year Xenophon prescribes Critobulus, you can hardly be cured of love in this time: some will hardly be weaned under. All this Heinsius merrily inculcates in an epistle to his friend Primerius: First, fast, then tarry, thirdly, change thy place, fourthly, think of an halter. If change of place, continuance of time, absence, will not wear it out with those precedent remedies, it will hardly be removed: but these commonly are of force.

Felix Plater had a baker to his patient, almost mad for the love of his maid, and desperate; by removing her from him, he was in a short space cured. Isaeus, a philosopher of Assyria, was a most dissolute liver in his youth, in love with all he met; but after he betook himself by his friends' advice to his study, and left women's company, he was so changed that he cared no more for plays, nor feasts, nor masks, nor songs, nor verses, fine clothes, nor on such love-toys: he became a new man upon a sudden (saith mine author), as if he had lost his former eyes. Peter Godefridus, in the last chapter of his third book, hath a story out of St Ambrose, of a young man, that meeting his old love after long absence, on whom he had extremely doted, would scarce take notice of her; she wondered at it, that he should so lightly esteem her, called him again, and told him who she was, I am so-and-so, said she; but he replied, he was not the same man; tore himself away, as Aeneas fled from Dido, not vouchsafing her any further parley, loathing his folly, and ashamed of that which formerly he had done. 'O Neaera, put your tricks, and practise hereafter, upon somebody else, you shall befool me no longer.'

Petrarch hath such another tale of a young gallant, that loved a wench with one eye, and for that cause by his parents was sent to travel into far countries; after some years he returned, and meeting the maid for whose sake he was sent abroad, asked her how and by what chance she lost her eye? 'No,' said she, 'I have lost none, but you have found yours'; signifying thereby that all lovers were blind, as Fabius saith, lovers cannot judge of beauty, nor scarce of anything else, as they will easily confess, after they return unto themselves by some discontinuance or better advice, wonder at their own folly, madness, stupidity, blindness, be much abashed, 'and laugh at love, and call't an idle thing', condemn themselves that ever they should be so besotted or misled, and be heartily glad they have so happily escaped.

If so be (which is seldom) that change of place will not effect this alteration, then other remedies are to be annexed, fair and foul means, as to persuade, promise, threaten, terrify, or to divert by some contrary passion, rumour, tales, news, or some witty invention to alter his affection, by some greater sorrow to drive out the less, saith Gordonius, as that his house is on fire, his best friends dead, his money stolen, that he is made some great governor, or hath some honour, office, some inheritance is befallen him, he shall be a knight, a baron; or by some false accusation, as they do to such as have the hiccup, to make them forget it.

St Jerome, in his epistle to Rusticus the monk, hath an instance of a young man of Greece, that lived in a monastery in Egypt, that by no labour, no continence, no persuasion could be diverted, but at last by this trick he was delivered. The abbot sets one of his convent to quarrel with him, and with some scandalous reproach or other to defame him before company, and then to come and complain first; the witnesses were likewise suborned for the plaintiff. The young man wept, and when all were against him the abbot cunningly took his part, lest he should be overcome with immoderate grief; but what need many words? By this invention he was cured, and alienated from his pristine love-thoughts.

Injuries, slanders, contempts, disgraces, 'the affront of slighted beauty' (Virgil), are very forcible means to withdraw men's affections. As Lucian saith, lovers reviled or neglected, contemned or misused, turn love to hate. 'Come back? Not if you ask me on your knees, I'll never love thee more.' So Zephyrus hated Hyacinthus because he scorned him, and preferred his corrival Apollo. He will not come again though he be invited. Tell him but how he was scoffed at behind his back ('tis the counsel of Avicenna), that his love is false, and entertains another, rejects him, cares not for him, or that she is a fool, a nasty quean, a slut, a vixen, a scold, a devil, or, which Italians commonly do, that he or she hath some loathsome filthy disease, gout, stone, strangury, falling sickness, and that they are hereditary, not to be avoided, he is subject to a consumption, hath the pox, that he hath three or four incurable tetters, issues; that she is bald, her breath stinks, she is mad by inheritance, and so are all the kindred, an hare-brain, with many other secret infirmities, which I will not so much as name, belonging to women. That he is an hermaphrodite, an eunuch, imperfect, impotent, a spendthrift, a gamester, a fool, a gull, a beggar, a whoremaster, far in debt, and not able to maintain her, a common drunkard, his mother was a witch, his father hanged, that he hath a wolf in his bosom, a sore leg, he is a leper, hath some incurable disease, that he will surely beat her, he cannot hold his water, that he cries out or walks in the night, will stab his bed-fellow, tell all his secrets in his sleep, and that nobody dare lie with him, his house is haunted with spirits, with such fearful and tragical things, able to avert and terrify any man or woman living. Gordonius offers this counsel: show him a menstruous rag, saying, 'Such is your goddess', and if he be not cured he is not a man. See Avicenna to the same effect on such distasteful things. Also Arculanus, Rhasis, etc.

Withal, as they do discommend the old, for the better effecting a more speedy alteration, they must commend another paramour, set him or her to be wooed, or woo some other that shall be fairer, of better note, better fortune, birth, parentage, much to be preferred: 'You'll find another lover if Alexis disdains you' (Virgil), by this means, which Jason Pratensis wisheth, to turn the stream of affection another way: 'The new love thrusts out the old' (Ovid); or, as Valesius adviseth, by subdividing to diminish it, as a great river cut into many channels runs low at last. If you suspect to be taken, be sure, saith the poet Ovid, to have two mistresses at once, or go from one to another; as he that goes from a good fire in cold weather is loth to depart from it, though in the next room there be a better which will refresh him as much; there's as much difference of women as fires; or bring him to some public shows, plays, meetings, where he may see variety, and he shall likely loathe his first choice: carry him but to the next town, yea peradventure to the next house, and as Paris lost Oenone's love by seeing Helena, and Cressida forsook Troilus by conversing with Diomede, he will dislike his former mistress, and leave her quite behind him, as Theseus left Ariadne fast asleep in the island of Dia, to seek her fortune, that was erst his loving mistress.

As he that looks himself in a glass forgets his physiognomy forthwith, this flattering glass of love will be diminished by remove; after a little absence it will be remitted, the next fair object will likely alter it. A young man in Lucian was pitifully in love, he came to the theatre by chance, and by seeing other fair objects there was fully recovered, and went merrily home, as if he had taken a dram of oblivion. A mouse (saith an apologer) was brought up in a chest, there fed with fragments of bread and cheese, thought there could be no better meat, till coming forth at last, and feeding liberally of other variety of viands, loathed his former life: moralize this fable by thyself.

Plato, in his seventh book, hath a pretty fiction of a city underground, to which by little holes some small store of light came; the inhabitants thought there could not be a better place, and at their first coming abroad they might not endure the light, but after they were accustomed a little to it, they deplored their fellows' misery that lived underground. A silly lover is in like state; none so fair as his mistress at first, he cares for none but her; yet after a while, when he hath compared her with others, he abhors her name, sight, and memory. 'Tis generally true; for one fire drives another; and such is women's weakness, that they love commonly him that is present.

And so do many men; as he confessed, he loved Amy, till he saw Floriat, and when he saw Cynthia, forgat them both; but fair Phyllis was incomparably beyond them all, Chloris surpassed her, and yet when he espied Amaryllis, she was his sole mistress; O divine Amaryllis! how lovely, how tall, how comely she was (saith Polemius) till he saw another, and then she was the sole subject of his thoughts.

In conclusion, her he loves best he saw last. Triton, the sea-god, first loved Leucothoe, till he came in presence of Milaene; she was the commandress of his heart, till he saw Galatea; but (as she complains) he loved another eftsoons, another, and another. 'Tis a thing, which by Jerome's report, hath been usually practised. Heathen philosophers drive out one love with another, as they do a peg, or pin with a pin; which those seven Persian princes did to Ahasuerus, that they might requite the desire of Queen Vashti with the love of others. Pausanias saith that therefore one Cupid was painted to contend with another, and to take the garland from him, because one love drives out another, and Tully, disputing with C. Cotta, makes mention of three several Cupids, all differing in office.

Felix Plater, in the first book of his Observations, boasts how he cured a widower in Basil, a patient of his, by this stratagem alone, that doted upon a poor servant his maid, when friends, children, no persuasion could serve to alienate his mind; they motioned him to another honest man's daughter in the town, whom he loved and lived with long after, abhorring the very name and sight of the first. After the death of Lucretia, Euryalus would admit of no comfort, till the Emperor Sigismund married him to a noble lady of his court, and so in short space he was freed.

XVII

*By counsel and persuasion, foulness of
the face, men's, women's faults, miseries
of marriage, events of lust, etc.*

As there be divers causes of this burning lust, or heroical love, so there be many good remedies to ease and help; among which, good counsel and persuasion, which I should have handled in the first place, are of great moment, and not to be omitted. Many are of opinion that in this blind headstrong passion counsel can do no good.

> *Which thing hath neither judgment, nor an end,*
> *How should advice or counsel it amend?*
>
> (TERENCE)

'What bounds can be set to love?' (Virgil). But, without question, good counsel and advice must needs be of great force, especially if it shall proceed from a wise, fatherly, reverend, discreet person, a man of authority, whom the parties do respect, stand in awe of, or from a judicious friend, of itself alone it is able to divert and suffice.

Gordonius the physician attributes so much to it, that he would have it by all means used in the first place. He would have some discreet men to dissuade them, after the fury of passion is a little spent, or by absence allayed; for it is as intempestive at first to give counsel, as to comfort parents when their children are in that instant departed; to no purpose to prescribe narcotics, cordials, nectarines, potions, Homer's nepenthes, or Helen's bowl, etc. She will not cease to beat her breast, she will lament and howl for a season: let passion have his course awhile, and then he may proceed, by foreshadowing the miserable events and dangers which will surely happen, the pains of hell, joys of Paradise, and the like, which by their preposterous courses they shall forfeit or incur; and 'tis a fit method, a very good means; for what Seneca said of vice, I say of love, 'tis learned of itself, but hardly left without a tutor.

'Tis not amiss therefore to have some such overseer, to expostulate and show them such absurdities, inconveniences, imperfections, discontents, as usually follow; which their blindness, fury, madness, cannot apply unto themselves, or will not apprehend through weakness; and good for them to disclose themselves, to give ear to friendly admonitions. 'Tell me, sweetheart,' saith Tryphaena to a lovesick Charmides in Lucian, 'what is it that troubles thee? peradventure I can ease thy mind, and further thee in thy suit'; and so, without question, she might, and so mayst thou, if the patient be capable of good counsel, and will hear at least what may be said.

If he love at all, she is either an honest woman or a whore. If dishonest, let him read or inculcate to him that fifth of Solomon's Proverbs, Ecclus. xxvi, Ambrose, in his book of Abel and Cain, Philo Judaeus, Platina's Dialogues on Love, Espencaeus, and those three books of Peter Haedus on the contempt of love, Aeneas Sylvius' tart epistle, which he wrote to his friend Nicholas of Wartburg, which he calls a cure for illicit love, etc. For what's a whore, as he saith, but a poller of youth, ruin of men, a destruction, a devourer of patrimonies, a downfall of honour, fodder for the devil, the gate of death, and supplement of hell? Such a love is a snare, etc., a bitter honey, sweet poison, delicate destruction, a voluntary mischief, sheer filth. And as Peter Aretine's Lucretia, a notable quean, confesseth: Gluttony, anger, envy, pride, sacrilege, theft, slaughter were all born that day that a whore began her profession; for, as she follows it, her pride is greater than a rich churl's, she is more envious than the pox, as malicious as melancholy, as covetous as hell. If from the beginning of the world any were bad, worse, worst, bad in the positive, comparative, superlative degree, 'tis a whore; how many have I undone, caused to be wounded, slain! 'O Antonia, thou seest what I am without, but within, God knows, a puddle of iniquity, a sink of sin, a pocky quean.'

Let him now that so dotes meditate on this; let him see the event and success of others, Samson, Hercules, Holofernes, etc. Those infinite mischiefs attend it: if she be another man's wife he loves, 'tis abominable in the sight of God and men; adultery is expressly forbidden in God's commandment, a mortal sin, able to endanger his soul; if he be such a one that fears God, or have any religion, he will eschew it, and abhor the loathsomeness of his own fact. If he love an honest maid, 'tis to abuse or marry her: if to abuse, 'tis fornication, a foul fact (though some make light of it), and almost equal to adultery itself. If to marry, let him seriously consider what he takes in hand, look before he leap, as the proverb is, or settle his affections, and examine first the party, and condition of his estate and hers, whether it be a fit match, for fortunes, years, parentage, and such other circumstances, whether it be likely to proceed; if not, let him wisely stave himself off at the first, curb in his inordinate passion and moderate his desire, by thinking of some other subject, divert his cogitations. Or if it be not for his good, as Aeneas, forewarned by Mercury in a dream, left Dido's love, and in all haste got him to sea: and although she did oppose with vows, tears, prayers, and imprecation, all her tears moved him not, her words fell on deaf ears.

Let thy Mercury, reason, rule thee against all allurements, seeming delights, pleasing inward or outward provocations. Thou mayst do this if thou wilt, a father dotes not on his own daughter, a brother on a sister; and why? because it is unnatural, unlawful, unfit. If he be sickly, soft, deformed, let him think of his deformities, vices, infirmities; if in debt, let him ruminate how to pay his debts; if he be in any danger, let him seek to avoid it; if he have any lawsuit or other business, he may do well to let his love-matters alone and follow it, labour in his vocation, whatever it is. But if he cannot so ease himself, yet let him wisely premeditate of both their estates; if they be unequal in years, she young and he old, what an unfit match must it needs be, an uneven yoke, how absurd and undecent a thing is it, as Lycinus in Lucian told Timolaus, for an old bald crook-nosed knave to marry a young wench? how odious a thing it is to see an old lecher! What should a bald fellow do with a comb, a dumb doter with a pipe, a blind man with a looking-glass, and thou with such a wife? How absurd it is for a young man to marry an old wife for a piece of good!

But put case she be equal in years, birth, fortunes, and other qualities correspondent, he doth desire to be coupled in marriage, which is an honourable estate, but for what respects? Her beauty belike, and comeliness of person, that is commonly the main object, she is a most absolute form, in his eye at least, she has the beauty of the Paphian, the elegance of the Graces; but do other men affirm as much? or is it an error in his judgement. Our eyes and other senses will commonly deceive us; it may be, to thee thyself upon a more serious examination, or after a little absence, she is not so fair as she seems. Compare her to another standing by, 'tis a touchstone to try, confer hand to hand, body to body, face to face, eye to eye, nose to nose, neck to neck, etc., examine every part of itself, then altogether, in all postures, several sites, and tell me how thou likest her. It may be not she that is so fair, but her coats, or put another in her clothes, and she will seem all out as fair; as the poet [Ovid] then prescribes, separate her from her clothes: suppose thou saw her in a base beggar's weed, or else dressed in some old hirsute attires out of fashion, foul linen, coarse raiment, besmeared with soot, colly [smut], perfumed with opoponax, sagapenum, assafoetida, or some such filthy gums, dirty, about some undecent action or other; or in such a case as Brassavola the physician found Malatesta, his patient, after a potion of hellebore which he had prescribed: hands on the ground, backside raised to heaven (like the Socratic in Aristophanes who while making geometric figures on the ground seemed to be rooting for truffles), the white wall blackened with his bile, the room and himself befouled, etc., all-to bewrayed, or worse; if thou saw'st her (I say), wouldst thou affect her as thou dost? Suppose thou beheldest her in a frosty morning, in cold weather, in some passion or perturbation of mind, weeping, chafing, etc., rivelled and ill-favoured to behold.

She many times that in a composed look seems so amiable and delicious, so elegant, if she do but laugh or smile, makes an ugly sparrow-mouthed face, and shows a pair of uneven, loathsome, rotten foul teeth: she hath a black skin, gouty legs, a deformed crooked carcass under a fine coat. It may be for all her costly tires she is bald, and though she seem so fair by dark, by candle-light, or afar off at such a distance, as Callicratides observed in Lucian, if thou should see her near, or in a morning, she would appear more ugly than a beast; if you reflect what issues from her mouth and nostrils and other orifices you will say that you have never seen worse filth.

Follow my counsel, see her undressed, see her, if it be possible, out of her attires, stripped of her borrowed colours, it may be she is like Aesop's jay, or Pliny's cantharides, she will be loathsome, ridiculous, thou wilt not endure her sight: or suppose thou saw'st her sick, pale, in a consumption, on her death-bed, skin and bones, or now dead, whose embrace was so pleasant, as Bernard saith, will be horrible to see. As a posy she smells sweet, is most fresh and fair one day, but dried up, withered, and stinks another. Beautiful Nireus, by that Homer so much admired, once dead, is more deformed than Thersites, and Solomon deceased as ugly as Marcolphus: thy lovely mistress that was erst dearer to thee than thine eyes, once sick or departed, is worse than any dirt or dunghill. Her embraces were not so acceptable as now her looks be terrible: thou hadst better behold a Gorgon's head than Helena's carcass.

Some are of opinion that to see a woman naked is able of itself to alter his affection; and it is worthy of consideration, saith Montaigne the Frenchman in his Essays, that the skilfullest masters of amorous dalliance appoint for a remedy of venerous passions, a full survey of the body; which the poet insinuates:

> *The love stood still, that ran in full career,*
> *When once it saw those parts should not appear.*

(OVID)

It is reported of Seleucus, King of Syria, that seeing his wife Stratonice's bald pate, as she was undressing her by chance, he could never affect her after. Raymond Lully, the physician, spying an ulcer or canker in his mistress' breast, whom he so dearly loved, from that day following abhorred the looks of her. Philip the French king, as Nubrigensis relates it, married the King of Denmark's daughter, and after he had used her as a wife one night, because her breath stunk, they say, or for some other secret fault, sent her back again to her father. Peter Matthaeus, in the life of Louis the Eleventh, finds fault with our English chronicles, for writing how Margaret, the King of Scots' daughter, and wife to Louis the eleventh French king, was because of her bad breath rejected by her husband. Many such matches are made for by-respects, or some seemly comeliness, which after honeymoon's past turn to bitterness; for burning lust is but a flash, a gunpowder passion, and hatred oft follows in the highest degree, dislike and contempt. When they wax old and ill-favoured they may commonly no longer abide them: begone; they grow stale, fulsome, loathsome, odious; thou art a beastly filthy quean, a face like one straining at the stool, thou art hind end of Saturn, withered and dry, savourless and old; wrinkled, ugly, and grey, I say begone, there's the door, go.

Yea, but you will infer, your mistress is complete, of a most absolute form in all men's opinions, no exceptions can be taken at her, nothing may be added to her person, nothing detracted, she is the mirror of women for her beauty, comeliness, and pleasant grace, unimitable, she is a mere magazine of natural perfections, she hath all the Loves and Graces, in each part absolute and complete, beautiful cheeks, rosy lips, languishing eyes; to be admired for her person, a most incomparable, unmatchable piece, a phoenix, a nymph, a fairy, like Venus herself when she was a maid, second to none, a mere quintessence, a breathing flower, a female prodigy: put case she be, how long will she continue? Every day detracts from her person, and this beauty is fragile, a mere flash, a Venice glass, quickly broken: Beauty to mortals is a short-lived boon, it will not last. As that fair flower Adonis, which we call an anemone, flourisheth but one month, this gracious all-commanding beauty fades in an instant. It is a jewel soon lost, the painter's goddess, a mere picture. 'Favour is deceitful, and beauty is vanity' (Prov. xxxi, 30).

> *A brittle gem, bubble, is beauty pale,*
> *A rose, dew, snow, smoke, wind, air, naught at all.*
>
> (BAUHUSIUS)

If she be fair, as the saying is, she is commonly a fool; if proud, scornful, or dishonest; can she be fair and honest too?

Aristo, the son of Agasicles, married a Spartan lass, the fairest lady in all Greece next to Helen, but for her conditions [character] the most abominable and beastly creature of the world. So that I would wish thee to respect, with Seneca, not her person but qualities. Will you say that's a good blade which hath a gilded scabbard, embroidered with gold and jewels? No, but that which hath a good edge and point, well-tempered mettle, able to resist. This beauty is of the body alone, and what is that but, as Gregory Nazianzen telleth us, a mock of time and sickness? or as Boethius, as mutable as a flower, and 'tis not nature so makes us, but most part the infirmity of the beholder? For ask another, he sees no such matter: 'I pray thee tell me how thou likest my sweetheart,' as she asked her sister in Aristaenetus, 'whom I so much admire; methinks he is the sweetest gentleman, the properest man that ever I saw; but I am in love, I confess, and am not ashamed to confess it, and cannot therefore well judge.'

But be she fair indeed, golden-haired, as Anacreon his Bathyllus (to examine particulars), she have sparkling eyes, a milk-white neck, a pure sanguine complexion, little mouth, coral lips, white teeth, soft and plump neck, body, hands, feet, all fair and lovely to behold, composed of all graces, elegancies, an absolute piece. Let Melita have Juno's eyes, Minerva's hands, breasts like Venus, a leg like Amphitrite; let her head be from Prague, paps out of Austria, belly from France, back from Brabant, hands out of England, feet from Rhine, buttocks from Switzerland, let her have the Spanish gait, the Venetian tire, Italian complement and endowments. Let her eyes shine like the stars, saith Petronius, her neck bloom like the rose, her hair brighter than gold, her lips be red of the sweetest hue; let her radiate beauty more than heavenly Venus, etc. Let her be such a one throughout, as Lucian deciphers in his Images, as Euphranor of old painted Venus, Aristaenetus describes Lais, another Helena, Chariclea, Leucippe, Lucretia, Pandora; let her have a box of beauty to repair herself still, such a one as Venus gave Phaon, when he carried her over the ford; let her use all helps art and nature can yield; be like her, and her, and whom thou wilt, or all these in one: a little sickness, a fever, small-pox, wound, scar, loss of an eye or limb, a violent passion, a distemperature of heat or cold, mars all in an instant, disfigures all;

child-bearing, old age, that tyrant time, will turn Venus to Erinnys; raging time, care, rivels her upon a sudden; after she hath been married a small while, and the black ox hath trodden on her toe, she will be so much altered, and wax out of favour, thou wilt not know her.

One grows too fat, another too lean, etc. Modest Matilda, pretty pleasing Peg, sweet-singing Susan, mincing merry Moll, dainty dancing Doll, neat Nancy, jolly Joan, nimble Nell, kissing Kate, bouncing Bess with black eyes, fair Phyllis with fine white hands, fiddling Frances, tall Tib, slender Sib, etc., will quickly lose their grace, grow fulsome, stale, sad, heavy, dull, sour, and all at last out of fashion. Where now the lively looks, the caressing ways, the captivating laugh, etc.? Those fair sparkling eyes will look dull, her soft coral lips will be pale, dry, cold, rough, and blue, her skin rugged, that soft and tender superficies will be hard and harsh, her whole complexion change in a moment, and as Matilda writ to King John:

> I am not now as when thou saw'st me last,
> That favour soon is vanished and past;
> That rosy blush lapt in a lily vale,
> Now is with morphew overgrown and pale.
>
> (DRAYTON)

'Tis so in the rest, their beauty fades as a tree in winter, which Deianira hath elegantly expressed in Seneca:

> And as a tree that in the greenwood grow,
> With fruit and leaves, and in the summer blows,
> In winter like a stock deformed shows:
> Our beauty takes his race and journey goes,
> And doth decrease, and lose, and come to naught,
> Admir'd of old, to this by child-birth brought:

And mother hath bereft me of my grace,
And crooked old age coming on apace.

To conclude with Chrysostom: When thou seest a fair and beautiful person, a brave bona-roba, who makes your mouth water, a merry maid, whom you can easily love, a comely woman, having bright eyes, a merry countenance, a shining lustre in her look, a pleasant grace, wringing thy soul and increasing thy concupiscence; bethink with thyself that it is but earth thou lovest, a mere excrement which so vexeth thee, which thou so admirest, and thy raging soul will be at rest. Take her skin from her face, and thou shalt see all loathsomeness under it, that beauty is a superficial skin and bones, nerves, sinews; suppose her sick, now rivelled, hoary-headed, hollow-cheeked, old; within she is full of filthy phlegm, stinking, putrid, excremental stuff: snot and snivel in her nostrils, spittle in her mouth, water in her eyes, what filth in her brains, etc.

Or take her at best, and look narrowly upon her in the light, stand near her, nearer yet, thou shalt perceive almost as much, and love less; as Cardan well writes, the sharp-eyed love less, though Scaliger deride him for it: if he see her near, or look exactly at such a posture, whosoever he is, according to the true rules of symmetry and proportion, those I mean of Albert Durer, Lomatius and Taisnier, examine him of her. If he be a connoisseur of beauty he shall find many faults in physiognomy, and ill colour: if form, one side of the face likely bigger than the other, or crooked nose, bad eyes, prominent veins, concavities about the eyes, wrinkles, pimples, red streaks, freckles, hairs, warts, moles, inequalities, roughness, scabredity, paleness, yellowness, and as many colours as are in a turkey-cock's neck, many indecorums in their other parts; some things lacking, others superfluous, one leers, another frowns, a third gapes, squints, etc. And 'tis true that Cardan saith, seldom shall you find an absolute face without fault, as I have often observed; not in the face alone is this defect or disproportion to be found, but in all the other parts, of body and mind; she is fair, indeed, but foolish; pretty, comely, and decent, of a majestical presence, but peradventure imperious, unhonest, self-willed; she is rich, but deformed; hath a sweet face, but bad carriage, no bringing up, a rude and wanton flirt; a neat body she hath, but it is a nasty quean otherwise, a very slut, of a bad kind.

As flowers in a garden have colour some, but no smell, others have a fragrant smell, but are unseemly to the eye; one is unsavoury to the taste as rue, as bitter as wormwood, and yet a most medicinal cordial flower, most acceptable to the stomach; so are men and women; one is well qualified, but of ill proportion, poor and base: a good eye she hath, but a bad hand and foot, a fine leg, bad teeth, a vast body, etc. Examine all parts of body and mind, I advise thee to inquire of all. See her angry, merry, laugh, weep, hot, cold, sick, sullen, dressed, undressed, in all attires, sites, gestures, passions, eat her meals, etc., and in some of these you will surely dislike. Yea, not her only let him observe, but her parents, how they carry themselves: for what deformities, defects, encumbrances of body or mind be in them at such an age, they will likely be subject to, be molested in like manner, they will take after father or mother.

And withal let him take notice of her companions (as Guevara prescribes), whom she converseth with. A man is known by the company he keeps. According to Thucydides, she is commonly the best that is least talked of abroad. For if she be a noted reveller, a gadder, a singer, a pranker, or dancer, then take heed of her. For what saith Theocritus? Ye merry girls, haste not to the dance; a rakish goat lies in wait for you. 'Young men will do it when they come to it' [Shakespeare: *Hamlet*], fauns and satyrs will certainly play wreeks [pranks], when they come in such wanton Bacchis' or Elenora's presence. Now when they shall perceive any such obliquity, indecency, disproportion, deformity, bad conditions, etc., let them still ruminate on that, and as Haedus adviseth out of Ovid, note their faults, vices, errors, and think of their imperfections; 'tis the next way to divert and mitigate love's furious headstrong passions, as a peacock's feet and filthy comb, they say, make him forget his fine feathers and pride of his tail; she is lovely, fair, well favoured, well qualified, courteous, and kind, 'But if she be not so to me, what care I how kind she be?' [Wither]. I say with Philostratus, beautiful to others, she is a tyrant to me, and so let her go. Besides these outward naeves [birth marks], or open faults, errors, there be many inward infirmities, secret, some private (which I will omit), and some more common to the sex, sullen fits, evil qualities, filthy diseases, in this case fit to be considered; first their menstrual uncleanness, of which Savonarola exposes, Platina dwells upon at length, and many other physicians mention. A lover in Calcagninus' Apologues wished with all his heart he were his mistress' ring, to hear, embrace, see, and do I know not what: 'O thou fool,' quoth the ring, 'if thou wer'st in my room, thou shouldst hear, observe, and see that which would make thee loathe and hate her, yea, peradventure, all women for her sake.'

I will say nothing of the vices of their minds, their pride, envy, inconstancy, weakness, malice, self-will, lightness, insatiable lust, jealousy; 'No malice to a woman's' (Ecclus xxv, 13), 'no bitterness like to hers' (Eccles. vii, 26), and as the same author urgeth (Prov. xxxi, 10), 'Who shall find a virtuous woman?' He makes a question of it. They know neither good nor bad, be it better or worse (as the comical poet hath it), beneficial or hurtful, they will do what they list. 'A snare to the human race, the affliction of life, the spoiler of the night, the bitterest cares by day, the torture of husbands, the ruin of youths' [Lochaeus]. And to that purpose were they first made, as Jupiter insinuates in the poet [Hesiod]:

> *The fire that bold Prometheus stole from me,*
> *With plagues call'd women shall revenged be,*
> *On whose alluring and enticing face,*
> *Poor mortals doting shall their death embrace.*

In fine, as Diogenes concludes in Nevisanus: they have all their faults.

> *Every each of them hath some vice,*
> *If one be full of villainy,*
> *Another hath a liquorish eye.*
> *If one be full of wantonness,*
> *Another is a chideress.*

(CHAUCER)

When Leander was drowned the inhabitants of Sestos consecrated Hero's lantern to Anteros, and he that had good success in his love should light the candle; but never any man was found to light it; which I can refer to naught but the inconstancy and lightness of women.

> *For in a thousand, good there is not one;*
> *All be so proud, unthankful, and unkind,*
> *With flinty hearts, careless of others' moan,*
> *In their own lusts carried most headlong blind,*
> *But more herein to speak I am forbidden:*
> *Sometimes for speaking truth one may be chidden.*

(ARIOSTO)

I am not willing, you see, to prosecute the cause against them, and therefore take heed you mistake me not, I honour the sex, with all good men, and as I ought to do, rather than displease them, I will voluntarily take the oath which Mercurius Britannicus took, never by word or deed to offend the most noble sex, etc. Let Simonides, Mantuan, Platina, Peter Aretine, and such women-haters bear the blame, if aught be said amiss; I have not writ a tenth of that which might be urged out of them and others; all satires against women could not be contained in one volume.

And that which I have said (to speak truth) no more concerns them than men, though women be more frequently named in this tract; to apologize once for all, I am neither partial against them, or therefore bitter; what is said of the one, changing the name, may most part be understood of the other. My words are like Pauso's picture in Lucian, of whom, when a good fellow had bespoke an horse to be painted with his heels upwards, tumbling on his back, he made him passant; now when the fellow came for his piece he was very angry, and said it was quite opposite to his mind; but Pauso instantly turned the picture upside down, showed him the horse at that site which he requested, and so gave him satisfaction. If any man take exception at my words, let him alter the name, read him for her, and 'tis all one in effect.

But to my purpose. If women in general be so bad (and men worse than they), what a hazard is it to marry! where shall a man find a good wife, or a woman a good husband? A woman a man may eschew, but not a wife: wedding is undoing (some say), marrying marring, wooing woeing: a wife is a fever hectic, as Scaliger calls her, and not to be cured but by death, as out of Meander, Athenaeus adds:

> *Thou wadest into a sea itself of woes;*
> *In Libyck and Aegean each man knows*
> *Of thirty not three ships are cast away,*
> *But on this rock not one escapes, I say.*

The wordy cares, miseries, discontents, that accompany marriage, I pray you learn of them that have experience, for I have none; For my part I'll not dissemble with him:

> *Away from me, ye nymphs, deceitful maids!*
> *No married life for me;*

many married men exclaim at the miseries of it, and rail at wives downright; I never tried, but as I hear some of them say, an Irish Sea is not so turbulent and raging as a litigious wife.

> *Scylla and Charybdis are less dangerous,*
> *There is no beast that is so noxious.*

(SENECA)

Which made the devil belike, as most interpreters hold, when he had taken away Job's goods, health, children, friends, to persecute him the more, leave his wicked wife, as Pineda proves out of Tertullian, Cyprian, Austin, Chrysostom, Prosper, Gaudentius, etc., to vex and gall him worse than all the fiends in hell, as knowing the conditions of a bad woman. Jupiter inflicted on man no more pestilent evil, saith Simonides; 'Better dwell with a dragon or a lion, than keep house with a wicked wife' (Ecclus, xxv, 16); 'Better dwell in a wilderness' (Prov. xxi, 19); 'No wickedness like to her' (Ecclus. xxv, 19); 'She makes a sorry heart, an heavy countenance, a wounded mind, weak hands, and feeble knees' (verse 25); 'A woman and death are the two bitterest things in the world. When he said, I must marry today, he seemed to say, Go home and hang yourself' [Terence].

And yet for all this we bachelors desire to be married; with that vestal virgin, we long for it: 'Happy ye brides! 'tis sweet to marry.' 'Tis the sweetest thing in the world, I would I had a wife, saith he,

For fain would I leave a single life,
If I could get me a good wife.

Heigh-ho for a husband! cries she; a bad husband, nay, the worst that ever was, is better than none: O blissful marriage! O most welcome marriage! and happy are they that are so coupled: we do earnestly seek it, and are never well till we have effected it. But with what fate? Like those birds in the emblem, that fed about a cage, so long as they could fly away at their pleasure, liked well of it; but when they were taken and might not get loose, though they had the same meat, pined away for sullenness, and would not eat: so we commend marriage: So long as we are wooers, may kiss and coll at our pleasure, nothing is so sweet, we are in heaven as we think; but when we are once tied, and have lost our liberty, marriage is an hell; Give me my yellow hose again; a mouse in a trap lives as merrily, we are in a purgatory some of us, if not hell itself. As the proverb is, 'tis fine talking of war, and marriage sweet in contemplation, till it be tried: and then as wars are most dangerous, irksome, every minute at death's door, so is, etc.

When those wild Irish peers, saith Stanyhurst, were feasted by King Henry the Second (at what time he kept his Christmas at Dublin), and had tasted of his prince-like cheer, generous wines, dainty fare, had seen his massy plate of silver, gold, enamelled, beset with jewels, golden candlesticks, goodly rich hangings, brave furniture, heard his trumpets sound, fifes, drums, and his exquisite music in all kinds; when they had observed his majestical presence as he sat in purple robes, crowned, with his sceptre, etc., in his royal seat, the poor men were so amazed, enamoured, and taken with the object that they were weary and ashamed of their own sordidity and manner of life. They would all be English forthwith, who but English! but when they had now submitted themselves, and lost their former liberty, they began to rebel some of them, others repent of what they had done, when it was too late.

'Tis so with us bachelors; when we see and behold those sweet faces, those gaudy shows that women make, observe their pleasant gestures and graces, give ear to their siren tunes, see them dance, etc., we think their conditions are as fine as their faces, we are taken with dumb signs, we rush to embrace them, we rave, we burn, and would fain be married. But when we feel the miseries, cares, woes, that accompany it, we make our moan many of us, cry out at length and cannot be released. If this be true now, as some out of experience will inform us, farewell wiving for my part, and, as the comical poet [Eubulus] merrily saith:

> *Foul fall him that brought the second match to pass,*
> *The first I wish no harm, poor man, alas!*
> *He knew not what he did, nor what it was.*

What shall I say to him that marries again and again? I pity him not, for the first time he must do as he may, bear it out sometimes by the head and shoulders, and let his next neighbour ride, or else run away, or as that Syracusan in a tempest, when all ponderous things were to be exonerated out of the ship, because she was his heaviest burden, fling his wife into the sea.

But this I confess is comically spoken, and so I pray you take it. In sober sadness, marriage is a bondage, a thraldom, a yoke, an hindrance to all good enterprises—'He hath married a wife and cannot come' [Luke xiv, 20]; a stop to all preferments, a rock on which many are saved, many impinge and are cast away: not that the thing is evil in itself or troublesome, but full of all contentment and happiness, one of the three things which please God, 'when a man and his wife agree together', an honourable and happy estate, who knows it not? If they be sober, wise, honest, as Euripides infers,

> *If fitly match'd be man and wife,*
> *No pleasure's wanting to their life.*

But to undiscreet sensual persons that as brutes are wholly led by sense, it is a feral plague, many times a hell itself, and can give little or no content, being that they are often so irregular and prodigious in their lusts, so diverse in their affections. As Aelius Vetus said, a wife is a name of honour, not of pleasure; she is fit to bear the office, govern a family, to bring up children, sit at board's end and carve, as some carnal men think and say; they had rather go to the stews, or have now and then a snatch as they can come by it, borrow of their neighbours, than have wives of their own; except they may, as some princes and great men do, keep as many courtesans as they will themselves, fly out with impunity, violate other men's wives; unless that polygamy of Turks, Lex Julia, which Caesar once enforced in Rome (though Levinus Torrentius and others suspect it) that every great man might marry and keep as many wives as he would, or Irish divorcement, were in use: but as it is, 'tis hard and gives not that satisfaction to these carnal men, beastly men as too many are. What, still the same? to be tied to one, be she never so fair, never so virtuous, is a thing they may not endure, to love one long.

Say thy pleasure, and counterfeit as thou wilt, as Parmeno told Thais, one man will never please thee; or one woman many men. But as Pan replied to his father Mercury, when he asked whether he was married, 'No, father, no, I am a lover still, and cannot be contented with one woman.' Pitys, Echo, the Maenades, and I know not how many besides were his mistresses, he might not abide marriage. Variety pleases, 'tis loathsome and tedious; what, one still? That which the satirist [Juvenal] said of Iberina is verified in most:

> *'Tis not one man will serve her by her will,*
> *As soon she'll have one eye as one man still.*

As capable of any impression as primal matter itself, that still desires new forms, like the sea their affections ebb and flow. Husband is a cloak for some to hide their villainy; once married she may fly out at her pleasure, the name of husband is a sanctuary to make all good. They are right and straight, as true Trojans as mine host's daughter, that Spanish wench in Ariosto, as good wives as Messalina. Many men are as constant in their choice, and as good husbands, as Nero himself; they must have their pleasure of all they see, and are in a word far more fickle than any woman.

> *For either they be full of jealousy,*
> *Or masterful, or loven novelty.*
>
> (CHAUCER)

Good men have often ill wives, as bad as Xantippe was to Socrates, Elenora to St Louis [an error: should be Louis VII], Isabella to our Edward the Second; and good wives are as often matched to ill husbands as Mariamne to Herod, Serena to Diocletian, Theodora to Theophilus, and Thyra to Gurmunde. But I will say nothing of dissolute and bad husbands, of bachelors and their vices; their good qualities are a fitter subject for a just volume, too well known already in every village, town, and city, they need no blazon; and lest I should mar any matches, or dishearten loving maids, for this present I will let them pass.

Being that men and women are so irreligious, depraved by nature, so wandering in their affections, so brutish, so subject to disagreement, so unobservant of marriage rites, what shall I say? If thou beest such a one, or thou light on such a wife, what concord can there be, what hope of agreement? as the reed and fern in the emblem, averse and opposite in nature; 'tis twenty to one thou wilt not marry to thy contentment; but as in a lottery forty blanks were drawn commonly for one prize, out of a multitude you shall hardly choose a good one: a small ease hence, then, little comfort.

> *If he or she be such a one,*
> *Thou hadst much better be alone.*
>
> (SIMONIDES)

If she be barren, she is not——, etc. If she have children, and thy state be not good, though thou be wary and circumspect, thy charge will undo thee, thou wilt not be able to bring them up, and what greater misery can there be than to beget children, to whom thou canst leave no other inheritance but hunger and thirst? They break their father's heart with their piteous cries; what so grievous as to turn them up to the wide world, to shift for themselves? No plague like to want; and when thou hast good means, and art very careful of their education, they will not be ruled. Think but of that old proverb, great men's sons seldom do well. 'Would that I had either remained single, or not had children,' Augustus exclaims in Suetonius. Jacob had his Reuben, Simeon, and Levi; David an Amnon, an Absalon, an Adonijah; wise men's sons are commonly fools, insomuch that Spartan concludes, they had been much better to have been childless: 'Tis too common in the middle sort; thy son's a drunkard, a gamester, a spendthrift; thy daughter a fool, a whore; thy servants lazy drones and thieves; thy neighbours devils, they will make thee weary of thy life.

If thy wife be froward when she may not have her will, thou hadst better be buried alive; she will be so impatient, raving still, and roaring like Juno in the tragedy, there's nothing but tempests, all is in an uproar. If she be soft and foolish, thou werst better have a block, she will shame thee and reveal thy secrets; if wise and learned, well qualified, there is as much danger on the other side, saith Nevisanus, she will be too insolent and peevish: 'I had rather have,' saith Juvenal, 'a Venusian wench than thee, Cornelia, mother of the Gracchi.'

Take heed; if she be a slut, thou wilt loathe her; if proud, she'll beggar thee, she'll spend thy patrimony in baubles, all Arabia will not serve to perfume her hair, saith Lucian; if fair and wanton, she'll make thee a cornuto; if deformed, she will paint. If her face be filthy by nature, she will mend it by art, which who can endure? If she do not paint, she will look so filthy, thou canst not love her, and that peradventure will make thee unhonest. Cromerus relates of Casimirus that he was unchaste because his wife Aleida, the daughter of Henry, Landgrave of Hesse, was so deformed. If she be poor, she brings beggary with her (saith Nevisanus), misery and discontent.

If you marry a maid it is uncertain how she proves: perhaps she will prove unsuitable for you. If young, she is likely wanton and untaught; if lusty, too lascivious; and if she be not satisfied, you know where and when, all is in an uproar, and there is little quietness to be had; if an old maid, 'tis a hazard she dies in childbed; if a rich widow, thou dost halter thyself, she will make all away beforehand, to her other children, etc. Who can endure a virago for a wife? she will hit thee still in the teeth with her first husband; if a young widow, she is often unsatiable and immodest. If she is rich, well descended, bring a great dowry, or be nobly allied, thy wife's friends will eat thee out of house and home, she will be so proud, so high-minded, so imperious. For there's nothing so intolerable as a rich wife; thou shalt be as the tassel of a goshawk, she will ride upon thee, domineer as she list, wear the breeches in her oligarchical government, and beggar thee besides. Rich wives expect submission, as Seneca hits them. They will have sovereignty, a tyrant for a wife, they will have attendance, they will do what they list. In taking a dowry thou losest thy liberty, hazardest thine estate, with many such inconveniences.

Say the best, she is a commanding servant; thou hadst better have taken a good housewife maid in her smock. Since then there is such hazard, if thou be wise keep thyself as thou art, 'tis good to match, much better to be free. 'Tis pleasant to beget children, but pleasanter to be free. Art thou young? then match not yet; if old, match not at all. And therefore, with that philosopher [Thales] still make answer to thy friends that importune thee to marry, 'tis yet unseasonable, and ever will be.

Consider withal how free, how happy, how secure, how heavenly, in respect, a single man is; as he said in the comedy, 'that which all my neighbours admire and applaud me for, account so great a happiness, I never had a wife;' consider how contentedly, quietly, neatly, plentifully, sweetly, and how merrily he lives! he hath no man to care for but himself, none to please, no charge, none to control him, is tied to no residence, no cure to serve, may go and come, when, whither, live where he will, his own master, and do what he list himself.

Consider the excellency of virgins; marriage replenisheth the earth, but virginity Paradise; Elias, Eliseus, John Baptist were bachelors: virginity is a precious jewel, a fair garland, a never-fading flower; for why was Daphne turned to a green bay-tree, but to show that virginity is immortal?

> *As the sequestered flower that grows within*
> *Some fenced-in garden, to the herd unknown,*
> *Ne'er turned up by the plough, fanned by the air,*
> *By the sun strengthened, by the shower reared,*
> *So is the virgin in her maiden state,*

Dear to her friends, but if the flower be ta'en,
She is undone and meets no more regard.

(CATULLUS)

Virginity is a fine picture, as Bonaventure calls it, a blessed thing in itself, and if you will believe a Papist, meritorious. And although there be some inconveniences, irksomeness, solitariness, etc., incident to such persons, want of those comforts (one to attend to him when he is ill, etc.), embracing, dalliance, kissing, colling, etc., those furious motives and wanton pleasures a new-married wife most part enjoys; yet they are but toys in respect, easily to be endured, if conferred to those frequent encumbrances of marriage. Solitariness may be otherwise avoided with mirth, music, good company, business, employment; in a word, he shall have less joy and less sorrow; for their good nights, he shall have good days. And methinks some time or other, among so many rich bachelors, a benefactor should be found to build a monastical college for old, decayed, deformed, or discontented maids to live together in, that have lost their first loves, or otherwise miscarried, or else are willing howsoever to lead a single life. The rest, I say, are toys in respect, and sufficiently recompensed by those innumerable contents and incomparable privileges of virginity.

Think of these things, confer both lives, and consider last of all these commodious prerogatives a bachelor hath, how well he is esteemed, how heartily welcome to all his friends, as Tertullian observes, with what counterfeit courtesies they will adore him, follow him, present him with gifts; it cannot be believed (saith Ammianus) with what humble service he shall be worshipped, how loved and respected. If he want children (and have means) he shall be often invited, attended on by princes, and have advocates to plead his cause for nothing, as Plutarch adds. Wilt thou then be reverenced, and had in estimation?

Live a single man, marry not, and thou shalt soon perceive how these legacy-hunters (for so they were called of old) will seek after thee, bribe and flatter thee for thy favour, to be thine heir or executor: Arruntius and Haterius, those famous parasites in this kind, as Tacitus and Seneca have recorded, shall not go beyond them. Periplectomenes, that good personate old man, well understood this in Plautus: for when Pleusides exhorted him to marry that he might have children of his own, he readily replied in this sort:

> *Whilst I have kin, what need I brats to have?*
> *Now I live well, and as I will, most brave.*
> *And when I die, my goods I'll give away*
> *To them that do invite me every day,*
> *That visit me, and send me pretty toys,*
> *And strive who shall do me most courtesies.*

This respect thou shalt have in like manner, living as he did, a single man.

But if thou marry once, bethink thyself what a slavery it is, what a heavy burden thou shalt undertake, how hard a task thou art tied to; for, as Jerome hath it, he that hath a wife is bound to serve her, and how continuate, what squalor attends it, what irksomeness, what charges, for wife and children are a perpetual bill of charges; besides a myriad of cares, miseries, and troubles; for as that comical Plautus merrily and truly said, he that wants trouble must get to be master of a ship, or marry a wife; and, as another seconds him, Wife and children have undone me; so many and such infinite encumbrances accompany this kind of life. Furthermore, a wife's a scold, or as he said in the comedy, 'I married, that was misery; children were born, that was worse.'

All gifts and invitations cease, no friend will esteem thee, and thou shalt be compelled to lament thy misery, and make thy moan with

Bartholomaeus Scheraeus, that famous poet laureate, and professor of Hebrew in Wittenberg: 'I had finished this work long since, but that (I use his own words), amongst many miseries which almost broke my back, a shrew to my wife, tormented my mind above measure, and beyond the rest. So shalt thou be compelled to complain, and to cry out at last, with Phoroneus the lawyer, How happy had I been, if I had wanted a wife!'

If this which I have said will not suffice, see more in Lemnius, Espencaeus, Kornmannus, Platina, Barbarus, Arnisaeus, and him that is best of all, Nevisanus the lawyer, almost in every page.

XVIII

Philters, Magical, and Poetical Cures.

WHERE PERSUASIONS and other remedies will not take place, many fly to unlawful means, philters, amulets, magic spells, ligatures, characters, charms, which, as a wound with the spear of Achilles, if so made and caused, must so be cured. If forced by spells and philters, saith Paracelsus, it must be eased by characters and by incantations. Fernelius hath some examples of such as have been so magically caused, and magically cured, and by witchcraft: so saith Baptista Condronchus. 'Tis not permitted to be done, I confess; yet often attempted: Cardan reckons up many magnetical medicines, as to piss through a ring, etc. Mizaldus, Baptista Porta, Jason Pratensis, Lobelius, Matthiolus, etc., prescribe many absurd remedies: mandrake root, parings from an ass's hoof, his beloved's excrement without her knowledge put under his pillow, its odour to kill his desire. An owl's egg encourages continence, says Isarca the Indian gymnosophist according to Philostratus. The blood of the beloved drunk removeth love; Faustina, wife of Marcus Aurelius, taken by love for a gladiator, was released, saith Julius Capitolinus, by a Chaldean maxim. Some of our astrologers will effect as much by characteristical images, seals of Hermes or Solomon, of Chael, etc. Our old poets and phantastical writers have many fabulous remedies for such as are lovesick, as that of Protesilaus' tomb in Philostratus, in his dialogue between Phoenix and Vinitor: Vinitor, upon occasion discoursing of the rare virtues of that shrine, telleth him that Protesilaus' altar and tomb cures almost all manner of diseases, consumptions, dropsies, quartan-agues, sore eyes; and among the rest, such as are lovesick shall there be helped.

But the most famous is Leucata Petra, that renowned rock in Greece, of which Strabo writes, not far from St Maura, saith Sands, from which rock if any lover flung himself down headlong, he was instantly cured. Venus after the death of Adonis, when she could take no rest for love, a raging fire burned in her heart, came to the temple of Apollo to know what she should do to be eased of her pain; Apollo sent her to Leucata Petra, where she precipitated herself, and was forthwith freed; and when she would needs know of him a reason of it, he told her again, that he had often observed Jupiter, when he was enamoured on Juno, thither go to ease and wash himself, and after him divers others. Cephalus for the love of Pelater, Desoneius' daughter, leaped down here; that Lesbian Sappho for Phaon, on whom she miserably doted, in love-frenzy, flung herself down, hoping thus to ease herself, and to be freed of her love-pangs.

> *Hither Deucalion came, when Pyrrha's love*
> *Tormented him, and leapt down to the sea,*
> *And had no harm at all, but by and by*
> *His love was gone and chased quite away.*

This medicine Joseph Scaliger speaks of, Salmuth, and other writers.

Pliny reports, that among the Cyziceni, there is a well consecrated to Cupid, of which if any lover taste, his passion is mitigated: and Anthony Verdurius saith that among the ancients there was a god presiding over Lethe; he took burning torches, and extinguished them in the river; his statue was to be seen in the temple of Venus Erycina, of which Ovid makes mention, and saith that all lovers of old went thither on pilgrimage, that would be rid of their love-pangs. Pausanias writes of a temple dedicated to Venus in the vault, at Naupactus in Achaia (now Lepanto), in which your widows that would have second husbands made their supplications to the goddess; all manner of suits concerning lovers were commenced, and their grievance helped. The same author tells as much of the River Selemnus in Greece; if any lover washed himself in it, by a secret virtue of that water (by reason of the extreme coldness belike) he was healed of love's torments: what that causes love's wound also heals it; which if it be so, that water, as he holds, is better than gold.

Where none of all these remedies will take place, I know no other but that all lovers must make an head and rebel, as they did in Ausonius, and crucify Cupid till he grant their request, or satisfy their desires.

XIX

The last and best Cure of Love-Melancholy
is, to let them have their Desire.

THE LAST REFUGE and surest remedy, to be put in practice in the utmost place, when no other means will take effect, is to let them go together, and enjoy one another, as saith Guianerius. Aesculapius himself, to this malady, cannot invent a better remedy (saith Jason Pratensis), than that a lover have his desire.

> *And let them both be joined in a bed,*
> *And let Aeneas fair Lavina wed.*

'Tis the special cure, to let them bleed in the hymenean vein, for love is a pleurisy, and if it be possible, so let it be, let them enjoy their longed-for bliss. Arculanus holds it the speediest and the best cure, 'tis Savonarola's last precept, a principal infallible remedy, the last, sole, and safest refuge.

> *Julia alone can quench my desire,*
> *With neither ice nor snow, but with like fire.*
>
> (PETRONIUS)

When you have all done, saith Avicenna, there is no speedier or safer course than to join the parties together according to their desires and wishes, the custom and form of law; and so we have seen him quickly restored to his former health, that was languished away to skin and bones; after his desire was satisfied, his discontent ceased, and we thought it strange; our opinion is therefore that in such cases nature is to be obeyed. Aretaeus, an old author, hath an instance of a young man, when no other means could prevail, was so speedily relieved. What remains then but to join them in marriage? They may then kiss and coll, lie and look babies in one another's eyes, as their sires before them did; they may then satiate themselves with love's pleasures, which they have so long wished and expected; they may rest together in one bed, their lips joined, and peacefully together.

Yea, but this cannot conveniently be done, by reason of many and several impediments. Sometimes both parties themselves are not agreed; parents, tutors, masters, guardians will not give consent; laws, customs, statutes hinder; poverty, superstition, fear, and suspicion; many men dote on one woman simultaneously; she dotes as much on him, or them, and in modesty must not, cannot woo, as unwilling to confess as willing to love; she dare not make it known, show her affection, or speak her mind. And hard is the choice (as it is in Euphues) when one is compelled either by silence to die with grief, or by speaking to live with shame. In this case almost was the fair Lady Elizabeth, Edward the Fourth his daughter, when she was enamoured on Henry the Seventh, that noble young prince, and new saluted king, when she brake forth into that passionate speech: 'O that I were worthy of that comely prince! but my father being dead, I want friends to motion such a matter. What shall I say? I am all alone, and dare not open my mind to any. What if I acquaint my mother with it? bashfulness forbids. What if some of the lords? audacity wants. O that I might but confer with him, perhaps in discourse I might let slip such a word that might discover mine intention!'

How many modest maids may this concern! I am a poor servant, what shall I do? I am a fatherless child, and want means, I am blithe and buxom, young and lusty, but I have never a suitor, as she said in

Celestina, a company of silly fellows looks belike that I should woo them and speak first: fain they would and cannot woo, how can I begin? being merely passive, they may not make suit, with many such lets and inconveniences, which I know not; what shall we do in such a case? sing Fortune my foe?

Some are so curious in this behalf, as those old Romans, our modern Venetians, Dutch, and French, that if two parties dearly love, the one noble, the other ignoble, they may not by their laws match, though equal otherwise in years, fortunes, education, and all good affection. In Germany, except they can prove their gentility by three descents, they scorn to match with them. A nobleman must marry a noblewoman; a baron, a baron's daughter; a knight, a knight's; a gentleman, a gentleman's: as slaters sort their slates, do they degrees and families. If she be never so rich, fair, well qualified otherwise, they will make him forsake her. The Spaniards abhor all widows; the Turks repute them old women if past five-and-twenty. But these are too severe laws, and strict customs, some concession must be made to love, we are all the sons of Adam, 'tis opposite to nature, it ought not to be so.

Again, he loves her most impotently, she loves not him, and so on the contrary Pan loved Echo, Echo Satyrus, Satyrus Lyda. They love and loathe of all sorts, he loves her, she hates him, and is loathed of him on whom she dotes. Cupid hath two darts, one to force love, all of gold, and that sharp; another blunt, of lead, and that to hinder. This we see too often verified in our common experience. Coresus dearly loved that virgin Callirrhoe, but the more he loved her, the more she hated him. Oenone loved Paris, but he rejected her; they are stiff of all sides, as if beauty were therefore created to undo or be undone. I give her all attendance, all observance, I pray and entreat, fair mistress, pity me, I spend myself, my time, friends, and fortunes to win her favour (as he complains in the eclogue), I lament, sigh, weep, and make my moan to her, but she is hard as flint, as fair and hard as a diamond, she will not respect or hear me: she flees, unmoved by my tears, deaf to my laments. What shall I do?

> *I wooed her as a young man should do,*
> *But Sir, she said, I love not you,*
> *Rock, marble, heart of oak with iron barr'd,*
> *Frost, flint or adamants, are not so hard.*
>
> (ANGERIANUS)

I give, I bribe, I send presents, but they are refused, Corydon in Virgil is but a lout; Alexis rejects his gifts. I protest, I swear, I weep, and she repays my love with hate, mocks my tears with laughter; she neglects me for all this, she derides me, contemns me, she hates me, 'Phillida flouts me': Eurydice is stiff, churlish, rocky still.

And 'tis most true, many gentlewomen are so nice, they scorn all suitors, crucify their poor paramours, and think nobody good enough for them, as dainty to please as Daphne herself in Ovid.

> *Many did woo her, but she scorn'd them still,*
> *And said she would not marry by her will.*
>
> (OVID)

One while they will not marry, as they say at least (whenas they intend nothing less), another while not yet, when 'tis their only desire, they rave upon it. She will marry at last, but not him: he is a proper man indeed, and well qualified, but he wants means; another of her suitors hath good means, but he wants wit; one is too old, another too young, too deformed, she likes not his carriage; a third too loosely given, he is rich, but baseborn: she will be a gentlewoman, a lady, as her sister is, as her mother is; she is all out as fair, as well brought up, hath as good a portion, and she looks for as good a match, as Matilda or Dorinda: if not, she is resolved as yet to tarry, so apt are young maids to boggle at every object, so soon won or lost with every toy, so quickly diverted, so hard to be pleased. In the meantime, how many has she tortured!; one suitor pines away, languisheth in love, how many have killed themselves!; another sighs and grieves, she cares not; and which Stroza objected to Ariadne,

> *Is no more mov'd with those sad sighs and tears,*
> *Of her sweetheart, than raging sea with prayers:*
> *Thou scorn'st the fairest youth in all our city,*
> *And mak'st him almost mad for love to die.*

They take a pride to prank up themselves, to make young men enamoured, to dote on them, and to run mad for their sakes,

> *Whilst niggardly their favours they discover.*
> *They love to be belov'd, yet scorn the lover.*
>
> (VIRGIL)

All suit and service is too little for them, and presents too base. As Atalanta, they must be overrun, or not won.

Many young men are as obstinate, and as curious in their choice, as tyrannically proud, insulting, deceitful, false-hearted, as irrefragable and peevish on the other side, Narcissus-like:

> *Young men and maids did to him sue,*
> *But in his youth, so proud, so coy was he,*
> *Young men and maids bade him adieu.*
>
> (OVID)

Echo wept and wooed him by all means above the rest, Love me for pity, or pity me for love, but he was obstinate: he would rather die than give consent. Psyche ran whining after Cupid:

> *Fair Cupid, thy fair Psyche to thee sues,*
> *A lovely lass a fine young gallant woos;*
>> (FRASCATORIUS)

but he rejected her nevertheless. Thus many lovers do hold out so long, doting on themselves, stand in their own light, till in the end they come to be scorned and rejected, as Stroza Gargiliana was,

> *Both young and old do hate thee scorned now,*
> *That once was all their joy and comfort too,*

as Narcissus was himself,

> *Who, despising many,*
> *Died ere he could enjoy the love of any.*

They begin to be contemned themselves of others, as he was of his shadow, and take up with a poor curate, or an old serving-man at last, that might have had their choice of right good matches in their youth; like that generous mare in Plutarch, which would admit of none but great horses, but when her tail was cut off and mane shorn close, and she now saw herself so deformed in the water when she came to drink, she was contented at last to be covered by an ass.

Yet this is a common humour, will not be left, and cannot be helped.

> *I love a maid, she loves me not: full fain*
> *She would have me, but I not her again;*

So love to crucify men's souls is bent:
But seldom doth it please or give content.

(AUSONIUS)

Their love danceth in a ring, and Cupid hunts them round about; he dotes, is doted on again, their affection cannot be reconciled. Oftentimes they may and will not, 'tis their own foolish proceeding that mars all, they are too distrustful of themselves, too soon dejected: say she be rich, thou poor; she young, thou old; she lovely and fair, thou most ill-favoured and deformed; she noble, thou base; she spruce and fine, but thou an ugly clown: there's hope enough yet: 'Nisa engaged to Mopsus, what may not we lovers hope for?' Put thyself forward once more, as unlikely matches have been and are daily made, see what will be the event. Many leave roses and gather thistles, loathe honey and love verjuice: our likings are as various as our palates. But commonly they omit opportunities, etc., they neglect the usual means and times.

He that will not when he may,
When he will he shall have nay.

They look to be wooed, sought after, and sued to. Most part they will and cannot, either for the above-named reasons, or for that there is a multitude of suitors equally enamoured, doting all alike; and where one alone must speed, what shall become of the rest?

Hero was beloved of many, but one did enjoy her; Penelope had a company of suitors, yet all missed of their aim. In such cases he or they must wisely and warily unwind themselves, unsettle his affections by those rules above prescribed—divert his cogitations, or else bravely bear it out, as Turnus did. Let Lavinia be your wife; when he could not get her, with a kind of heroical scorn he bid Aeneas take her, or with a milder farewell, let her go, have Phyllis for yourself, take her to you, God give you joy, sir. The fox in the emblem would eat no grapes, but why? because he could not get them; care not then for that which may not be had.

Many such inconveniences, lets, and hindrances there are, which cross their projects, and crucify poor lovers, which sometimes may, sometimes again cannot, be so easily removed. But put case they be reconciled all, agreed hitherto, suppose this love or good liking be betwixt two alone, both parties well pleased, there is mutual love and great affection, yet their parents, guardians, tutors, cannot agree; thence all is dashed, the match is unequal: one rich, another poor; an hard-hearted, unnatural, a covetous father will not marry his son, except he have so much money, everybody is mad for money, as Chrysostom notes, nor join his daughter in marriage, to save her dowry, or for that he cannot spare her for the service she doth him, and is resolved to part with nothing while he lives, not a penny; though he may peradventure well give it, he will not till he dies, and then, as a pot of money broke, it is divided among them that gaped after it so earnestly.

Or else he wants means to set her out, he hath no money, and though it be to the manifest prejudice of her body and soul's health, he cares not, he will take no notice of it, she must and shall tarry. Many slack and careless parents measure their children's affections by their own, they are now cold and decrepit themselves, past all such youthful conceits, and they will therefore starve their children's genius, have them be old before they are young, as he said in the comedy, they must not marry; they will stifle nature, their young bloods must not participate of youthful pleasures, but be as they are themselves, old on a sudden. And 'tis a general fault among most parents in bestowing of their children; the father wholly respects wealth; when through his folly, riot, indiscretion, he hath embezzled his estate, to recover himself he confines and prostitutes his eldest son's love and affection to some fool, or ancient or deformed piece, for money: 'He shall marry the daughter of Phanocrates, red-haired, blear-eyed, big mouth, hooked nose'; and though his son utterly dislike, with Clitipho in the comedy of Terence, 'Father, I cannot'; if she be rich (he replies), he must and shall have her, she is fair enough, young enough; if he look or hope to inherit his lands, he shall marry, not when or whom he loves, but whom his father commands, when and where he likes, his affection must dance attendance upon him. His daughter is in the same predicament forsooth; as an empty boat she must carry what, where, when, and whom her father will. So that in these businesses the father is still for the best advantage; now the mother respects good kindred, most part the son a proper woman. All which Livy exemplifies; a gentleman and a yeoman wooed a wench in Rome (contrary to that statute that the gentry and commonalty must not match together); the matter was controverted: the gentleman was preferred by the mother's voice, who wanted a brilliant match for her daughter; the overseers stood for him that was most worth, etc.

But parents ought not to be so strict in this behalf; beauty is a dowry of itself all-sufficient. Rachel was so married to Jacob, and Bonaventure denies that he so much as venially sins that marries a maid for comeliness of person. The Jews (Deut. xxi, 11), if they saw among the captives a beautiful woman, some small circumstances observed, might take her to wife. They should not be too severe in that kind, especially if there be no such urgent occasion, or grievous impediment. 'Tis good for a commonwealth, Plato holds, that in their contracts young men should never avoid the affinity of poor folks, or seek after rich. Poverty and base parentage may be sufficiently recompensed by many other good qualities, modesty, virtue, religion, and choice bringing up. 'I am poor, I confess, but am I therefore contemptible, and an abject? Love itself is naked, the Graces, the stars, and Hercules clad in a lion's skin.' Give something to virtue, love, wisdom, favour, beauty, person; be not all for money.

Besides, you must consider that love cannot be compelled, they must affect as they may; as the saying is, marriage and hanging goes by destiny, matches are made in heaven.

> *It lies not in our power to love or hate,*
> *For will in us is overrul'd by fate.*
>
> (MARLOWE)

A servant maid in Aristaenetus loved her mistress' minion, which when her dame perceived, in a jealous humour she dragged her about the house by the hair of the head, and vexed her sore. The wench cried out, 'O mistress, fortune hath made my body your servant, but not my soul!' Affections are free, not to be commanded. Moreover, it may be to restrain their ambition, pride, and covetousness, to correct those hereditary diseases of a family, God in His just judgement assigns and permits such matches to be made. For I am of Plato and Bodine's mind, that families have their bounds and periods as well as kingdoms, beyond which for extent or continuance they shall not exceed, six or seven hundred years, as they there illustrate by a multitude of examples, and which Peucer and Melancthon approve, but in a perpetual tenor (as we see by many pedigrees of knights, gentlemen, yeomen) continue as they began, for many descents with little alternation.

Howsoever, let them, I say, give something to youth, to love; they must not think they can fancy whom they appoint; this is a free passion, as Pliny said in a panegyric of his, and may not be forced. Love craves liking, as the saying is, it requires mutual affections, a correspondency: it can be given nor taken away against one's will, it may not be learned, Ovid himself cannot teach us how to love,

Solomon describe, Apelles paint, or Helena express it. They must not therefore compel or intrude (as Fabius urgeth), for who can love against the grain? But consider withal the miseries of enforced marriages, take pity upon youth; and such above the rest as have daughters to bestow, should be very careful and provident to marry them in due time. Siracides [Ecclesiasticus vii, 25] calls it a weighty matter to perform, so to marry a daughter to a man of understanding in due time. As Lemnius admonisheth, virgins must be provided for in season, to prevent many diseases, of which Rodericus Castro and Lodovic Mercatus have both largely discoursed. And therefore as well to avoid these feral maladies, 'tis good to get them husbands betimes, as to prevent some other gross inconveniences, and for a thing that I know besides; at the marriageable age, as Chrysostom adviseth, let them not defer it; they perchance will marry themselves else, or do worse. If Nevisanus the lawyer do not impose, they may do it by right; for as he proves out of Curtius and some other civilians, a maid past twenty-five years of age, against her parents' consent, may marry such a one as is unworthy of, and inferior to her, and her father by law must be compelled to give her a competent dowry.

Mistake me not in the meantime, or think that I do apologize here for any headstrong, unruly, wanton flirts. I do approve that of St Ambrose which he hath written touching Rebecca's spousals: A woman should give unto her parents the choice of her husband, lest she be reputed to be malapert and wanton, if she take upon her to make her own choice; for she should rather seem to be desired by a man than to desire a man herself. To those hard parents alone I retort that of Curtius, in the behalf of modester maids, that are too remiss and careless of their due time and riper years. For if they tarry longer, to say truth, they are past date, and nobody will respect them. A woman with us in Italy (saith Aretine's Lucretia), twenty-four years of age, is old already, past the best, of no account. An old fellow, as Lysistrata confesseth in Aristophanes, 'tis no news for an old fellow to marry a young wench; but as he follows it, a woman's chance does not last long; who cares for an old maid? she may sit and wait. A virgin, as the poet holds, is like a flower, a rose withered on a sudden.

> *She that was erst a maid as fresh as May,*
> *Is now an old crone, time so steals away.*
>
> (AUSONIUS)

Let them take them while they may, make advantage of youth, and as Catullus prescribes,

> *Fair maids, go gather roses in the prime,*
> *And think that as a flower so goes on time.*
>
> (AUSONIUS)

Let's all love, while we are in the flower of years, fit for love-matters, and while time serves; for

> *Suns that set may rise again,*
> *But if once we lose this light,*
> *'Tis with us perpetual night.*
>
> (CATULLUS TRANSLATED BY JONSON)

Time past cannot be recalled.

But we need no such exhortation, we are all commonly too forward: yet if there be any escape, and all be not as it should, as Diogenes struck the father when the son swore, because he taught him no better, if a maid or young man miscarry, I think their parents oftentimes, guardians, overseers, governors (saith Chrysostom) are in as much fault, and as severely to be punished as their children, in providing for them no sooner.

Now for such as have free liberty to bestow themselves, I could wish that good counsel of the comical old man [Plautus] were put in practice,

> *That rich men would marry poor maidens some,*
> *And that without dowry, and so bring them home,*
> *So would much concord be in our city,*
> *Less envy should we have, much more pity.*

If they would care less for wealth, we should have much more content and quietness in a commonwealth. Beauty, good bringing up, methinks, is a sufficient portion of itself, beauty is the maiden's dower, and he doth well that will accept of such a wife. Eubulides, in Arisaenetus, married a poor man's child; of a merry countenance and heavenly visage, in pity of her estate, and that quickly. Acontius, coming to Delos to sacrifice to Diana, fell in love with Cydippe, a noble lass, and wanting means to get her love, flung a golden apple into her lap, with this inscription upon it:

> *I swear by all the rites of Diana,*
> *I'll come and be thy husband if I may.*

She considered of it, and upon some small inquiry of his person and estate, was married unto him.

> *Blessed is the wooing,*
> *That is not long a-doing,*

as the saying is; when the parties are sufficiently known to each other, what needs such scrupulosity, so many circumstances? dost thou know her conditions, her bringing-up, like her person? let her means be what they will, take her without any more ado.

Dido and Aeneas were accidentally driven by a storm both into one cave, they made a match upon it; Masinissa was married to that fair captive Sophonisba, King Syphax' wife, the same day that he saw her first, to prevent Scipio and Laelius, lest they should determine otherwise of her. If thou lovest the party, do as much: good education and beauty is a competent dowry, stand not upon money. Men once had hearts of gold (saith Theocritus), in the golden world men did so (in the reign of Ogyges belike, before staggering Ninus began to domineer), if all be true that is reported: and some few nowadays will do as much, here and there one; 'tis well done, methinks, and all happiness befall them for so doing. Leontius, a philosopher of Athens, had a fair daughter called Athenais (saith mine author), of a comely carriage, he gave her no portion but her bringing-up, out of some secret foreknowledge of her fortune, bestowing that little which he had among his other children. But she, thus qualified, was preferred by some friends to Constantinople, to serve Pulcheria, the emperor's sister, of whom she was baptized and called Eudocia. Theodosius, the emperor, in short space took notice of her excellent beauty and good parts, and a little after, upon his sister's sole commendation, made her his wife: 'twas nobly done of Theodosius.

Rhodope was the fairest lady in her days in all Egypt; she went to wash herself, and by chance (her maids meanwhile looking but carelessly to her clothes), an eagle stole away one of her shoes, and laid it in Psammetichus the King of Egypt's lap at Memphis; he wondered at the excellency of the shoe and pretty foot, but more at the manner of the bringing of it, and caused forthwith proclamation to be made, that she that owned that shoe should come presently to his court; the virgin came, and was forthwith married to the king. I say this was heroically done, and like a prince; I commend him for it, and all such as have means, that will either do (as he did) themselves, or so for love, etc., marry their children.

If he be rich, let him take such a one as wants, if she be virtuously given; for as Siracides [Ecclus. vii. 19], adviseth, 'Forgo not a wise and good woman; for her grace is above gold.' If she have fortunes of her own, let her make a man. Danaus of Lacedaemon had a many daughters to bestow, and means enough for them all; he never stood inquiring after great matches, as others used to do, but sent for a company of brave young gallants home to his house, and bid his daughters choose every one one, whom she liked best, and take him for her husband, without any more ado. This act of his was much approved in those times. But in this iron age of ours we respect riches alone (for a maid must buy her husband now with a great dowry, if she will have him), covetousness and filthy lucre mars all good matches, or some such by-respects. Crales, a Servian prince (as Nicephorus Gregoras relates it), was an earnest suitor to Eudocia, the emperor's sister; though her brother much desired it, yet she could not abide him, for he had three former wives, all basely abused; but the emperor still desiring the friendship of Crales, because he was a great prince and a troublesome neighbour, much desired his affinity, and to that end betrothed his own daughter Simonida to him, a little girl five years of age, he being forty-five, and five years older than the emperor himself: such disproportionable and unlikely matches can wealth and a fair fortune make.

And yet not that alone, it is not only money, but sometimes vainglory, pride, ambition, do as much harm as wretched covetousness itself in another extreme. If a yeoman have one sole daughter, he must over-match her, above her birth and calling, to a gentleman forsooth, because of her great portion, too good for one of her own rank, as he supposeth; a gentleman's daughter and heir must be married to a knight baronet's eldest son at least; and a knight's only daughter to a baron himself, or an earl, and so upwards, her great dower deserves it. And thus striving for more honour to their wealth, they undo their children, many discontents follows, and oftentimes they ruinate their families.

Paulus Jovius gives instance in Galeatius the Second, that heroical Duke of Milan who made alliances abroad which conferred on him a royal pomp, but which proved detrimental and almost ruinous to him and his descendants; he married his eldest son John Galeatius to Isabella the King of France his sister, but she was a burden to him, her entertainment at Milan was so costly that it almost undid him. His daughter Violanta was married to Lionel, Duke of Clarence, the youngest son to Edward the Third, King of England, but, he was welcomed with such incredible magnificence that a king's purse was scarce able to bear it; for besides many rich presents of horses, arms, plate, money, jewels, etc., he made one dinner for him and his company, in which were thirty-two messes, and as much provision left, as would serve ten thousand men; but a little after Lionel died, through riotous living, etc., and to the duke's great loss, the solemnity was ended. So can titles, honours, ambition make many brave but unfortunate matches of all sides for by-respects, though both crazed in body and mind, most unwilling, averse, and often unfit; so love is banished, and we feel the smart of it in the end. But I am too lavish peradventure in this subject.

Another let or hindrance is strict and severe discipline, laws and rigorous customs that forbid men to marry at set times and in some places; as prentices, servants, collegiates, states of lives in copyholds, or in some base inferior offices; you may desire in such cases, you cannot have, as Apuleius said. They see but as prisoners through a grate, they covet and catch, as Tantalus snatches at the water, etc.

Their love is lost, and vain it is in such an estate to attempt. 'Tis a grievous thing to love and not enjoy. They may indeed, I deny not, marry if they will, and have free choice some of them; but in the meantime their case is desperate, they hold a wolf by the ears, they must either burn or starve. 'Tis a sophistical dilemma, hard to resolve: if they marry they forfeit their estates, they are undone, and starve themselves through beggary and want; if they do not marry, in this heroical passion they furiously rage, are tormented, and torn in pieces by their predominate affections.

Every man hath not the gift of continence; let him pray for it then, as Beza adviseth in his tract, because God hath so called him to a single life, in taking away the means of marriage. Paul would have gone from Mysia to Bithynia, but the spirit suffered him not and thou wouldst peradventure be a married man with all thy will, but that protecting angel holds it not fit. The devil too sometimes may divert by his ill suggestions, and mar many good matches, as the same Paul was willing to see the Romans, but hindered of Satan he could not.

There be those that think they are necessitated by fate, their stars have so decreed, and therefore they grumble at their hard fortune; they are well inclined to marry, but one rub or other is ever in the way. I know what astrologers say in this behalf, what Ptolemy, Leovitius, which Sextus ab Heminga takes to be the horoscope of Hieronymus Wolfius, what Pezelius, Origanus, and Leovitius his illustrator Garcaeus, what Junctine, Pontarius, Campanella, what the rest (to omit those Arabian conjectures on marriage, lasciviousness, the triple Venus, and those resolutions upon a question, etc.), determine in this behalf, viz., whether he is destined to marry, whether he will get a wife easily or not, how many wives he shall have and what they shall be like, when he shall marry them, whether they shall love one another, both in men's and women's genitures, by the examination of the seventh house, the almutens, lords, and planets there; with many such, too tedious to relate. Yet let no man be troubled, or find himself grieved with such predictions; as Hieronymus Wolfius well saith in his astrological dialogue, they be but conjectures, the stars incline, but not enforce: 'The stars have power over our bodies which are base clay; they cannot force the rational mind, for that is under the control of God alone.' Wisdom, diligence, discretion may mitigate if not quite alter such decrees: fate depends on a man's own character; those who are cautious and prudent obtain their desires, etc. Let no man then be terrified or molested with such astrological aphorisms, or be much moved, either to vain hope or fear, from such predictions, but let every man follow his own free will in this case, and do as he sees cause. Better it is indeed to marry than burn for their souls' health, but for their present fortunes by some other means to pacify themselves and divert the stream of this fiery torrent, to continue as they are, rest satisfied, deploring their misery with that eunuch in Libanius, since there is no help or remedy, and with Jephtha's daughter to bewail their virginities.

Of like nature is superstition, those rash vows of monks and friars, and such as live in religious orders, but far more tyrannical and much worse. Nature, youth, and his furious passion forcibly inclines, and rageth on the one side; but their order and vow checks them on the other. What merits and indulgences they heap unto themselves by it, what commodities, I know not; but I am sure, from such rash vows and inhuman manner of life proceed many inconveniences, many diseases, many vices, mastupration, satyriasis, priapismus, melancholy, madness, fornication, adultery, buggery, sodomy, theft, murder, and all manner of mischiefs: read but Bale's catalogue of sodomites, at the visitation of abbeys here in England, Henry Stephanus his Apology for Herodotus, that which Ulricus writes in one of his epistles, that Pope Gregory, when he saw 6,000 skulls and bones of infants taken out of a fish-pond near a nunnery, thereupon retracted that degree of priests' marriages which was the cause of such a slaughter, was much grieved at it, and purged himself by repentance. Read many such, and then ask what is to be done, is this vow to be broke or not? No, saith Bellarmine, better turn, or fly out, than to break thy vow. And Coster saith it is absolutely a greater sin for a priest to marry than to keep a concubine at home. Gregory de Valence maintains the same, as those Essenes and Montanists of old. Insomuch that many votaries, out of a false persuasion of merit and holiness in this kind, will sooner die than marry, though it be the saving of their lives. In the year 1419 Pius II Pope, James Rossa, nephew to the King of Portugal, and then elect Archbishop of Lisbon, being very sick at Florence, when his physicians told him that his disease was such he must either lie with a wench, marry, or die, cheerfully chose to die.

Now they commended him for it; but St Paul teacheth otherwise, 'Better marry than burn', and as St Jerome gravely delivers it, there's a difference betwixt God's ordinances and men's laws: and therefore Cyprian boldly denounceth, it is abominable, impious, adulterous, and sacrilegious, what men make and ordain after their own furies to cross God's laws. Georgius Wicelius, one of their own arch-divines, exclaims against it, and all such rash monastical vows, and would have such persons seriously to consider what they do, whom they admit, lest they repent it at last. For either, as he follows it, you must allow them concubines or suffer them to marry, for scarce shall you find three priests of three thousand that are not troubled with burning lust. Wherefore, I conclude, it is an unnatural and impious thing to bar men of this Christian liberty, too severe and inhuman an edict.

> *The silly wren, the titmouse also,*
> *The little redbreast have their election,*
> *They fly I saw and together gone,*
> *Whereas hem list, about environ*

> *As they of kind have inclination,*
> *And as nature impress and guide,*
> *Of everything list to provide.*
> *But man alone, alas, the hard stond,*
> *Full cruelly by kind's ordinance*
> *Constrained is, and by statutes bound,*
> *And debarred from all such pleasance:*
> *What meaneth this, what is this pretence*
> *Of laws, I wis, against all right of kind*
> *Without a cause, so narrow men to bind?*

(LYDGATE IN CHAUCER'S FLOWER OF CURTESIE)

Many laymen repine still at priests' marriages above the rest, and not at clergymen only, but of all the meaner sort and condition; they would have none marry but such as are rich and able to maintain wives, because their parish belike shall be pestered with orphans, and the world full of beggars; but these are hard-hearted, unnatural, monsters of men, shallow politicians, they do not consider that a great part of the world is not yet inhabited as it ought, how many colonies into America, Terra Australis Incognita, Africa, may be sent. Let them consult with Sir William Alexander's *Book of Colonies,* Orpheus Junior's *Golden Fleece,* Captain Whitbourne, Mr Hagthorpe, etc., and they shall surely be otherwise informed.

Those politic Romans were of another mind, they thought their city and country could never be too populous. Hadrian the emperor said he had rather have men than money. Augustus Caesar made an oration in Rome to bachelors, to persuade them to marry; some countries compelled them to marry of old, as Jews, Turks, Indians, Chinese among the rest in these days, who much wonder at our discipline to suffer so many idle persons to live in monasteries, and often marvel how they can live honest. In the Isle of Maragnan the governor and petty king there did wonder at the Frenchmen, and admire how so many friars and the rest of their company could live without wives, they thought it a thing unpossible, and would not believe it. If these men should but survey our multitudes of religious houses, observe our numbers of monasteries all over Europe, 18 nunneries in Padua, in Venice 34 cloisters of monks, 28 of nuns, etc., 'tis to this proportion in all other provinces and cities, what would they think, do they live honest? Let them dissemble as they will, I am of Tertullian's mind, that few can continue but by compulsion. O chastity (saith he), thou art a rare goddess in the world, not so easily got, seldom continuate; thou mayst now and then be compelled, either for defect of nature, or if discipline persuade, decrees enforce; or for some such by-respects, sullenness, discontent, they have lost their first loves, may not have whom they will themselves, want of means, rash vows, etc. But can he willingly contain? I think not.

Therefore, either out of commiseration of human imbecility in policy, or to prevent a far worse inconvenience, for they hold some of them as necessary as meat and drink, and because vigour of youth, the state and temper of most men's bodies do so furiously desire it, they have heretofore in some nations liberally admitted polygamy and stews, as hundred thousand courtesans in Grand Cairo in Egypt, as Radzivilius observes, are tolerated, besides boys: how many at Fez, Rome, Naples, Florence, Venice, etc.? and still in many other provinces and cities of Europe they do as much, because they think young men, churchmen, and servants among the rest, can hardly live honest. The consideration of this belike made Vibius, the Spaniard, when his friend Crassus, that rich Roman gallant, lay hid in the cave, to gratify him the more, send two lusty lasses to accompany him all that while he was there imprisoned; and Surenas, the Parthian general, when he warred against the Romans, to carry about with him 20 concubines, as the Swiss soldiers do now commonly their wives.

But, because this course is not generally approved, but rather contradicted as unlawful and abhorred, in most countries they do much encourage them to marriage, give great rewards to such as have many children, and mulct those that will not marry, and in A. Gellius, Aelian, Valerius, we read that three children freed the father from painful offices, and five from all contribution. A woman shall be saved by bearing children. Epictetus would have all marry, and as Plato will, he that marrieth not before thirty-five years of his age, must be compelled and punished, and the money consecrated to Juno's temple, or applied to public uses. They account him, in some countries, unfortunate that dies without a wife, a most unhappy man, as Boethius infers, and if at all happy, yet unhappy in his supposed happiness. They commonly deplore his estate, and much lament him for it: 'O my sweet son', etc.

Yet, notwithstanding, many with us are of the opposite part, they are married themselves, and for others, let them burn, fire and flame, they care not, so they be not troubled with them. Some are too curious, and some too covetous, they may marry when they will both for ability and means, but so nice, that except, as Theophilus the emperor was presented by his mother Euphrosyne with all the rarest beauties of the empire in the great chamber of his palace at once, and bid to give a golden apple to her he liked best, if they might so take and choose whom they list out of all the fair maids their nation affords, they could happily condescend to marry; otherwise, etc.

Why should a man marry? saith another Epicurean rout, what's matrimony but a matter of money? why should free nature be entrenched on, confined, or obliged to this or that man or woman, with these manacles of body and goods? etc. There are those too that dearly love, admire, and follow women all their lives long, Penelope's suitors, never well but in their company, wistly gazing on their beauties, observing close, hanging after them, dallying still with them, and yet dare not, will not marry. Many poor people, and of the meaner sort, are too distrustful of God's providence, they will not, dare not for such worldly respects, fear of want, woes, miseries, or that they shall light, as Lemnius saith, on a scold, a slut, or a bad wife. And therefore, they spend their youth sadly, they are resolved to live single, as Epaminondas did: he says there is nothing to surpass a single life, and ready with Hippolytus to adjure all women: 'I detest all of them, loathe, shun, execrate them,' etc. But, alas, poor Hippolytus, thou knowest not what thou sayest, 'tis otherwise, Hippolytus.

Some make a doubt, whether a scholar should marry; if she be fair she will bring him back from his grammar to his horn-book, or else with kissing and dalliance she will hinder his study; if foul, with scolding; he cannot well intend to both, as Philippus Beroaldus, that great Bolognian doctor, once writ, but he recanted at last, and in a solemn sort with true-conceived words he did ask the world and all women forgiveness. But you shall have the story as he relates himself, in his Commentaries on the Sixth of Apuleius: 'For a long time I lived a single life, I could not abide marriage, but as a rambler, I took a snatch where I could get it; nay more, I railed at marriage downright, and in a public auditory, when I did interpret that sixth Satire of Juvenal, out of Plutarch and Seneca, I did heap up all the dicteries I could against women; but now recant with Stesichorus, I approve of marriage, I am glad I am a married man, I am heartily glad I have a wife, so sweet a wife, so noble a wife, so young, so chaste a wife, so loving a wife, and I do wish and desire all other men to marry; and especially scholars, that as of old Martia did by Hortensius, Terentia by Tullius, Calphurnia to Plinius, Pudentilla to Apuleius, hold the candle whilst their husbands did meditate and write, so theirs may do them, and as my dear Camilla doth to me.'

Let other men be averse, rail then and scoff at women, and say what they can to the contrary, a single man is a happy man, etc., but this is a toy: Reject not in your prime, saith Horace, the sweets of love or of the dance. These men are too distrustful, and much to blame to use such speeches. They must not condemn all for some. As there be many bad, there be some good wives; as some be vicious, some be virtuous. Read what Solomon hath said in their praises (Prov. xxxi, and Siracides [Ecclesiasticus] (xxvi and xxx), 'Blessed is the man that hath a virtuous wife, for the number of his days shall be double. A virtuous woman rejoiceth her husband, and she shall fulfil the years of his life in peace. A good wife is a good portion (xxxvi), an help, a pillar of rest.'

Who takes a wife takes a brother and sister [Aphranius]. He that hath no wife wandereth to and fro mourning. Women are the sole, only joy, and comfort of a man's life, born for man's help and pleasure and for founding a family.

> *Joy of the human race, solace in life,*
> *By night caressing, and by day the object*
> *Of pleasant care, the strong desire of men,*
> *The hope of lads.*
>
> (LOECHAEUS)

'A wife is a young man's mistress, a middle-age's companion, an old man's nurse' [Bacon], a partner of his joys and sorrows, a prop, an help, etc.

> *Man's best possession is a loving wife,*
> *She tempers anger and diverts all strife.*
>
> (EURIPIDES)

There is no joy, no comfort, no sweetness, no pleasure in the world like to that of a good wife: When a loving wife and a faithful husband live together—what harmony, saith our Latin Homer; she is still the same in sickness and in health, his eye, his hand, his bosom friend, his partner at all times, his other self, not to be separated by any calamity, but ready to share all sorrow, discontent, and as the Indian women do, live and die with him, nay more, to die presently for him.

Admetus, King of Thessaly, when he lay upon his deathbed, was told by Apollo's oracle, that if he could get anybody to die for him, he should live longer yet, but when all refused, his parents, friends, and followers forsook him, Alcestis his wife, though young, most willingly undertook it; what more can be desired or expected? And although on the other side there be an infinite number of bad husbands (I should rail downright against some of them) able to discourage any women; yet there be some good ones again, and those most observant of marriage rites. An honest country fellow (as Fulgosus relates it) in the kingdom of Naples, at plough by the sea-side, saw his wife carried away by Mauritanian pirates; he ran after in all haste, up to the chin first, and when he could wade no longer, swam, calling to the governor of the ship to deliver his wife, or if he must not have her restored, to let him follow as a prisoner, for he was resolved to be a galley-slave, his drudge, willing to endure any misery, so that he might enjoy his dear wife. The Moors, seeing the man's constancy, and relating the whole matter to their governor at Tunis, set them both free, and gave them an honest pension to maintain themselves during their lives.

I could tell many stories to this effect; but put case it often prove otherwise, because marriage is troublesome, wholly therefore to avoid it is no argument. He that will avoid trouble must avoid the world. Some trouble there is in marriage, I deny not; yet there be many things to sweeten it, saith Erasmus, a pleasant wife, pretty children, the chief delight of the sons of men (Eccles. ii, 8), etc. And howsoever, though it were all troubles, it must willingly be undergone for public good's sake.

> *Hear me, O my countrymen, saith Susarion,*
> *Women are naught, yet no life without one.*
>
> (STOBAEUS)

They are evils but necessary evils, and for our own ends we must make use of them to have issue, and to propagate the Church. For to what end is a man born? why lives he, but to increase the world? and how shall he do that well, if he do not marry? Matrimony, saith Nevisanus, makes us immortal, and, according to Tacitus, 'tis the sole and chief prop of an empire.

Pelopidas objected to Epaminondas, he was an unworthy member of a commonwealth that left not a child after him to defend it; and as Trismegistus to his son Tatius, 'Have no commerce with a single man,' holding belike that a bachelor could not live honestly as he should; and with Georgius Wicelius, a great divine and holy man, who of late by twenty-six arguments commends marriage as a thing most necessary for all kind of persons, most laudable and fit to be embraced: and is persuaded withal that no man can live and die religiously and as he ought, without a wife, he is false, an enemy to the commonwealth, injurious to himself, destructive to the world, an apostate to nature, a rebel against heaven and earth. Let our wilful, obstinate, and stale bachelors ruminate of this. If we could live without wives, as Marcellus Numidicus said in A. Gellius, we would all want them; but because we cannot, let all marry, and consult rather to the public good than their own private pleasure or estate. It were an happy thing, as wise Euripides hath it, if we could buy children with gold and silver, and be so provided without women's company; but that may not be:

> *Earth, air, sea, land eftsoon would come to naught,*
> *The world itself should be to ruin brought.*
>
> (SENECA)

Necessity therefore compels us to marry.

But what do I trouble myself, to find arguments to persuade to, or commend marriage? behold a brief abstract of all that which I have said, and much more, succinctly, pithily, pathetically, perspicuously, and elegantly delivered in twelve motions to mitigate the miseries of marriage, by Jacobus de Voragine.

1. Hast thou means? thou hast one to keep and increase it. 2. Hast none? thou hast one to help to get it. 3. Art in prosperity? thine happiness is double. 4. Art in adversity? she'll comfort, assist, bear a part of thy burden to make it more tolerable. 5. Art at home? she'll drive away melancholy. 6. Art abroad? she looks after thee going from home, wishes for thee in thine absence, and joyfully welcomes thy return. 7. There's nothing delightsome without society, no society so sweet as matrimony. 8. The band of conjugal love is adamantine. 9. The sweet company of kinsmen increaseth, the number of parents is doubled, of brothers, sisters, nephews. 10. Thou are made a father by a fair and happy issue. 11. Moses curseth the barrenness of matrimony, how much more a single life? 12. If nature escape not punishment, surely thy will shall not avoid it.

All this is true, say you, and who knows it not? but how easy a matter is it to answer these motives, and to make an antiparody quite opposite unto it! To exercise myself I will essay:

1. Hast thou means? thou hast one to spend it. 2. Hast none? thy beggary is increased. 3. Art in prosperity? thy happiness is ended. 4. Art in adversity? like Job's wife she'll aggravate thy misery, vex thy soul, make thy burden intolerable. 5. Art at home? she'll scold thee out of doors. 6. Art abroad? If thou be wise, keep thee so, she'll

perhaps graft horns in thine absence, scowl on thee coming home. 7. Nothing gives more content than solitariness, no solitariness like this of a single life. 8. The band of marriage is adamantine, no hope of losing it, thou art undone. 9. Thy number increaseth, thou shalt be devoured by thy wife's friends. 10. Thou art made a cornuto by an unchaste wife, and shalt bring up other folks' children instead of thine own. 11. Paul commends marriage, yet he prefers a single life. 12. Is marriage honourable? What an immortal crown belongs to virginity.

So Siracides (Ecclesiasticus) himself speaks as much as may be for and against women, so doth almost every philosopher plead pro and con, every poet thus argues the case, though what cares the common herd what they say? so can I conceive peradventure, and so canst thou: when all is said, yet since some be good, some bad, let's put it to the venture. I conclude therefore with Seneca: Why dost thou lie alone, let thy youth and best days to pass away? Marry whilst thou mayest, whilst thou are yet able, yet lusty, choose one to whom thou canst say, 'Thee alone I love', make thy choice, and that freely forthwith, make no delay, but take thy fortune as it falls. 'Tis true, unlucky he who lights upon a bad wife, happy he who finds a good one. 'Tis an hazard both ways I confess, to live single or to marry, it may be bad, it may be good; as it is a cross and calamity on the one side, so 'tis a sweet delight, an incomparable happiness, a blessed estate, a most unspeakable benefit, a sole content, on the other; 'tis all in the proof.

Be not then so wayward, so covetous, so distrustful, so curious and nice, but let's all marry. Take me to thee, and thee to me, tomorrow is St Valentine's Day, let's keep it holiday for Cupid's sake, for that great god Love's sake, for Hymen's sake, and celebrate Venus' vigil with our ancestors for company together, singing as they did:

> *Tomorrow let him love who ne'er loved yet,*
> *Nor let him who e'er loved before forget.*

> *'Tis tuneful spring, the world's new-born in spring,*
> *It is love's season, birds then pairing sing.*
> *'Tis then the woods renew their annual green.*

Let him that is averse from marriage read more in Barbarus, Lemnius, P. Godefridus, Nevisanus, Alex, ab. Alexandro, Tunstall, Erasmus' tracts, etc., and I doubt not but in the end he will rest satisfied, recant with Beroaldus, do penance for his former folly, singing some penitential ditties, desire to be reconciled to the deity of this great god Love, go a pilgrimage to his shrine, offer to his image, sacrifice upon his altar, and be as willing at last to embrace marriage as the rest. There will not be found, I hope, no, not in that severe family of Stoics, who shall refuse to submit his grave beard and supercilious looks to the clipping of a wife, or disagree from his fellows in this point. For what more willingly (as Varro holds) can a proper man see than a fair wife, a sweet wife, a loving wife? Can the world afford a better sight, sweeter content, a fairer object, a more gracious aspect?

Since then this of marriage is the last and best refuge and cure of heroical love, all doubts the cleared, and impediments removed; I say again, what remains, but that according to both their desires they be happily joined, since it cannot otherwise be helped? God send us all good wives, every man his wish in this kind, and me mine!

> *And God that all this world hath y-wrought*
> *Send him his love that hath it so dere y-bought.*

(CHAUCER)

If all parties be pleased, ask their banns, 'tis a match. Rhodanthe and Dosicles shall go together, Clitiphon and Leucippe, Theagenes and Chariclea, Poliarchus hath his Argenis, Lysander Calista (to make up the mask), and young Iphis enjoys his Ianthe.

And Troilus in lust and in quiet
Is with Creseid, his own heart sweet.

(CHAUCER)

And although they have hardly passed the pikes, through many difficulties and delays brought the match about, yet let them take this of Aristaenetus (that so marry) for their comfort; 'After many troubles and cares, the marriages of lovers are more sweet and pleasant.' As we commonly conclude a comedy with a wedding and shaking of hands, let's shut up our discourse, and end all with an epithalamium.

To bride, bridegroom, happiness, God give them joy together, Hymen, lead them home. 'Tis well done, 'tis an happy conjunction, a fortunate match, an even couple, they both excel in gifts of body and mind, are both equal in years, youth, vigour, alacrity, she is fair and lovely as Lais or Helen, he as another Cleinias or Alcibiades:

Then modestly go sport and toy,
And let's have every year a boy.

(CATULLUS)

'Go give a sweet smell as incense, and bring forth flowers as the lily' [Ecclus, xxxix, 14], that we may say hereafter: 'I' faith, a pretty boy is born to Pamphilus'. In the meantime I say,

Gentle youths, go sport yourselves betimes,
Let not the doves outpass your murmurings,
Or ivy clasping arms, or oyster kissings.

(GALLIENUS)

And in the morn betime, as those Lacedaemonian lasses saluted Helena and Menelaus, singing at their windows, and wishing good success, do we at yours:

> *Good morrow, master bridegroom, and mistress bride,*
> *Many fair lovely bairns to you betide!*
> *Let Venus to you mutual love procure,*
> *Let Saturn give you riches to endure,*
> *Long may you sleep in one another's arms,*
> *Inspiring sweet desire, and free from harms.*

(THEOCRITUS)

Even all your lives long,

> *The loves of turtles hap to you,*
> *And ravens' years still to renew.*

(ERASMUS)

Let the Muses sing (as he said), the Graces dance, not at their weddings only but all their days long: 'so couple their hearts, that no irksomeness or anger ever befall them. Let him never call her other name than my joy, my light, or she call him otherwise than sweetheart. To this happiness of theirs let not old age any whit detract, but as their years, so let their mutual love and comfort increase.' And when they depart this life,

> *Because they have so sweetly liv'd together,*
> *Let not one die a day before the other,*
> *He bury her, she him, with even fate,*
> *One hour their souls let jointly separate.*

(OVID)

O happy both! if that my lines have power
No time shall ever make your memory fade.

(VIRGIL)

We have now said enough on the subject of love, under correction, as Kornmannus saith, of any one who knows better. He who would learn more of the remedies for love may consult Jason Pratensis, etc.; among the poets, Ovid, our own Chaucer, etc., with whom I conclude.

For my words here and every part,
I speak hem all under correction,
Of you that feeling have in love's art,
And put it all in your discretion,
To entreat or make diminution,
Of my language, that I you beseech:
But now to purpose of my rather speech.

XX

*Jealousy, its Equivocations, Name, Definition,
Extent, several kinds; of Princes, Parents,
Friends. In Beasts, Men: before marriage,
as Corrivals; or after, as in this place.*

VALESCUS DE TARANTA, Aelian Montaltus, Felix Platerus, Guianerius put jealousy for a cause of melancholy, others for a symptom; because melancholy persons, among these passions and perturbations of the mind, are most obnoxious to it. But methinks for the latitude it hath, and that prerogative above other ordinary symptoms, it ought to be treated of as a species apart, being of so great and eminent note, so furious a passion, and almost of as great extent as love itself; as Benedetto Varchi holds, no love without a mixture of jealousy. For these causes I will dilate and treat of it by itself, as a bastard branch or kind of love-melancholy, which, as heroical love goeth commonly before marriage, doth usually follow, torture, and crucify in like sort, deserves therefore to be rectified alike, requires as much care and industry in setting out the several causes of it, prognostics and cures. Which I have more willingly done, that he that is or hath been jealous may see his error as in a glass; he that is not, may learn to detest, avoid it himself, and dispossess others that are anywise affected with it.

Jealousy is described and defined to be a certain suspicion which the lover hath of the party he chiefly loveth, lest he or she should be enamoured of another; or any eager desire to enjoy some beauty alone, to have it proper to himself only: a fear or doubt lest any foreigner should participate or share with him in his love. Or (as Scaliger adds) a fear of losing her favour whom he so earnestly affects. Cardan calls it a zeal for love, and a kind of envy lest any man should beguile us. Ludovicus Vives defines it in the very same words, or little differing in sense.

There be many other jealousies, but improperly so called all; as that of parents, tutors, guardians over their children, friends whom they love, or such as are left to their wardship or protection: 'Storax, Aeschinus has not returned from supper, nor any of the slaves who went to meet him', as the old man in the comedy [Terence's Adelphi] cried out in a passion, and from a solicitous fear and care he had of his adopted son; not of beauty, but lest they should miscarry, do amiss, or anyway discredit, disgrace (as Vives notes), or endanger themselves and us. Aegeus was so solicitous for his son Theseus (when he went to fight with the Minotaur), of his success, lest he should be foiled. We are still apt to suspect the worst in such doubtful cases, as many wives in their husbands' absence, fond mothers in their children's, lest if absent they should be misled or sick, and are continually expecting news from them, how they do fare, and what is become of them, they cannot endure to have them long out of their sight: Oh, my sweet son! oh, my dear child! etc.

Paul was jealous over the Church of Corinth, as he confesseth (2 Cor. xi, 2, 3), 'with a godly jealousy, to present them a pure virgin to Christ'; and he was afraid still, lest, as the serpent beguiled Eve through his subtility, so their minds should be corrupt from the simplicity that is in Christ. God himself, in some sense, is said to be jealous: 'I am a jealous God, and will visit'; so Psalm lxxix, 5: 'Shall thy jealousy burn like fire for ever?' But these are improperly called jealousies, and by a metaphor, to show the care and solicitude they have of them. Although some jealousies express all the symptoms of this which we treat of, fear, sorrow, anguish, anxiety, suspicion, hatred, etc., the object only varied. That of some fathers is very eminent to their sons and heirs; for though they love them dearly being children, yet now coming towards man's estate they may not well abide them; the son and heir is commonly sick of the father, and the father again may not well brook his eldest son, thence quarrels, strife, and enmity.

But that of princes is most notorious, as when they fear córrivals (if I may so call them), successors, emulators, subjects, or such as they have offended. They are still suspicious, lest their authority should be diminished, as one observes; and as Commines hath it, it cannot be expressed what slender causes they have of their grief and suspicion, a secret disease, that commonly lurks and breeds in princes' families. Sometimes it is for their honour only, as that of Hadrian the emperor, that killed all his emulators. Saul envied David; Domitian Agricola, because he did excel him, obscure his honour, as he thought, eclipse his fame. Juno turned Proetus' daughters into kine, for that they contended with her for beauty; the Cyparissae, King Etoecles' children, were envied of the goddesses for their excellent good parts, and dancing among the rest, saith Constantine, and for that cause flung headlong from heaven, and buried in a pit, but the earth took pity of them, and brought out cypress trees to preserve their memories. Niobe, Arachne, and Marsyas can testify as much.

But it is most grievous when it is for a kingdom itself, or matters of commodity, it produceth lamentable effects, especially among tyrants, and such as are more feared than beloved of their subjects, that get and keep their sovereignty by force and fear, as Phalaris, Dionysius, Periander held theirs. For though fear, cowardice, and jealousy, in Plutarch's opinion, be the common causes of tyranny, as in Nero, Caligula, Tiberius, yet most take them to be symptoms. For what slave, what hangman (as Bodine well expresseth this passion) can so cruelly torture a condemned person as this fear and suspicion?

Fear of death, infamy, torments are those furies and vultures that vex and disquiet tyrants, and torture them day and night with perpetual terrors and affrights; envy, suspicion, fear, desire of revenge, and a thousand such disagreeing perturbations turn and affright the soul out of the hinges of health, and more grievously wound and pierce than those cruel masters can exasperate and vex their prentices or servants with clubs, whips, chains, and tortures.

Many terrible examples we have in this kind, among the Turks especially, many jealous outrages; Selimus killed Cornutus his youngest brother, five of his nephews, Mustapha Bassa, and divers others. Bajazet, the second Turk, jealous of the valour and greatness of Achmet Bassa, caused him to be slain. Solyman the Magnificent murdered his own son Mustapha; and 'tis an ordinary thing among them, to make away their brothers, or any competitors, at the first coming to the crown: 'tis all the solemnity they use at their fathers' funerals. What mad pranks in his jealous fury did Herod of old commit in Jewry, when he massacred all the children of a year old! Valens the emperor in Constantinople, whenas he left no man alive of quality in his kingdom that had his name begun with Theo! Theodoti, Theognosti, Theodosii, Theoduli, etc., they went all to their long home, because a wizard told him that name should succeed in his empire. And what furious designs hath John Basilius [Ivan the Terrible], that Muscovian tyrant, practised of late!

It is a wonder to read that strange suspicion which Suetonius reports of Claudius Caesar and of Domitian, they were afraid of every man they saw; and which Herodian reports of Antoninus and Geta, those two jealous brothers, the one could not endure so much as the other's servants, but made away him, his chiefest followers, and all that belonged to him or were his well-wishers. Maximinus, perceiving himself to be odious to most men, because he was come to that height of honour out of base beginnings, and suspecting his mean parentage would be objected to him, caused all the senators that were nobly descended to be slain in a jealous humour, turned all the servants of Alexander his predecessor out of doors, and slew many of them, because they lamented their master's death, suspecting them to be traitors for the love they bare to him. When Alexander in his fury had made Clitus his dear friend to be put to death, and saw now (saith Curtius) an alienation in his subjects' hearts, none durst talk with him, he began to be jealous of himself, lest they should attempt as much on him, and said they lived like so many wild beasts in a wilderness, one afraid of another.

Our modern stories afford us many notable examples. Henry the Third of France, jealous of Henry of Lorraine, Duke of Guise, *anno* 1588, caused him to be murdered in his own chamber. Louis the Eleventh was so suspicious, he durst not trust his children, every man about him he suspected for a traitor; many strange tricks Commines telleth of him. How jealous was our Henry the Fourth of King Richard the Second, so long as he lived, after he was deposed! and of his own son Henry in his later days! which the prince well perceiving, came to visit his father in his sickness, in a watchet velvet gown, full of oilet-holes, and with needles sticking in them (as an emblem of jealousy), and so pacified his suspicious father, after some speeches and protestations which he had used to that purpose. Perpetual imprisonment, as that of Robert Duke of Normandy, in the days of Henry the First, forbidding of marriage to some persons, with such-like edicts and prohibitions, are ordinary in all states. In a word, as he [Robert Tofte in the Blason of Jealousie] said, three things cause jealousy, a mighty state, a rich treasure, a fair wife; or where there is a cracked title, much tyranny, and many exactions. In our state, as being freed from all these fears and miseries, we may be most secure and happy under the reign of our fortunate prince.

> *His fortune hath indebted him to none,*
> *But to all his people universally;*
> *And not to them but for their love alone,*
> *Which they account as placed worthily.*
> *He is so set, he hath no cause to be*
> *Jealous, or dreadful of disloyalty;*
> *The pedestal whereon his greatness stands,*
> *Is held of all our hearts, and all our hands.*

(DANIEL)

But I rove, I confess. These equivocations, jealousies, and many such, which crucify the souls of men, are not here properly meant, or in this distinction of ours included, but that alone which is for beauty, tending to love, and wherein they can brook no corrival, or endure any participation: and this jealousy belongs as well to brute beasts as men. Some creatures, saith Vives, swans, doves, cocks, bulls, etc., are jealous as well as men, and as much moved, for fear of communion.

> *In Venus' cause what mighty battles make*
> *Your raving bulls, and stirs for their herd's sake:*
> *And harts and bucks, that are so timorous,*
> *Will fight and roar, if once they be but jealous.*

(SENECA)

In bulls, horses, goats this is most apparently discerned; bulls especially: he will not admit another bull to feed in the same pasture, saith Oppian: which Stephanus Bathorius, late King of Poland, used as an impress, with that motto, a throne will not hold two. Robert Tofte, in his Blazon of Jealousy, telleth a story of a swan about Windsor, that finding a strange cock with his mate, did swim I know not how many miles after to kill him, and when he had so done, came back and killed his hen; a certain truth, he saith, done upon Thames, as many watermen and neighbour gentlemen can tell. For my part, I do believe it may be true; for swans have ever been branded with that epithet of jealousy.

> *The jealous swanne against his death that singeth,*
> *And eke the owle that of death bode bringeth.*

(CHAUCER)

Some say as much of elephants, that they are more jealous than any other creatures whatsoever; and those old Egyptians, as Pierius informeth us, express in their hieroglyphics the passion of jealousy by a camel; because that, fearing the worst still about matters of venery, he loves solitudes, that he may enjoy his pleasure alone, he will quarrel and fight with whosoever comes next, man or beast, in his jealous fits. I have read as much of crocodiles; and if Peter Martyr's authority be authentic, you shall have a strange tale to that purpose confidently related. Another story of the jealousy of dogs, see in Hieronymus Fabricius.

But this furious passion is most eminent in men, and is as well among bachelors as married men. If it appear among bachelors we commonly call them rivals or corrivals, a metaphor derived from a river, for as a river, saith Acron and Donatus, divides a common ground betwixt two men, and both participate of it, so is a woman indifferent between two suitors, both likely to enjoy her; and thence comes this emulation, which breaks out many times into tempestuous storms, and produceth lamentable effects, murder itself, with much cruelty, many single combats. They cannot endure the least injury done unto them before their mistress, and in her defence will bite off one another's noses; they are most impatient of any flout, disgrace, least emulation, or participation in that kind. Memmius the Roman (as Tully tells the story), being corrival with Largus at Terracina, bit him by the arm, which fact of his was so famous, that it afterwards grew to a proverb in those parts. Phaedria could not abide his corrival Thraso; for when Parmeno demanded whether he would command him any more service: No more (saith he) but to speak in his behalf, and to drive away his corrival if he could.

Constantine, in the eleventh book of his Husbandry, hath a pleasant tale of the pine-tree; she was once a fair maid, whom Phineus and Boreas, two corrivals, dearly sought; but jealous Boreas broke her neck, etc. And in his eighteenth chapter he telleth another tale of Mars, that in his jealousy slew Adonis. Petronius calleth this passion a furious emulation; and their symptoms are well expressed by Sir Geoffrey Chaucer in his first Canterbury Tale. It will make the nearest and dearest friends fall out; they will endure all other things to be common, goods, lands, moneys, participate of each other's pleasures, and take in good part any disgraces, injuries in another kind; but as Propertius well describes it in an elegy of his, in this they will suffer nothing, have no corrivals.

> *Stab me with sword, or poison strong*
>   *Give me to work my bane:*
> *So thou court not my lass, so thou*
>   *From mistress mine refrain.*
> *Command myself, my body, purse,*
>   *As thine own goods take all,*
> *And as my ever dearest friend,*
>   *I ever use thee shall.*
> *O spare my love, to have alone*
>   *Her to myself I crave,*
> *Nay, Jove himself I'll not endure*
>   *My rival for to have.*

This jealousy which I am to treat of, is that which belongs to married men, in respect of their own wives; to whose estate, as no sweetness, pleasure, happiness, can be compared in the world, if they live quietly and lovingly together; so if they disagree or be jealous, those bitter pills of sorrow and grief, disastrous mischiefs, mischances, tortures, gripings, discontents are not to be separated from them. A most violent passion it is where it taketh place, an unspeakable torment, a hellish torture, an infernal plague, as Ariosto calls it, a fury, a continual fever, full of suspicion, fear, and sorrow, a martyrdom, a mirth-marring monster. The sorrow and grief of heart of one woman jealous of another, is heavier than death (Ecclus, xxvi, 6), as Peninnah did Hannah, vex her and upbraid her sore. 'Tis a main vexation, a most intolerable burden, a corsive to all content, a frenzy, a madness itself; as Benedetto Varchi proves out of that select sonnet of Giovanni de la Casa, that reverend lord, as he styles him.

XXI

Causes of Jealousy. Who are most apt.
Idleness, Melancholy, Impotency, long
Absence, Beauty, Wantonness, naught
themselves. Allurements from time,
place, persons, bad usage, Causes.

ASTROLOGERS MAKE the stars a cause or sign of this bitter passion, and out of every man's horoscope will give a probable conjecture whether he will be jealous or no, and at what time, by direction of the significators to their several promissors: their aphorisms are to be read in Albubater, Pontanus, Scheiner, Junctine, etc. Bodine ascribes a great cause to the country or clime, and discourseth largely there of this subject, saying, that southern men are more hot, lascivious, and jealous than such as live in the north; they can hardly contain themselves in those hotter climes, but are most subject to prodigious lust. Leo Afer telleth incredible things almost of the lust and jealousy of his countrymen of Africa, and especially such as live about Carthage, and so doth every geographer of them in Asia, Turkey, Spaniards, Italians. Germany hath not so many drunkards, England tobacconists, France dancers, Holland mariners, as Italy alone hath jealous husbands. And in Italy some account them of Piacenza more jealous than the rest.

In Germany, France, Britain, Scandia, Poland, Muscovy, they are not so troubled with this feral malady, although Damianus à Goes, which I do much wonder at, in his topography of Lapland, and Herbastein of Russia, against the stream of all other geographers, would fasten it upon those northern inhabitants. Altomarus, Poggius, and Munster, in his description of Baden, reports that men and women of all sorts go commonly into the baths together, without all suspicion; the name of jealousy (saith Munster) is not so much as once heard of among them. In Friesland the women kiss him they drink to, and are kissed again of those they pledge. The virgins in Holland go hand-in-hand with young men from home, glide on the ice, such is their harmless liberty, and lodge together abroad without suspicion, which rash Sansovinus, an Italian, makes a great sign of unchastity. In France, upon small acquaintance, it is usual to court other men's wives, to come to their houses, and accompany them arm-in-arm in the streets, without imputation. In the most northern countries young men and maids familiarly dance together, men and their wives, which, Siena only excepted, Italians may not abide.

The Greeks, on the other side, have their private baths for men and women, where they must not come near, nor so much as see one another; and as Bodine observes, the Italians could never endure this, or a Spaniard, the very conceit of it would make him mad; and for that cause they lock up their women, and will not suffer them to be near men, so much as in the church, but with a partition between. He telleth, moreover, how that when he was ambassador in England, he heard Mendoza the Spanish legate finding fault with it, as a filthy custom for men and women to sit promiscuously in churches together; but Dr Dale, the Master of the Requests, told him again that it was indeed a filthy custom in Spain, where they could not contain themselves from lascivious thoughts in their holy places, but not with us.

Baronius in his Annals, out of Eusebius, taxeth Licinius the emperor for a decree of his made ordering that men and women should not sit together in church: for being prodigiously naughty himself, he so esteemed others. But we are far from any such strange conceits, and will permit our wives and daughters to go to the tavern with a friend, as Aubanus saith, and suspect nothing, to kiss coming and going, which, as Erasmus write in one of his epistles, they cannot endure. England is a paradise for women, and hell for horses: Italy a paradise for horses, hell for women, as the diverb goes. Some make a question whether this headstrong passion rage more in women than men, as Montaigne. But sure it is more outrageous in women, as all other melancholy is, by reason of the weakness of their sex. Scaliger concludes against women: Besides their inconstancy, treachery, suspicion, dissimulation, superstition, pride (for all women are by nature proud), desire of sovereignty, if they be great women (he gives instance in Juno), bitterness and jealousy are the most remarkable affections.

> *Tiger, boar, bear, viper, lioness,*
> *A woman's fury cannot express.*
>
> (OVID)

Some say red-headed women, pale-coloured, black-eyed, and of a shrill voice, are most subject to jealousy.

> *High colour in a woman choler shows,*
> *Naught are they, peevish, proud, malicious;*
> *But worst of all, red, shrill, and jealous.*
>
> (ROBERT TOFTE)

Comparisons are odious, I neither parallel them with others nor debase them any more: men and women are both bad, and too subject to this pernicious infirmity. It is most part a symptom and cause of melancholy, as Plater and Valescus teach us: melancholy men are apt to be jealous, and jealous apt to be melancholy.

Pale jealousy, child of insatiate love,
Of heart-sick thoughts which melancholy bred,
A hell-tormenting fear, no faith can move,
By discontent with deadly poison fed;
With heedless youth and error vainly led.
A mortal plague, a virtue-drowning flood,
A hellish fire not quenched but with blood.

(DRAYTON)

If idleness concur with melancholy, such persons are most apt to be jealous; 'tis Nevisanus' note, An idle woman is presumed to be lascivious, and often jealous, and 'tis not unlikely, for they have no other business to trouble their heads with.

More particular causes be these which follow. Impotency first, when a man is not able of himself to perform those dues which he ought unto his wife: for though he be an honest liver, hurt no man, yet Trebatius the lawyer may make a question, whether he gives everyone their own; and therefore when he takes notice of his wants, and perceives her to be more craving, clamorous, unsatiable, and prone to lust than is fit, he begins presently to suspect, that wherein he is defective, she will satisfy herself, she will be pleased by some other means. Cornelius Gallus hath elegantly expressed this humour in an epigram to his Lycoris:

Now seeks she other youths and other loves,
Calls me a worn-out, good-for-naught old man.

For this cause is most evident in old men, that are cold and dry by nature, and married to young wanton wives; with old doting Janivere in Chaucer, they begin to mistrust all is not well:

> *She was young and he was old,*
> *And therefore he feared to be a cuckold.*

And how should it otherwise be? Old age is a disease of itself, loath-some, full of suspicion and fear; when it is at best, unable, unfit for such matters. As welcome to a young woman as snow in harvest, saith Nevisanus; marry a lusty maid and she will surely graft horns on thy head. All women are slippery, often unfaithful to their husbands (as Aeneas Sylvius seconds him), but to old men most treacherous: they had rather lie with a corpse than such a one: 'boys hate him, women despise him'.

On the other side, many men, said Hieronymus, are suspicious of their wives, if they be lightly given, but old folks above the rest. Insomuch that she did not complain without a cause in Apuleius, of an old bald bedridden knave she had to her goodman. 'Poor woman as I am, what shall I do? I have an old grim sire to my husband, as bald as a coot, as little and as unable as a child, a bedful of bones, he keeps all the doors barred and locked upon me, woe is me, what shall I do?' He was jealous, and she made him a cuckold for keeping her up: suspicion without a cause, hard usage is able of itself to make a woman fly out, that was otherwise honest, bad usage aggravates the matter. As Nevisanus holds, when a woman thinks her husband watcheth her she will sooner offend; rough handling makes them worse: as the Goodwife of Bath in Chaucer brags,

> *In his own grease I made him frie*
> *For anger and for very jealousie.*

Of two extremes, this of hard usage is the worst. 'Tis a great fault (for some men are uxorious to be too fond of their wives, to dote on them as Senior Deliro on his Fallace [characters in Ben Jonson's

Everyman Out of His Humour], to be too effeminate, or as some do, to be sick for their wives, breed children for them, and like the Tiberini lie in for them; as some birds hatch eggs by turns, they do all women's offices: Caelius Rhodiginus makes mention of a fellow out of Seneca, that was so besotted on his wife, he could not endure a moment out of her company, he wore her scarf when he went abroad next his heart, and would never drink but in that cup she began first. We have many such fondlings that are their wives' packhorses and slaves, as the comical poet hath it, there's no greater misery to a man than to let his wife's domineer), to carry her muff, dog, and fan, let her wear the breeches, lay out, spend, and do what she will, go and come whither, when she will, they give consent:

> *Here, take my muff, and, do you hear, good man,*
> *Now give me Pearl, and carry you my fan, etc.*
>
> (CHALONER)

Many brave and worthy men have trespassed in this kind, and many noble senators and soldiers (as Pliny notes) have lost their honour, in being uxorious, so sottishly overruled by their wives; and therefore Cato in Plutarch made a bitter jest on his fellow-citizens, the Romans: 'We govern all the world abroad, and our wives at home rule us.'

These offend in one extreme; but too hard and too severe are far more offensive on the other. As just a cause may be long absence of either party, when they must of necessity be much from home, as lawyers, physicians, mariners, by their professions; or otherwise make frivolous, impertinent journeys, tarry long abroad to no purpose, lie out, and are gadding still, upon small occasions, it must needs yield matter of suspicion, when they use their wives unkindly in the meantime, and never tarry at home, it cannot use but engender some such conceit.

If thou be absent long, thy wife then thinks,
Th' art drunk, at ease, or with some pretty minx,
'Tis well with thee, or else beloved of some,
Whilst she, poor soul, doth fare full ill at home.

(TERENCE)

Hippocrates the physician had a smack of this disease; for when he was to go from home as far as Abdera and some other remote cities of Greece, he writ to his friend Dionysius (if at least those Epistles be his) to oversee his wife in his absence (as Apollo set a raven to watch his Coronis), although she lived in his house with her father and mother, whom he knew would have a care of her; yet that would not satisfy his jealousy, he would have his special friend Dionysius to dwell in his house with her all the time of his peregrination, and to observe her behaviour, how she carried herself in her husband's absence, and that she did not lust after other men. For a woman had need to have an overseer to keep her honest; they are bad by nature, and lightly given all, and if they be not curbed in time, as an unpruned tree, they will be full of wild branches, and degenerate of a sudden. Especially in their husbands' absence. Though one Lucretia were trusty, and one Penelope, yet Clytemnestra made Agamemnon cuckold; and no question there be too many of her conditions. If their husbands tarry too long abroad upon unnecessary business, well they may suspect: or if they run one way, their wives at home will fly out another, quid pro quo. Or if present, and give them not that content which they ought, they cannot endure to lie alone, or to fast long. Peter Godefridus, in his second book of Love, and sixth chapter, hath a story out of St Anthony's life, of a gentleman, who, by that good man's advice, would not meddle with his wife in the Passion Week, but for his pains she set a pair of horns on his head. Such another he hath out of Abstemius: one persuaded a new-married man to forbear the three first nights, and he should all his lifetime after be fortunate in cattle, but his impatient wife would not tarry so long: well he might speed in cattle, but not in children.

Such a tale hath Heinsius of an impotent and slack scholar, a mere student, and a friend of his, that seeing by chance a fine damsel sing and dance, would needs marry her; the match was soon made, for he was young and rich, smooth-cheeked, well educated, and rich, like that Apollo in Apuleius. The first night, having liberally taken his liquor (as in that country they do), my fine scholar was so fuzzled, that he no sooner was laid in bed but he fell fast asleep, never waked till morning, and then much abashed, when the fair morn with purple hue 'gan shine, he made an excuse, I know not what, out of Hippocrates Cous, etc., and for that time it went current; but whenas afterwards he did not play the man as he should do, he fell in league with a good fellow and while he sat up late at his study about those criticisms, mending so hard places in Festus or Pollux, came cold to bed, and would tell her still what he had done, she did not much regard what he said, etc. She would have another matter mended much rather, which he did not conceive was corrupt: thus he continued at his study late, she at her sport somewhere else, hating all scholars for his sake, till at length he began to suspect, and turned a little yellow, as well he might; for it was his own fault; and if men be jealous in such cases (as oft it falls out) the mends is in their own hands, they must thank themselves.

Who will pity them, saith Neander, or be much offended with such wives, if they deceive those that cozened them first? A lawyer's wife in Aristaenetus, because her husband was negligent in his business, threatened to cornute him, and did not stick to tell Philinna, one of her gossips, as much, and that aloud for him to hear: 'If he follow other men's matters and leave his own, I'll have an orator shall plead my cause, I care not if he know it.'

A fourth eminent cause of jealousy may be this, when he that is deformed and, as Pindarus of Vulcan, not favoured by nature, hirsute, ragged, yet virtuously given, will marry some fair nice piece, or light housewife, begins to misdoubt (as well he may) she doth not affect him. Beauty and honesty have ever been at odds. Abraham was jealous of his wife because she was fair: so was Vulcan of his Venus, when he made her creaking shoes, saith Philostratus, that he might hear by them when she stirred, which Mars was not well pleased with. Good cause had Vulcan to do as he did, for she was no honester than she should be. Your fine faces have commonly this fault; and it is hard to find, saith Francis Philelphus in an epistle to Saxola his friend, a rich man honest, a proper woman not proud or unchaste. Can she be fair and honest too?

He that marries a wife that is snout-fair alone, let him look, saith Barbarus, for no better success than Vulcan had with Venus, or Claudius with Messalina. And 'tis impossible almost in such cases the wife should contain, or the good man not be jealous: for when he is so defective, weak, ill-proportioned, unpleasing in those parts which women most affect, and she most absolutely fair and able on the other side, if she be not very virtuously given, how can she love him? and although she be not fair, yet if he admire her and think her so, in his conceit she is absolute, he holds it unpossible for any man living not to dote as he doth, to look on her and not lust, not to covet, and if he be in company with her, not to lay siege to her honesty: or else out of a deep apprehension of his infirmities, deformities, and other men's good parts, out of his own little worth and desert, he distrusts himself (for what is jealousy but distrust?), he suspects she cannot afford him, or be not so kind and loving as she should, she certainly loves some other man better than himself.

Nevisanus will have barrenness to be a main cause of jealousy. If her husband cannot play the man, some other shall, they will leave no remedies unassayed, and thereupon the good man grows jealous; I could give an instance, but be it as it is.

I find this reason given by some men, because they have been formerly naughty themselves, they think they may be so served by others; they turned up trump before the cards were shuffled, they shall have therefore like for like.

> *Wretch as I was, I taught her bad to be,*
> *And now mine own sly tricks are put upon me.*
>
> (TIBULLUS)

Ill dispositions cause ill suspicion, as the saying is,

> *There is none jealous, I durst pawn my life,*
> *But he that hath defiled another's wife,*
> *And for that he himself hath gone astray,*
> *He straightway thinks his wife will tread that way.*
>
> (WITHER)

To these two above-named causes, or incendiaries of this rage, I may very well annex those circumstances of time, place, persons, by which it ebbs and flows, the fuel of this fury, as Vives truly observes: and such-like accidents or occasions, proceeding from the parties themselves or others, which much aggravate and intend this suspicious humour. For many men are so lasciviously given, either out of a depraved nature or too much liberty, which they do assume unto themselves by reason of their greatness, in that they are noblemen (for licence to sin and company of sinners are great motives), though their own wives be never so fair, noble, virtuous, honest, wise, able, and well given, they must have change.

> *Who being match'd to wives most virtuous,*
> *Noble, and fair, fly out lascivious.*
>
> (MARULLUS)

That which is ordinary is unpleasant. Nero (saith Tacitus) abhorred Octavia his own wife, a noble virtuous lady, and loved Acte, a base quean in respect. Cerinthus rejected Sulpicia, a nobleman's daughter, and courted a poor servant maid, for that stolen waters be more pleasant: or, as Vitellius the emperor was wont to say, like stolen venison, still the sweetest is that love which is most difficultly attained: they like better to hunt by stealth in another man's walk, than to have the fairest course that may be at game of their own.

> *As sun and moon in heaven change their course,*
> *So they change loves, though often to the worse.*
>
> (PROPERTIUS)

Or that some fair object so forcibly moves them, they cannot contain themselves; be it heard or seen, they will be at it. Nessus, the centaur, was by agreement to carry Hercules and his wife over the River Evenus; no sooner had he set Deianira on the other side but he would have offered violence unto her, leaving Hercules to swim over as he could: and though her husband was a spectator, yet he would not desist till Hercules with a poisoned arrow shot him to death. Neptune saw by chance that Thessalian Tyro, Enipeus' wife; he forthwith in the fury of his lust counterfeited her husband's habit, and made him cuckold. Tarquin heard Collatine commend his wife, and was so far enraged that in the midst of the night to her he went. Theseus stole Ariadne, carried off that Troezenian Anaxo, Antiope, and now being old, Helena, a girl not yet ready for a husband.

Great men are most part thus affected all, as a horse they neigh, saith Jeremiah, after their neighbours' wives: and if they be in company with other women, though in their own wives' presence, they must be courting and dallying with them. Juno in Lucian complains of Jupiter that he was still kissing Ganymede before her face, which did not a little offend her: and besides, he was a counterfeit Amphitruo, a bull, a swan, a golden shower, and played many such bad pranks, too long, too shameful to relate.

Or that they care little for their own ladies, and fear no laws, they dare freely keep whores at their wives' noses. 'Tis too frequent with noblemen to be dishonest; as Seneca said long since, piety, chastity, and such-like virtues are for private men: not to be much looked after in great courts: and which Suetonius said of the good princes of his time, they might be all engraven in one ring, we may truly hold of chaste potentates of our age. For great personages will familiarly run out in this kind, and yield occasion of offence. Montaigne, in his Essays, gives instance in Caesar, Mahomet the Turk, that sacked Constantinople, and Ladislaus, King of Naples, that besieged Florence: great men, and great soldiers, are commonly great, etc.; it is a known fact, they are good doers. Mars and Venus are equally balanced in their actions:

> *A dove within a head-piece made her nest,*
> *'Twixt Mars and Venus see an interest.*
>
> (PETRONIUS)

Especially if they be bald, for bald men have ever been suspicious (read more in Aristotle, as Galba, Otho, Domitian, and remarkable Caesar among the rest: 'Citizens, look to your wives, we bring along a bald gallant.' Besides, this bald Caesar, saith Curio in Suetonius, ran after every woman; he made love to Eunoe, Queen of Mauritania;

to Cleopatra; to Posthumia, wife to Sergius Sulpicius; to Lollia, wife to Gabinius; to Tertulla, of Crassus; to Mucia, Pompey's wife, and I know not how many besides: and well he might, for, if all be true that I have read, he had a licence to lie with whom he list).

Every private history will yield such variety of instances; otherwise good, wise, discreet men, virtuous and valiant, but too faulty in this. Priamus had fifty sons, but seventeen alone lawfully begotten. Philippus Bonus left fourteen bastards. Lorenzo de' Medici, a good prince and a wise, but, saith Machiavel, prodigiously lascivious. None so valiant as Castruccius Castrucanus, but, as the said author hath it, none so incontinent as he was. And 'tis not only predominant in grandees, this fault; but, if you will take a great man's testimony, 'tis familiar with every base soldier in France (and elsewhere, I think). 'This vice (saith mine author) is so common with us in France, that he is of no account, a mere coward, not worthy the name of a soldier, that is not a notorious whoremaster.' In Italy he is not a gentleman that besides his wife hath not a courtesan and mistress. 'Tis no marvel, then, if poor women in such cases be jealous, when they shall see themselves manifestly neglected, contemned, loathed, unkindly used; their disloyal husbands to entertain others in their rooms, and many times to court ladies to their faces; other men's wives to wear their jewels: how shall a poor woman in such a case moderate her passion?

How, on the other side, shall a poor man contain himself from this feral malady, when he shall see so manifest signs of his wife's inconstancy? whenas, like Milo's wife, she dotes upon every young man she sees, or, as Martial's Sota, deserting her husband, following Clitus. Though her husband be proper and tall, fair and lovely to behold, able to give contentment to any one woman, yet she will taste of the forbidden fruit: Juvenal's Iberina to a hair, she is as well pleased with one eye as one man. If a young gallant come by chance into her presence, a Fastidius Brisk [a character in Ben Jonson's *Every Man Out of His Humour*], that can wear his clothes well in fashion, with a lock, jingling spur, a feather, that can cringe, and withal compliment, court a gentlewoman, she raves upon him: O what a lovely proper man he was, another Hector, an Alexander, a goodly man, a demigod, how sweetly he carried himself, with how comely a grace, how neatly he did wear his clothes! how bravely did he discourse, ride, sing, and dance, etc.; and then she begins to loathe her husband's kisses, to hate him and his filthy beard, his goatish complexion, as Doris said of Polyphemus, he is a rammy fulsome fellow, a goblin-faced fellow, he smells, he stinks of onions and garlic, how like a dizzard, a fool, an ass, he looks, how like a clown he behaves himself! she will not come near him by her own good will, but wholly rejects him, as Venus did her fulginous Vulcan at last. So did Lucretia, a lady of Senae, after she had but seen Euryalus, she would not hold her eyes off him in his presence, and in his absence could think of none but him, she loathed her husband forthwith, might not abide him:

> *All against the laws of matrimony,*
> *She did abhor her husband's phis'nomy;*

and sought all opportunity to see her sweetheart again.

Now when the good man shall observe his wife so lightly given to be free and familiar with every gallant, her immodesty and wantonness (as Camerarius notes), it must needs yield matter of suspicion to him, when she still pranks up herself beyond her means and fortunes, makes impertinent journeys, unnecessary visitations, stays out so long, with such and such companions, so frequently goes to plays, masks, feasts, and all public meetings, shall use such immodest gestures, free speeches, and withal show some distaste of her own husband; how can he choose, though he were another Socrates, but be suspicious, and instantly jealous? more especially when he shall take notice of their more secret and sly tricks which to cornute their husbands they commonly use, they pretend love, honour, chastity, and seem to respect them before all men living; saints in show, so cunningly can they dissemble, they will not so much as look upon another man in his presence, so chaste, so religious, and so devout, they cannot endure the name or sight of a quean, an harlot, out upon her! and in their outward carriage are most loving and officious, will kiss their husband, and hang about his neck (dear husband, sweet husband), and with a composed countenance salute him, especially when he comes home; or if he go from home, weep, sigh, lament, and take upon them to be sick and swoon (like Jocundo's wife in Ariosto, when her husband was to depart), and yet arrant, etc., they care not for him:

> *Ay me, the thought (quoth she) makes me so 'fraid,*
> *That scarce the breath abideth in my breast;*
> *Peace, my sweet love and wife, Jocundo said,*
> *And weeps as fast, and comforts her his best, etc.*
> *All this might not assuage the woman's pain,*
> *Needs must I die before you come again,*
> *Nor how to keep my life I can devise,*
> *The doleful days and nights I shall sustain,*
> *From meat my mouth, from sleep will keep mine eyes, etc.*
> *That very night that went before the morrow,*
> *That he had pointed surely to depart,*
> *Jocundo's wife was sick, and swoon'd for sorrow*
> *Amid his arms, so heavy was her heart.*

And yet for all these counterfeit tears and protestations, Jocundo coming back in all haste for a jewel he had forgot,

> *His chaste and faithful yoke-fellow he found*
> *Yoked with a knave, all honesty neglected,*
> *The adulterer sleeping very sound,*
> *Yet by his face was easily detected;*
> *A beggar's brat bred by him from his cradle,*
> *And now was riding on his master's saddle.*

Thus can they cunningly counterfeit, as Platina describes their customs, kiss their husbands, whom they had rather see hanging on a gallows, and swear they love him dearer than their own lives, whose soul they would not ransom for their little dog's.

Many of them seem to be precise and holy forsooth, and will go to such a church, to hear such a good man by all means, an excellent man, when 'tis for no other intent (as he follows it) than to see and to be seen, to observe what fashions are in use, to meet some pander, bawd, monk, friar, or to entice some good fellow. For they persuade themselves, as Nevisanus shows, that it is neither sin nor shame to lie with a lord or a parish priest, if he be a proper man; and though she kneel often, and pray devoutly, 'tis (saith Platina) not for her husband's welfare, or children's good, or any friend, but for her sweetheart's return, her pander's health. If her husband would have her go, she feigns herself sick, her head aches, and she cannot stir; but if her paramour ask as much, she is for him in all seasons, at all hours of the night.

In the kingdom of Malabar, and about Goa in the East Indies, the women are so subtile that, with a certain drink they give them to drive away cares as they say, they will make them sleep for twenty-four hours, or so intoxicate them that they can remember naught of that they saw done or heard, and, by washing of their feet, restore them again, and so make their husbands cuckolds to their faces. Some are ill disposed at all times to all persons they like, others more wary to some few, at such and such seasons, as Augusta Livia carried a passenger only in a full boat. But as he [Ariosto] said:

> *No pen could write, no tongue attain to tell,*
> *By force of eloquence, or help of art,*
> *Of women's treacheries the hundredth part.*

Both, to say truth, are often faulty; men and women give just occasion in this humour of discontent, aggravate and yield matter of suspicion; but most part of the chief causes proceed from other adventitious accidents and circumstances, though the parties be free, and both well given themselves. The undiscreet carriage of some lascivious gallant (or of some light woman) by his often frequenting of an house, bold unseemly gestures, may make a breach, and by his over-familiarity, if he be inclined to yellowness, colour him quite out. If he be poor, basely born, saith Benedetto Varchi, and otherwise unhandsome, he suspects him the less; but if a proper man, such as was Alcibiades in Greece, and Castruccius Castrucanus in Italy, well descended, commendable for his good parts, he taketh on the more, and watcheth his doings. Theodosius the emperor gave his wife Eudocia a golden apple when he was a suitor to her, which she long after bestowed upon a young gallant in the court, of her especial acquaintance. The emperor, espying this apple in his hand, suspected forthwith, more than was, his wife's dishonesty, banished him the court, and from that day following forbare to accompany her any more. A rich merchant had a fair wife; according to his custom he went to travel; in his absence a good fellow tempted his wife; she denied him; yet he, dying a little after, gave her a legacy for the love he bore her. At his return, her jealous husband, because she had got more by land than he had done by sea, turned her away upon suspicion.

Now when those other circumstances of time and place, opportunity and importunity, shall concur, what will they not effect?

> *Fair opportunity can win the coyest she that is,*
> *So wisely he takes time, as he'll be sure he will not miss:*
> *Then he that loves her gamesome vein, and tempers toys with art,*
> *Brings love that swimmeth in her eyes to dive into her heart.*

As at plays, masks, great feasts, and banquets, one singles out his wife to dance, another courts her in his presence, a third tempts her, a fourth insinuates with a pleasing compliment, a sweet smile, ingratiates himself with an amphibological speech as that merry companion in the satirist Juvenal did to his Glycerium, sitting by her and stroking her palm: Take what is in my garden if you'll give me what is in yours; with many such, etc., and then, as Chaucer saith,

> *She may no while in chastity abide,*
> *That is assailed on every side.*

For after a great feast, a woman knows not her own husband. Noah (saith Jerome) showed his nakedness in his drunkenness, which for six hundred years he had covered in soberness. Lot lay with his daughters in his drink, as Cinyras with Myrrha, for what, asks Propertius, scruples has love when flown with wine? The most continent may be overcome, or if otherwise they keep bad company, they that are modest of themselves, and dare not offend, confirmed by others, grow impudent, and confident, and get an ill habit. One, saith Euripides, breaks her marriage vow for gain, another seduces others to have companions in guilt. Or if they dwell in suspected places, as in an infamous inn, near some stews, near monks, friars, Nevisanus adds, where be many tempters and solicitors, idle persons that frequent their companies, it may give just cause of suspicion. Martial of old inveighed against them that counterfeited a disease to go to the baths; for so, many times a chaste Penelope returns a wanton Helen.

Aeneas Sylvius puts in a caveat against princes' courts, because there be so many brave suitors to tempt, etc. If you leave her in such a place you shall likely find her in company you like not; either they come to her or she is gone to them. Kornmannus makes a doubting jest in his lascivious country: Can a girl remain a virgin with so many students about? And Baldus the lawyer scoffs on; when a scholar talks with a maid or another man's wife in private, it is presumed he saith not a paternoster. Or if I shall see a monk or a friar climb up a ladder at midnight into a virgin's or widow's chamber-window, I shall hardly think he then goes to administer the sacraments, or to take her confession. These are the ordinary causes of jealousy, which are intended or remitted as the circumstances vary.

XXII

*Symptoms of Jealousy: Fear, Sorrow,
Suspicion, strange Actions, Gestures, Outrages,
Locking Up, Oaths, Trials, Laws, etc.*

O F ALL PASSIONS, as I have already proved, love is most violent, and of those bitter potions which this love-melancholy affords, this bastard jealousy is the greatest, as appears by those prodigious symptoms which it hath, and that it produceth. For besides fear and sorrow, which is common to all melancholy, anxiety of mind, suspicion, aggravation, restless thoughts, paleness, meagreness, neglect of business, and the like, these men are farther yet misaffected, and in a higher strain. 'Tis a more vehement passion, a more furious perturbation, bitter pain, a fire, a pernicious curiosity, a gall corrupting the honey of our life, madness, vertigo, plague, hell, they are more than ordinarily disquieted, they lose the blessing of peace, as Chrysostom observes; and though they be rich, keep sumptuous tables, be nobly allied, yet they are most miserable, they are more than ordinarily discontent, more sad, more than ordinarily suspicious. Jealousy, saith Vives, begets unquietness in the mind, night and day: he hunts after every word he hears, every whisper, and amplifies it to himself (as all melancholy men do in other matters) with a most unjust calumny of others; he misinterprets everything is said or done, most apt to mistake or misconster, he pries into every corner, follows close, observes to a hair. 'Tis proper to jealousy so to do,

> *Pale hag, infernal fury, pleasure's smart,*
> *Envy's observer, prying in every part.*
>
> (DANIEL)

Besides those strange gestures of staring, frowning, grinning, rolling of eyes, menacing, ghastly looks, broken pace, interrupt, precipitate half-turns. He will sometimes sigh, weep, sob for anger, swear and belie, slander any man, curse, threaten, brawl, scold, fight; and sometimes again flatter and speak fair, ask forgiveness, kiss and coll, condemn his rashness and folly, vow, protest, and swear he will never do so again; and then eftsoons, impatient as he is, rave, roar, and lay about him like a madman, thump her sides, drag her about perchance, drive her out of doors, send her home, he will be divorced forthwith, she is a whore, etc., by and by with all submiss compliment entreat her fair, and bring her in again, he loves her dearly, she is his sweet, most kind and loving wife, he will not change, nor leave her for a kingdom; so he continues off and on, as the toy takes him, the object moves him, but most part brawling, fretting, unquiet he is accusing and suspecting not strangers only, but brothers and sisters, father and mother, nearest and dearest friends, and through fear conceives unto himself things almost incredible and impossible to be effected.

As a heron when she fishes, still prying on all sides, or as a cat doth a mouse, his eye is never off hers; he gloats on him, on her, accurately observing on whom she looks, who looks at her, what she saith, doth, at dinner, at supper, sitting, walking, at home, abroad, he is the same, still inquiring, maundering, gazing, listening, affrighted with every small object; why did she smile, why did she pity him, commend him? why did she drink twice to such a man? why did she offer to kiss, to dance? etc., a whore, a whore, an arrant whore. All this he confesseth in the poet Propertius:

> *Each thing affrights me, I do fear,*
> *Ah pardon me my dear,*
> *I doubt a man is hid within*
> *The clothes that thou dost wear.*

Is't not a man in woman's apparel? is not somebody in that great chest, or behind the door, or hangings, or in some of those barrels? may not a man steal in at the window with a ladder of ropes, or come down the chimney, have a false key, or get in when he is asleep? If a mouse do but stir, or the wind blow, a casement clatter, that's the villain, there he is; by his good will no man shall see her, salute her, speak with her, she shall not go forth of his sight, so much as to do her needs. Argus did not so keep his cow, that watchful dragon the golden fleece, or Cerberus the coming in of hell, as he keeps his wife. If a dear friend or near kinsman come as a guest to his house, to visit him, he will never let him be out of his own sight and company, lest peradventure, etc. If the necessity of his business be such that he must go from home, he doth either lock her up or commit her with a deal of injunctions and protestations to some trusty friends, him and her he sets and bribes to oversee: one servant is set in his absence to watch another, and all to observe his wife, and yet all this will not serve; though his business be very urgent, he will when he is half-way come back again in all post-haste, rise from supper, or at midnight, and be gone, and sometimes leave his business undone, and as a stranger court his own wife in some disguised habit. Though there be no danger at all, no cause of suspicion, she live in such a place where Messalina herself could not be dishonest if she would, yet he suspects her as much as if she were in a bawdy-house, some prince's court, or in a common inn, where all comers might have free access. He calls her on a sudden all to naught, she is a strumpet, a light housewife, a bitch, an arrant whore. No persuasion, no protestation can divert this passion, nothing can ease him, secure or give him satisfaction.

It is most strange to report what outrageous acts by men and women have been committed in this kind, by women especially, that will run after their husbands into all places and companies, as Jovianus Pontanus' wife did by him, follow him whithersoever he went, it matters not, or upon what business, raving like Juno in the tragedy, miscalling, cursing, swearing, and mistrusting everyone she sees. Gomesius in his third book of the life and deeds of Francis Ximenes, sometime Archbishop of Toledo, hath a strange story of that incredible jealousy of Joan Queen of Spain, wife of King Philip, mother of Ferdinand and Charles the Fifth, emperors: when her husband Philip, either for that he was tired with his wife's jealousy or had some great business, went into the Low Countries, she was so impatient and melancholy upon his departure, that she would scarce eat her meat, or converse with any man; and though she were with child, the season of the year very bad, the wind against her, in all haste she would to sea after him. Neither Isabella her queen mother, the archbishop, or any other friend could persuade her to the contrary, but she would after him. When she was now come into the Low Countries, and kindly entertained by her husband, she could not contain herself, but in a rage ran upon a yellow-haired wench, with whom she suspected her husband to be naught, cut off her hair, did beat her black and blue, and so dragged her about. It is an ordinary thing for women in such cases to scratch the faces, slit the noses of such as they suspect; as Henry the Second's importune Juno did by Rosamund at Woodstock: for she complains in a modern poet [Daniel], she scarce spake,

But flies with eager fury to my face,
Offering me most unwomanly disgrace.

> *Look how a tigress, etc.*
> *So fell she on me in outrageous wise,*
> *As could disdain and jealousy devise.*

Or if it be so they dare not or cannot execute any such tyrannical injustice, they will miscall, rail and revile, bear them deadly hate and malice, as Tacitus observes, 'The hatred of a jealous woman as inseparable against such as she suspects.'

> *Winds, weapons, flames make not such hurly-burly,*
> *As raving women turn all topsy-turvy.*

> (SENECA)

So did Agrippina by Lollia, and Calpurnia in the days of Claudius.

But women are sufficiently curbed in such cases; the rage of men is more eminent, and frequently put in practice. See but with what rigour those jealous husbands tyrannize over their poor wives in Greece, Spain, Italy, Turkey, Africa, Asia, and generally over all those hot countries. Mahomet in his Alcoran gives this power to men: your wives are as your land, till them, use them, entreat them fair or foul, as you will yourselves. They lock them still in their houses, which are so many prisons to them, will suffer nobody to come at them, or their wives to be seen abroad. They must not so much as look out. And if they be great persons, they have eunuchs to keep them, as the Grand Seignior among the Turks, the Sophies of Persia, those Tartarian Mogors, and Kings of China. They geld innumerable infants, saith Riccius, to this purpose; the King of China maintains 10,000 eunuchs in his family to keep his wives.

The Xeriffs of Barbary keep their courtesans in such a strict manner, that if any man come but in sight of them he dies for it; and if they chance to see a man, and do not instantly cry out, though from their windows, they must be put to death. The Turks have I know not how many black, deformed eunuchs (for the white serve for other ministries) to this purpose sent commonly from Egypt, deprived in their childhood of all their privities, and brought up in the seraglio at Constantinople to keep their wives; which are so penned up they may not confer with any living man, or converse with younger women, have a cucumber or carrot sent into them for their diet, but sliced, for fear, etc., and so live and are left alone to their unchaste thoughts all the days of their lives. The vulgar sort of women, if at any time they come abroad, which is very seldom, to visit one another or to go to their baths, are so covered that no man can see them, as the matrons were in old Rome, in a litter or chair, so Dion and Seneca record, they go completely veiled, which Alexander ab Alexandro relates of the Parthians, which, with Andreas Tiraquellus his commentator, I rather think should be understood of Persians.

I have not yet said all; they do not only lock them up but lock up their pudenda as well: hear what Bembus relates in his Venetian history of those inhabitants that dwell about Quiloa in Africa. The Lusitanians adjoin certain tribes who at birth sew up their female infants, leaving passage only for urine; when they marry it is for the husband to part the maiden's lower lips. In some parts of Greece at this day, like those old Jews, they will not believe their wives are honest unless on the first night they see blood on the sheets: our countryman Sands in his Peregrinations saith it is severely observed in Zazynthus, or Zante: and Leo Afer in his time at Fez, in Africa, saith they will not believe in virginity without the bloody evidence; the girl is sent back to her parents. Otherwise those sheets are publicly shown by the parents, and kept as a sign of incorrupt virginity. The Jews of old examined their maids for the membrane called hymen, which Laurentius and others copiously confute; 'tis no sufficient trial, they contend. And yet others again defend it, Gaspar Bartholinus,

Pinaeus of Paris, Albertus Magnus, etc., and think they speak too much in favour of women. Ludovicus Boncialus maintains that the natural construction of the labia can be restored by astringents; if deflowered, wise women, he says, can make maids again. The same in Alsarius Crucius Genuensis, Avicenna, Rhasis, etc.

An old bawdy nurse in Aristaenetus (like that Spanish Caelestina), when a fair maid of her acquaintance wept and made her moan to her, how she had been deflowered, and, now ready to be married, was afraid it would be perceived, comfortably replied: 'Fear not, daughter, I'll teach thee a trick to help it.' To what end are all those astrological questions, whether a virgin, chaste, yet a woman? and such strange absurd trials in Albertus Magnus, in Wecker, by stones, perfumes, to make them piss, and confess I know not what in their sleep; some jealous brain was the first founder of them.

And to what passion may we ascribe those severe laws against jealousy (Num. v, 14), adulterers (Deut. xxii, 22), as among the Hebrews, among the Egyptians (read Bohemus, of the Carthaginians, of Turks), among the Athenians of old, Italians at this day, wherein they are to be severely punished, cut in pieces, burned, buried alive, with several expurgations, etc., are they not as so many symptoms of incredible jealousy? We may say the same of those vestal virgins that fetched water in a sieve, as Tatia did in Rome, in the year 800, before senators; and Aemilia, innocent virgin, that ran over hot irons, as Emma, Edward the Confessor's mother, did, the king himself being a spectator, with the like.

We read in Nicephorus, that Cunegunda, the wife of Henricus Bavarus, emperor, suspected of adultery, trod upon red-hot coulters, and had no harm: such another story we find in Regino; in Aventinus and Signonius, of Charles the Third and his wife Richarda, in 887, that was so purged with hot irons. Pausanias saith that he was once an eyewitness of such a miracle at Diana's temple, a maid without any harm at all walked upon burning coals. Pius Secundus, in his description of Europe, relates as much, that it was commonly practised at Diana's temple, for women to go barefoot over hot coals, to try their honesties; Plinius, Solinus, and many writers make mention of Feronia's temple, and Dioysius Halicarnasseus, of Memnon's statue, which were used to this purpose, Tatius, of Pan his cave (much like old St Wilfrid's needle in Yorkshire), wherein they did use to try maids, whether they were honest; when Leucippe went in a sweet sound was heard.

St Augustine relates many such examples, all which Lavater contends to be done by the illusion of devils; though Thomas ascribes it to good angels. Some, saith Austin, compel their wives to swear they be honest, as if perjury were a lesser sin than adultery; some consult oracles, as Pheron, that blind king of Egypt. Others reward, as those old Romans used to do; if a woman were contented with one man, she had a crown of chastity bestowed on her. When all this will not serve, saith Alexander Gaguinus, the Muscovites, if they suspect their wives, will beat them till they confess, and if that will not avail, like those wild Irish, be divorced at their pleasures, or else knock them on the heads, as the old Gauls have done in former ages.

XXIII

Prognostics of Jealousy, Despair, Madness,
to make away themselves and others.

THOSE WHICH ARE jealous, most part, if they be not otherwise relieved, proceed from suspicion to hatred, from hatred to frenzy, madness, injury, murder, and despair.

> *A plague by whose most damnable effect,*
> *Divers in deep despair to die have sought.*
> *By which a man to madness near is brought,*
> *As well with causeless as with just suspect.*
>
> (ARIOSTO)

In their madness many times, saith Vives, they make away themselves and others. Which induceth Cyprian to call it a fruitful mischief, the seminary of offences, and fountain of murders. Tragical examples are too common in this kind, both new and old, in all ages, as of Cephalus and Procris, Pheron of Egypt, Tereus, Atreus, and Thyestes. Alexander Pheraeus was murdered of his wife, on suspicion, Tully saith. Antoninus Verus was so made away by Lucilla; Demetrius the son of Antigonus, and Nicanor, by their wives; Hercules poisoned by Deianira, Caecinna murdered by Vespasian, Justina, a Roman lady, by her husband. Amestris, Xerxes' wife, because she found her husband's cloak in Masista his house, cut off Masista his wife's paps, and gave them to the dogs, flayed her besides, and cut off her ears, lips, tongue, and slit the nose of Artaynta her daughter. Our late writers are full of such outrages.

Paulus Aemilius, in his History of France, hath a tragical story of Chilpericus the First his death, made away by Fredegunde his queen. In a jealous humour he came from hunting, and stole behind his wife, as she was dressing and coming her head in the sun, gave her a familar touch with his wand, which she mistaking for her lover, said, 'Ah, Landre, a good knight should strike before, and not behind'; but when she saw herself betrayed by his presence, she instantly took order to make him away. Hierome Osorius, in the eleventh book of the deeds of Emanuel, King of Portugal, to this effect hath a tragical narration of one Ferdinandus Calderia, that wounded Gotherinus, a noble countryman of his, at Goa in the East Indies, and cut off one of his legs, for that he looked, as he thought, too familiarly upon his wife, which was afterwards a cause of many quarrels and much bloodshed. Guianerius speaks of a silly jealous fellow, that seeing his child new-born included in a kell [caul], thought sure a Franciscan that used to come to his house was the father of it, it was so like the friar's cowl, and thereupon threatened the friar to kill him: Fulgosus, of a woman in Narbonne, that cut off her husband's privities in the night, because she thought he played false with her. The story of Jonuses Bassa, and fair Manto his wife, is well known to such as have read the Turkish History; and that of Joan of Spain, of which I treated in my former section. Her jealousy, saith Gomesius, was the cause of both their deaths: King Philip died for grief a little after, as Martian his physician gave it out, and she for her part after a melancholy discontented life, mis-spent in lurking-holes and corners, made an end of her miseries.

Felix Plater, in the first book of his Observations, hath many such instances, of a physician of his acquaintance, that was first mad through jealousy, and afterwards desperate; of a merchant that killed his wife in the same humour, and after precipitated himself; of a doctor of law that cut off his man's nose; of a painter's wife in Basil, in the year 1600, that was mother of nine children and had been twenty-seven years married, yet afterwards jealous, and so impatient that she became desperate, and would neither eat or drink in her own house, for fear her husband should poison her. 'Tis a common sign this; for when once the humours are stirred, and the imagination misaffected, it will vary itself in divers forms; and many such absurd symptoms will accompany, even madness itself. Sckenkius hath an example of a jealous woman that by this means had many fits of the mother; and in his first book of some that through jealousy ran mad: of a baker that gelded himself to try his wife's honesty, etc. Such examples are too common.

XXIV

*Cure of Jealousy: by avoiding Occasions, not
to be Idle; by Good Counsel; to contemn it, not
to watch or lock them up; to dissemble it, etc.*

As of all other melancholy, some doubt whether this malady may be cured or no, they think 'tis like the gout, or Switzers, whom we commonly call Walloons, those hired soldiers, if once they take possession of a castle they can never be got out.

> *This is the cruel wound, against whose smart,*
> *No liquor's force prevails, or any plaster,*
> *No skill of stars, no depth of magic art,*
> *Devised by that great clerk Zoroaster;*
> *A wound that so infects the soul and heart,*
> *As all our sense and reason it doth master;*
> *A wound whose pang and torment is so durable,*
> *As it may rightly called be incurable.*

(ARIOSTO)

Yet what I have formerly said of other melancholy, I will say again, it may be cured, or mitigated at least, by some contrary passion, good counsel and persuasion, if it be withstood in the beginning, maturely resisted, and as those ancients hold, the nails of it be pared before they grow too long. No better means to resist or repel it than by avoiding idleness, to be still seriously busied about some matters of importance, to drive out those vain fears, foolish fantasies, and irksome suspicions out of his head, and then to be persuaded by his judicious friends to give ear to their good counsel and advice, and wisely to consider how much he discredits himself, his friends, dishonours his children, disgraceth his family, publisheth his shame, and, as a trumpeter of his own misery, divulgeth, macerates, grieves himself and others; what an argument of weakness it is, how absurd a thing in its own nature, how ridiculous, how brutish a passion, how sottish, how odious; for as Jerome well hath it, others hate him, and at last he hates himself for it; how hare-brain a disease, mad and furious. If he will but hear them speak, no doubt he may be cured.

Joan, Queen of Spain, of whom I have formerly spoken, under pretence of changing air was sent to Complutum, or Alcala de las Henares, where Ximenes the Archbishop of Toledo then lived, that by his good counsel (as for the present she was) she might be eased. For a disease of the soul, if concealed, tortures and overturns it, and by no physic can sooner be removed than by a discreet man's comfortable speeches. I will not here insert any consolatory sentences to this purpose, or forestall any man's invention, but leave it everyone to dilate and amplify as he shall think fit in his own judgement: let him advise with Siracides [Ecclus. ix, 1]: 'Be not jealous over the wife of thy bosom'; read that comfortable and pithy speech to this purpose of Ximenes, in the author himself, as it is recorded by Gomesius; consult with Chaloner or Caelia in her Epistles, etc.

Only this I will add, that if it be considered aright, which causeth this jealous passion, be it just or unjust, whether with or without cause, true or false, it ought not so heinously to be taken; 'tis no such real or capital matter, that it should make so deep a wound. 'Tis a blow that hurts not, an insensible smart, grounded many times upon false suspicion alone, and so fostered by a sinister conceit. If she be not dishonest, he troubles and macerates himself without a cause; or put case, which is the worst, he be a cuckold, it cannot be helped, the more he stirs in it, the more he aggravates his own misery. How much better were it in such a case to dissemble or contemn it! why should that be feared which cannot be redressed? Many women, saith Vives, when they see there is no remedy, have been pacified; and shall men be more jealous than women?

'Tis some comfort in such a case to have companions. Who can say he is free? Who can assure himself he is not one in the past, or secure himself for the future? If it were his case alone, it were hard; but being as it is almost a common calamity, 'tis not so grievously to be taken. If a man have a lock which every man's key will open as well as his own, why should he think to keep it private to himself? In some countries they make nothing of it, saith Leo Afer, in many parts of Africa (if she be past fourteen) there's not a nobleman that marries a maid, or that hath a chaste wife; 'tis so common; as the moon gives horns once a month to the world, do they to their husbands at least. And 'tis most part true which that Caledonian lady, Argentcoxus a British prince his wife, told Julia Augusta, which she took her up for dishonesty: 'We Britons are naught at least with some few choice men of the better sort, but you Romans lie with every base knave, you are a company of common whores.' Severus the emperor in his time made laws for the restraint of this vice; and as Dion Nicaeus relates in his life, three thousand cuckold-makers, or as Philo calls them, false coiners, and clippers of nature's money, were summoned into the court at once. And yet, the miller sees not all the water that goes by his mill; no doubt but, as in our days, these were of the commonalty, all the great ones were not so much as called in question for it.

Martial's epigram, I suppose, might have been generally applied in those licentious times: thy goods, lands, money, wits are thine own, but, neighbour Candidus, your wife is common. Husband and cuckold in that age, it seems, were reciprocal terms; the emperors themselves did wear Actaeon's badge; how many Caesars might I reckon up together, and what a catalogue of cornuted kings and princes in every story! Agamemnon, Menelaus, Philippus of Greece, Ptolemaeus of Aegypt, Lucullus, Caesar, Pompeius, Cato, Augustus, Antonius, Antoninus, etc., that wore fair plumes of bull's feathers in their crests. The bravest soldiers and most heroical spirits could not avoid it. They have been active and passive in this business, they have either given or taken horns. King Arthur, whom we call one of the Nine Worthies, for all his great valour, was unworthily served by Mordred, one of his Round-Table knights: and Guithera, or Helena Alba, his fair wife, as Leland interprets it, was an arrant honest woman. I could willingly wink, saith mine author, at a fair lady's faults, but that I am bound by the laws of history to tell the truth: against his will, God knows, did he write it, and so do I repeat it.

I speak not of our times all this while; we have good, honest, virtuous men and women, whom fame, zeal, fear of God, religion, and superstition contains: and yet for all that, we have many knights of this order, so dubbed by their wives, many good women abused by dissolute husbands. In some places, and such persons, you may as soon enjoin them to carry water in a sieve as to keep themselves honest. What shall a man do now in such a case? What remedy is to be had? how shall he be eased? By suing a divorce? this is hard to be effected: they carry the matter so cunningly, that though it be as common as simony, as clear and as manifest as the nose in a man's face, yet it cannot be evidently proved, or they likely taken in the fact: they will have a knave Gallus to watch, or with that Roman Sulpicia, all made fast and sure, 'Lest he should see her lying naked with Calenus.' She will hardly be surprised by her husband, be he never so wary.

Much better then to put it up; the more he strives in it, the more he shall divulge his own shame; make a virtue of necessity, and conceal it. Yea, but the world takes notice of it, 'tis in every man's mouth: let them talk their pleasure, of whom speak they not in this sense? From the highest to the lowest they are thus censured all; there is no remedy then but patience. It may be 'tis his own fault, and he hath no reason to complain, 'tis quid pro quo, she is bad, he is worse. Bethink thyself, hast thou not done as much for some of thy neighbours? why dost thou require that of thy wife, which thou wilt not perform thyself? Thou rangest like a town bull, why are thou so incensed if she tread awry?

> *Be it that some woman break chaste wedlock's laws,*
> *And leaves her husband and becomes unchaste:*
> *Yet commonly it is not without cause,*
> *She sees her man in sin her goods to waste,*
> *She feels that he his love from her withdraws,*
> *And hath on some perhaps less worthy placed,*
> *Who strike with sword, the scabbard them may strike,*
> *And sure love craveth love, like asketh like.*
>
> (ARIOSTO)

She will study, saith Nevisanus, to have her own back; she will quit if she can. And therefore, as well adviseth Siracides [Ecclus. ix, 1], 'teach her not an evil lesson against thyself', which, as Jansenius, Lyranus, on this text, and Carthusianus interpret, is no otherwise to be understood than that she do thee not a mischief. I do not excuse her in accusing thee; but if both be naught, mend thyself first; for as the old saying is, a good husband makes a good wife.

Yea, but, thou repliest, 'tis not the like reason betwixt man and woman, through her fault my children are bastards, I may not endure it; let her scold, brawl, and spend, I care not, so she be honest, I could easily bear it; but this I cannot, I may not, I will not; my faith, my fame, mine eye must not be touched, as the diverb is, I say the same of my wife, touch all, use all, take all but this. I acknowledge that of Seneca to be true, there is no sweet content in the possession of any good thing without a companion, this only excepted, I say, *this*. And why this? Even this which thou so much abhorrest, it may be for thy progeny's good, better be any man's son than thine, to be begot of base Irus, poor Seius, or mean Maevius, the town's swineherd's, a shepherd's son: and well is he, that like Hercules he hath any two fathers; for thou thyself hast peradventure more diseases than an horse, more infirmities of body and mind, a cankered soul, crabbed conditions; make the worst of it, as it is incurable, so it is insensible. But art thou sure it is so? does he do thy business for thee? doth he so indeed?

It may be thou art over-suspicious, and without a cause as some are: if it be born at eight months, or like him, and him, they fondly suspect he got it; if she speak or laugh familiarly with such or such men, then presently she is naught with them; such is thy weakness: whereas charity, or a well-disposed mind, would interpret all unto the best. St Francis, by chance seeing a friar familiarly kissing another man's wife, was so far from misconceiving it, that he presently kneeled down and thanked God there was so much charity left; but they, on the other side, will ascribe nothing to natural causes, indulge nothing to familiarity, mutual society, friendship; but out of a sinister suspicion, presently lock them close, watch them, thinking by those means to prevent all such inconveniences, that's the way to help it; whereas by such tricks they do aggravate the mischief. 'Tis but in vain to watch that which will away.

> *None can be kept resisting for her part;*
> *Though body be kept close, within her heart*
> *Advoutry lurks, t'exclude it there's no art.*

(OVID)

Argus with an hundred eyes cannot keep her, even he was deceived, and by love alone, as in Ariosto:

> *If all our hearts were eyes, yet sure, they said,*
> *We husbands of our wives should be betrayed.*

Jerome holds, to what end is all your custody? A dishonest woman cannot be kept, an honest woman ought not to be kept, necessity is a keeper not to be trusted. That which many covet can hardly be preserved, as Sarisburiensis thinks. I am of Aeneas Sylvius' mind; those jealous Italians do very ill to lock up their wives; for women are of such a disposition, they will most covet that which is denied most, and offend least when they have free liberty to trespass. It is in vain to lock her up if she be dishonest; as our great master Aristotle calls it, too tyrannical a task, most unfit; for when she perceives her husband observes her and suspects, she sins more freely, saith Nevisanus. The adulterous wife poisoned her jealous husband; she is exasperated, seeks by all means to vindicate herself, and will therefore offend, because she is unjustly suspected. The best course then is to let them have their own wills, give them free liberty, without any keeping.

> *In vain our friends from this do us dehort,*
> *For beauty will be where is most resort.*
>
> (DANIEL)

If she be honest as Lucretia to Collatinus, Laodamia to Protesilaus, Penelope to her Ulysses, she will so continue her honour, good name, credit; and as Phocias' wife in Plutarch, called her husband her wealth, treasure, world, joy, delight, orb, and sphere, she will hers. The vow she made unto her goodman, love, virtue, religion, zeal, are better keepers than all those locks, eunuchs, prisons; she will not be moved:

> *First I desire the earth to swallow me,*
> *Before I violate mine honesty,*
> *Or thunder from above drive me to hell,*
> *With those pale ghosts and ugly night to dwell.*
>
> (VIRGIL)

She is resolved with Dido to be chaste; though her husband be false, she will be true; and as Octavia writ to her Antony:

> *These walls that here do keep me out of sight,*
> *Shall keep me all unspotted unto thee,*
> *And testify that I will do thee right,*
> *I'll never stain thine house, though thou shame me.*
>
> (DANIEL)

Turn her loose to all those Tarquins and satyrs, she will not be tempted.

In the time of Valence, the emperor, saith St Augustine, one Archidamus, a consul of Antioch, offered an hundred pounds of gold to a fair young wife, and besides to set her husband free, who was then a dark prisoner, for one night with her; but the chaste matron would not accept of it. When one commended Theano's fine arm to his fellows, she took him up short: Sir, 'tis not common; she is wholly reserved to her husband. Bilia had an old man to her spouse, and his breath stunk, so that nobody could abide it abroad; coming home one day he reprehended his wife, because she did not tell him of it: she vowed unto him, she had told him, but she thought every man's breath had been as strong as his. Tigranes and Armenia his lady were invited to supper by King Cyrus: when they came home Tigranes asked his wife how she liked Cyrus, and what she did especially commend in him; she swore she did not observe him; when he replied again, what then she did observe, whom she looked on, she made an answer, her husband that said he would die for her sake.

Such are the properties and conditions of good women; and if she be well given, she will so carry herself; if otherwise she be naught, use all the means thou canst, she will be naught. Not the will but the lover is lacking, she hath so many lies, excuses, as an hare hath muses, tricks, panders, bawds, shifts to deceive, 'tis to no purpose to keep her up, or to reclaim her by hard usage. Fair means peradventure may do somewhat. Men and women are both in a predicament in this behalf, so sooner won, and better pacified: led, not forced. Though she be as arrant a scold as Xantippe, as cruel as Medea, as clamorous as Hecuba, as lustful as Messalina, by such means (if at all) she may be reformed. Many patient Grizels, by their obsequiousness in this kind, have reclaimed their husbands from their wandering lusts. In Nova Francia and Turkey (as Leah, Rachel, and Sarah did to Abraham and Jacob) they bring their fairest damsels to their husbands' beds; Livia seconded the lustful appetites of Augustus; Stratonice, wife to King Deiotarus, did not only bring Electra, a fair maid, to her goodman's bed, but brought up the children begot on her as carefully as if they had been her own. Tertius Aemilius' wife, Cornelia's mother, perceiving her husband's intemperance, dissimulated and made much of the maid, and would take no notice of it. A new-married man, when a pickthank friend of his, to curry favour, had showed him his wife familiar in private with a young gallant, courting and dallying, etc., 'Tush,' said he, 'let him do his worst, I dare trust my wife, though I dare not trust him.'

The best remedy then is by fair means; if that will not take place, to dissemble it as I say, or turn it off with a jest: for if you take exceptions at everything your wife doth, Solomon's wisdom, Hercules' valour, Homer's learning, Socrates' patience, Argus' vigilancy will not serve turn. Therefore a less mischief, Nevisanus holds, to dissemble, to be a buyer of cradles, as the proverb is, than to be too solicitous. A good fellow, when his wife was brought to bed before her time, bought half a dozen cradles beforehand for so many children, as if his wife should continue to bear children every two months. Pertinax the emperor, when one told him a fiddler was too familiar with his empress, made no reckoning of it. And when that Macedonian Philip was upbraided with his wife's dishonesty, a conqueror of kingdoms could not tame his wife (for she thrust him out of doors), he made a jest of it.

Wise men, saith Nevisanus, bear their horns in their hearts, fools on their foreheads. Eumenes, King of Pergamus, was at deadly feud with Perseus of Macedonia, insomuch that Perseus, hearing of a journey he was to take to Delphi, set a company of soldiers to intercept him in his passage; they did it accordingly, and as they supposed, left him stoned to death. The news of this fact was brought instantly to Pergamus; Attalus, Eumenes' brother, proclaimed himself king forthwith, took possession of the crown, and married Stratonice the queen. But by and by, when contrary news was brought, that King Eumenes was alive and now coming to the city, he laid by his crown, left his wife, as a private man went to meet him and congratulate his return. Eumenes, though he knew all particulars passed, yet dissembling the matter, kindly embraced his brother, and took his wife into his favour again, as if no such matter had been heard of or done. Jocundo, in Ariosto, found his wife in bed with a knave, both asleep, went his ways, and would not so much as wake them, much less reprove them for it. An honest fellow, finding in like sort his wife had played false at tables, and borne a man too many, drew his dagger, and swore if he had not been his very friend, he would have killed him. Another hearing one had done that for him which no man desires to be done by a deputy, followed in a rage with his sword drawn, and having overtaken him, laid adultery to his charge; the offender, hotly pursued, confessed it was true; with which confession he was satisfied, and so left him, swearing that if he had denied it he would not have put it up.

How much better is it to do thus than to macerate himself, impatiently to rave and rage, to enter an action (as Arnoldus Tilius did in the court of Toulouse against Martin Guerre his fellow-soldier, for that he counterfeited his habit and was too familiar with his wife), so to divulge his own shame, and to remain for ever a cuckold on record! How much better be Cornelius Tacitus than Publius Cornutus, to contemn in such cases, or take no notice of it! Better be a wittol and put it up, than to trouble himself to no purpose. And though he will not sleep for everyone, be an ass, as he is an ox, yet to wink at it as many do is not amiss at some times, in some cases, to some parties, if it be for his commodity, or some great man's sake, his landlord, patron, benefactor (as Galba the Roman, saith Plutarch, did by Maecenas, and Phayllus of Argos did by King Philip, when he promised him an office on that condition he might lie with his wife), and so let it pass. It never troubles me (said Amphitruo) to be cornuted by Jupiter; let it not molest thee then; be friends with her; let it, I say, make no breach of love between you. Howsoever, the best way is to contemn it, which Henry II, King of France, advised a courtier of his, jealous of his wife and complaining of her unchasteness, to reject it, and comfort himself; for he that suspects his wife's incontinency, and fears the Pope's curse, shall never live a merry hour or sleep a quiet night; no remedy but patience.

When all is done, according to that counsel of Nevisanus, if it may not be helped, it must be endured. Forgive and forget, 'tis Sophocles' advice, keep it to thyself, and (which Chrysostom calls a school of philosophy), put it up. There is no other cure but time to wear it out, as if they had drunk a draught of Lethe in Trophonius' den. To conclude, age will bereave her of it, time and patience must end it.

> *The mind's affections patience will appease,*
> *It passion kills, and healeth each disease.*

(TOFTE)

XXV

By prevention before or after marriage,
Plato's Community, marry a Courtesan,
Philters, Stews, to marry one equal in
years, fortunes, of a good family, education,
good place, to use them well, etc.

O F SUCH MEDICINES as conduce to the cure of this malady I
have sufficiently treated; there be some good remedies remaining,
by way of prevention, precautions, or admonitions, which, if
rightly practised, may do much good. Plato, in his Commonwealth,
to prevent this mischief belike, would have all things common, wives
and children, all as one: and which Caesar in his Commentaries
observed of those old Britons that first inhabited this land, they had
ten or twelve wives allotted to such a family, or promiscuously to be
used by so many men; not one to one, as with us, or four, five, or
six to one, as in Turkey. The Nicholaites, a sect that sprung, saith St
Augustine, from Nicholas the Deacon, would have women indifferent;
and the cause of this filthy sect was Nicholas the Deacon's jealousy,
for which when he was condemned, to purge himself of his offence
he broached his heresy that it was lawful to lie with one another's
wives, and for any man to lie with his: like to those Anabaptists in
Munster, that would consort with other men's wives as the spirit
moved them: or as Mahomet, the seducing prophet, would needs
use women as he list himself, to beget prophets; two hundred and
five, their Alcoran saith, were in love with him, and he was able as
forty men.

Among the old Carthaginians, as Bohemus relates out of Sabellicus, the king of the country lay with the bride the first night, and once in a year they went promiscuously all together. Munster ascribes the beginning of this brutish custom (unjustly) to one Picardus, a Frenchman, that invented a new sect of Adamites, to go naked as Adam did, and to use promiscuous venery at set times. When the priest repeated that of Genesis, 'Increase and multiply', out went the candles in the place where they met, and without all respect of age, persons, conditions, catch that catch may, every man took her that came next, etc. Some fasten this on those ancient Bohemians and Russians: others on the inhabitants of Mambrium, in the Lucerne valley in Piedmont; and, as I read, it was practised in Scotland among Christians themselves until King Malcolm's time, the king or the lord of the town had their maidenheads.

In some parts of India in our age, and those Icelanders, as among the Babylonians of old, they will prostitute their wives and daughters (which Chalcocondylas, a Greek modern writer, for want of better intelligence, puts upon us Britons) to such travellers or seafaring men as come among them by chance, to show how far they were from this feral vice of jealousy, and how little they esteemed it. The kings of Calicut, as Lod. Vertomannus relates, will not touch their wives till one of their Biarmi or high priests have lain first with them, to sanctify their wombs. But those Essenes and Montanists, two strange sects of old, were in another extreme, they would not marry at all, or have any society with women, because of their intemperance, they held them all to be naught. Nevisanus the lawyer would have him that is inclined to this malady, to prevent the worst, marry a quean; the advantage is so that at least he is not deceived, he knows what she is; which cannot be said of others.

A fornicator in Seneca constuprated two wenches in a night; for satisfaction, the one desired to hang him, the other to marry him.

Hieronymus, King of Syracuse in Sicily, espoused himself to Peitho, keeper of the stews; and Ptolemy took Thais, a common whore, to be his wife, had two sons, Leontiscus and Lagus, by her, and one daughter Irene: 'tis therefore no such unlikely thing. A citizen of Eugubine gelded himself to try his wife's honesty, and to be freed from jealousy; so did a baker in Basil, to the same intent.

But of all other precedents in this kind, that of Combabus is most memorable; who to prevent his master's suspicion, for he was a beautiful young man, and sent by Seleucus his lord and king, with Stratonice the queen to conduct her into Syria, fearing the worst, gelded himself before he went, and left his genitals behind him in a box sealed up. His mistress by the way fell in love with him, but he, not yielding to her, was accused to Seleucus of incontinency (as that Bellerophon was in like case falsely traduced by Sthenoboea) to King Proetus her husband, when he would not go to bed with her, and that by her, and was therefore at his coming home cast into prison: the day of hearing appointed, he was sufficiently cleared and acquitted, by showing his privities, which to the admiration of the beholders he had formerly cut off. The Lydians used to geld women whom they suspected, saith Leonicus, as well as men. To this purpose Saint Francis, because he used to confess women in private, to prevent suspicion, and prove himself a maid, stripped himself before the Bishop of Assisi and others: and Friar Leonard for the same cause went through Viterbio in Italy without any garments.

Our pseudo-Catholics, to help these inconveniences which proceed from jealousy, to keep themselves and their wives honest, make severe laws: against adultery, present death; and withal fornication, a venial sin, as a sink to convey that furious and swift stream of concupiscence, they appoint and permit stews, those punks and pleasant sinners, the more to secure their wives in all populous cities, for they hold them as necessary as churches; and howsoever unlawful, yet to avoid a greater mischief to be tolerated in policy, as usury, for the hardness of men's hearts; and for this end they have whole colleges of courtesans in their towns and cities. Of Cato's mind, belike, that would have his servants familiar with some such feminine creatures, to avoid worse mischiefs in his house, and made allowance for it. They hold it unpossible for idle persons, young, rich, and lusty, so many servants, monks, friars, to live honest, too tyrannical a burden to compel them to be chaste, and most unfit to suffer poor men, younger brothers, and soldiers at all to marry, as those diseased persons, votaries, priests, servants. Therefore, as well to keep and ease the one as the other, they tolerate and wink at these kind of brothel-houses and stews.

Many probable arguments they have to prove the lawfulness, the necessity, and a toleration of them, as of usury; and without question in policy they are not to be contradicted: but altogether in religion. Others prescribe philters, spells, charms to keep men and women honest. That a woman may not admit any but her husband, take a goat's gallbladder, dry it, boil it in oil, and she will love none other. In Aexis, Porta, etc., many and more absurd than this; also in Rhasis, to prevent admittance of other than husband and make her love only him, etc. But these are most part pagan, impious, irreligious, and ridiculous devices.

The best means to avoid these and like inconveniences are to take away the cause and occasions. To this purpose Varro writ Satiram Menippeam, but it is lost. Patricius prescribes four rules to be observed in choosing of a wife (which whoso will may read); Fonseca the Spaniard sets down six special cautions for men, four for women; Neander, out of Schonbernerus, five for men, five for women; Anthony Guevara many good lessons; Cleobulus two alone, others otherwise; as first to make a good choice in marriage, to invite Christ to their wedding, and which St Ambrose adviseth, and to pray to Him for her; a prudent wife is the gift of God, Prov. xix, not to be too rash and precipitate in his election, to run upon the first he meets, or dote on every snowt-fair piece he sees, but to choose her as much by his ears as eyes, to be well advised whom he takes, of what age, etc., and cautelous in his proceedings. An old man should not marry a young woman, nor a young woman an old man: such matches must needs minister a perpetual cause of suspicion, and be distasteful to each other.

> *Night-crows on tombs, owl sits on carcass dead,*
> *So lies a wench with Sophocles in bed.*
>
> (ALCIATE)

For Sophocles, as Athenaeus describes him, was a very old man, as cold as January, a bed-fellow of bones, and doted yet upon Archippe, a young courtesan, than which nothing can be more odious. An old man is a most unwelcome guest to a young wench, unable, unfit: 'Maidens shun their embraces; Love, Venus, and Hymen all abhor them' [Portanus]. And as in like case a good fellow that had but a peck of corn weekly to grind, yet would needs build a new mill for it, found his error eftsoons, for either he must let his mill lie waste, pull it quite down, or let others grind at it: so these men, etc.

Seneca therefore disallows all such unseasonable matches. And as Tully farther inveighs, 'tis unfit for any, but ugly and filthy in old age. In the old love is unseemly, one of the three things God hateth. Plutarch rails downright at such kind of marriages, which are attempted by old men, who, being impotent and past pleasure, sin only in their minds, and makes a question whether in some cases it be tolerable at least for such a man to marry, that is now past those venerous exercises, 'as a gelded man lies with a virgin and sighs' (Ecclus, xxx, 20), and now complains with him in Petronius, that is dead and buried which was once, he is quite done, though once an Achilles in the field of love. But the question is whether he may delight himself as those priapeian Popes, which, in their decrepit age, lay commonly between two wenches every night, fondling their beauties; and as many doting sires do to their own shame, their children's undoing, and their families' confusion: he abhors it, it must be avoided as a bedlam-master, and not obeyed. 'Alecto herself holds the torch at the nuptials, and Hymen makes wail'; the devil himself makes such matches.

Levinus Lemnius reckons up three things which generally disturb the peace of marriage: the first is when they marry intempestive or unseasonably, as many mortal men marry precipitately and inconsiderately when they are effete and old; the second, when they marry unequally for fortunes and birth; the third, when a sick impotent person weds one that is sound; many dislikes instantly follow. Many doting dizzards, it may not be denied, as Plutarch confesseth, recreate themselves with such obsolete, unseasonable, and filthy remedies (so he calls them), with a remembrance of their former pleasures; against nature they stir up their dead flesh; but an old lecher is abominable; a woman that marries a third time, Nevisanus holds, may be presumed to be no honester than she should. Of them both, thus Ambrose concludes in his Comment upon Luke: They that are coupled together, not to get children, but to satisfy their lust, are not husbands, but fornicators; with whom St Augustine consents: matrimony without hope of children is not a wedding but a jumbling or coupling together. In a word, except they wed for mutual society, help and comfort one of another, in which respects, though Tiberius deny it, without question old folks may well marry; for sometimes a man hath most need of a wife, according to Puccius, when he hath no need of a wife; otherwise it is most odious, when an old Acherontic dizzard, that hath one foot in the grave, shall flicker after a young wench that is blithe and bonny, lustful as a sparrow in spring or snow-white dove. What can be more detestable?

> *Thou old goat, hoary lecher, naughty man,*
> *With stinking breath, art thou in love?*
> *Must thou be slavering? she spews to see*
> *Thy filthy face, it doth so move.*
>
> (PLAUTUS)

Yet, as some will, it is much more tolerable for an old man to marry a young woman (Our Lady's match they call it), for she will be a woman tomorrow, as he said in Tully. Cato the Roman, Critobulus in Xenophon, Traquellus of late, Julius Scaliger, etc., and many famous precedents we have in that kind; but not to the contrary; 'tis not held fit for an ancient woman to match with a young man. For as Varro will, when an old woman disports herself she makes Death merry, 'tis Charon's match between Cascus and Casca, and the devil himself is surely well pleased with it. And therefore, as Martial inveighs, thou old Vetustilla, bed-ridden quean, that art now skin and bones,

> *That hast three hairs, four teeth, a breast*
> *Like grasshopper, an emmet's crest,*
> *A skin more rugged than thy coat,*
> *And dugs like spider's web to boot.*

Must thou marry a youth again? And yet they want to marry again though they have buried a hundred husbands: howsoever it is, as Apuleius gives out of his Meroe, a pestilent match, abominable, and not to be endured. In such case how can they otherwise choose but be jealous? how should they agree one with another? This inequality is not in years only, but in birth, fortunes, conditions, and all good qualities: If you would marry fitly, wed your equal [Ovid], 'Tis my counsel, saith Anthony Guevara, let a citizen match with a citizen, a gentleman with a gentlewoman; he that observes not this precept (saith he) instead of a fair wife shall have a fury, for a fit son-in-law a mere fiend, etc. Examples are too frequent.

Another main caution fit to be observed is this, that though they be equal in years, birth, fortunes, and other conditions, yet they do not omit virtue and good education, which Musonius and Antipater so much inculcate in Stobaeus. If, as Plutarch adviseth, one must eat a bushel of salt with him before he choose a friend, what care should be had in choosing a wife, his second self, how solicitous should he be to know her qualities and behaviour! and when he is assured of them, not to prefer birth, fortune, beauty, before bringing up, and good conditions. Cocuage, god of cuckolds, as one [Rabelais] merrily said, accompanies the goddess Jealousy, both follow the fairest, by Jupiter's appointment, and they sacrifice them together: beauty and honesty seldom agree; straight personages have often crooked manners; fair faces, foul vices; good complexions, ill conditions.

Beauty (saith Chrysostom) is full of treachery and suspicion: he that hath a fair wife cannot have a worse mischief and yet most covet it, as if nothing else in marriage but that and wealth were to be respected. Francis Sforza, Duke of Milan, was so curious in this behalf that he would not marry the Duke of Mantua's daughter, except he might see her naked first: which Lycurgus appointed in his laws, and Morus [Thomas More] in his Utopian commonwealth approves. In Italy, as a traveller observes, if a man have three or four daughters, or more, and they prove fair, they are married eftsoons: if deformed, they change their lovely names of Lucia, Cynthia, Camaena, call them Dorothy, Ursula, Bridget, and so put them into monasteries, as if none were fit for marriage, but such as are eminently fair; but these are erroneous tenents: a modest virgin, well conditioned, to such a fair snot piece is much to be preferred.

If thou wilt avoid them, take away all causes of suspicion and jealousy, marry a coarse piece, fetch her from Cassandra's temple, which was wont in Italy to be a sanctuary of all deformed maids, and so thou shalt be sure that no man will make thee cuckold, but for spite. A citizen of Byzance in Thrace had a filthy, dowdy, deformed slut to his wife, and finding her in bed with another man, cried out as one amazed: 'O thou wretch, what necessity brought thee hither?' as well he might; for who can affect such a one? But this is warily to be understood, most offend in another extreme, they prefer wealth before beauty, and so she be rich, they care not how she look; but these are all out as faulty as the rest. Regard your wife, Sarisburiensis adviseth, lest some other woman make you despise her, as the knight in Chaucer that was married to an old woman,

> *And all day after hid him as an owl,*
> *So woe was him and his wife looked so foul.*

Have a care of thy wife's complexion, lest while thou seest another, thou loathest her, she prove jealous, thou naught: 'If your wife be ugly, your maid beautiful, abstain from the maid.'

I can perhaps give instance. It is a misery to possess that which no man likes: on the other side, it is difficult to guard what many covet. And as the bragging soldier vaunted in the comedy, it is a misery to be so handsome. Scipio did never so hardly besiege Carthage as these young gallants will beset thine house, one with wit or person, another with wealth, etc. If she be fair, saith Guazzo, she will be suspected howsoever. Both extremes are naught, the one is soon beloved, the other loves; one is hardly kept, because proud and arrogant, the other not worth keeping; what is to be done in this case? Ennius adviseth thee as a friend to take one of a middle size, neither too fair nor too foul: with old Cato, though fit, let her beauty be not too elegant, nor without charm, between both. This I approve; but of the other two I resolve with Sarisburiensis, both rich alike, endowed alike, I had rather marry a fair one, and put it to the hazard, than be troubled with a blowze; but do thou as thou wilt, I speak only of myself.

Howsoever, I would advise thee this much, be she fair or foul, to choose a wife out of a good kindred, parentage, well brought up, in an honest place. He that marries a wife out of a suspected inn or alehouse, buys a horse in Smithfield, and hires a servant in Paul's, as the diverb is, shall likely have a jade to his horse, a knave for his man, an arrant honest woman to his wife. Such a mother, saith Nevisanus, such a daughter; like crow, like egg, cat to her kind. If the mother be dishonest, in all likelihood the daughter will take after her in all good qualities. If the dam trot, the foal will not amble. My last caution is that a woman do not bestow herself upon a fool, or an apparent melancholy person; jealousy is a symptom of that disease, and fools have no moderation. Justina, a Roman lady, was much persecuted, and after made away by her jealous husband, she caused and enjoined this epitaph, as a caveat to others, to be engraven on her tomb:

> *Learn parents all, and by Justina's case,*
> *Your children to no dizzards for to place.*

After marriage, I can give no better admonitions than to use their wives well, and which a friend of mine told me that was a married man, I will tell you as good cheap, saith Nicostratus in Stobaeus: to avoid future strife, and for quietness' sake, when you are in bed, take heed of your wife's flattering speeches overnight, and curtain sermons in the morning. Let them do their endeavour likewise to maintain them to their means, which Patricius ingeminates, and let them have liberty with discretion, as time and place requires: many women turn queans by compulsion, as Nevisanus observes, because their husbands are so hard, and keep them so short in diet and apparel, poverty and hunger, want of means, makes them dishonest, or bad usage; their churlish behaviour forceth them to fly out, or bad examples, they do it to cry quittance.

In the other extreme some are too liberal, as the proverb is, they make a rod for their own tails, as Candaules did to Gyges in Herodotus, commend his wife's beauty himself, and besides would needs have him see her naked. While they give their wives too much liberty to gad abroad, and bountiful allowance they are accessory to their own miseries; as Plautus jibes, they have deformed souls, and by their painting and colours procure their husband's hate, especially when they smear their poor husband's lips with paint. Besides, their wives (as Basil notes) impudently thrust themselves into other men's companies, and by their indecent wanton carriage provoke and tempt the spectators. Virtuous women should keep house; and 'twas well performed and ordered by the Greeks, that a woman should not be seen in public without her husband; which made Phidias belike at Elis paint Venus treading on a tortoise, a symbol of women's silence and housekeeping. For a woman abroad and alone is like a deer broke out of park, whom every hunter follows; and besides in such places she cannot so well vindicate herself, but as that virgin Dinah (Gen. xxxiv, 2), 'going for to see the daughters of the land', lost her virginity, she may be defiled and overtaken of a sudden.

And therefore I know not what philosopher he was, that would have women come but thrice abroad all their time, to be baptized, married, and buried; but he was too straitlaced. Let them have their liberty in good sort, and go in good sort, as a good fellow said, so that they look not twenty years younger abroad than they do at home; they be not spruce, neat, angels abroad, beasts, dowdies, sluts at home; but seek by all means to please and give content to their husbands: to be quiet above all things, obedient, silent, and patient; if they be incensed, angry, chide a little, their wives must not cample again [answer back], but take it in good part.

An honest woman, I cannot now tell where she dwelt, but by report an honest woman she was, hearing one of her gossips by chance complain of her husband's impatience, told her an excellent remedy for it, and gave her withal a glass of water, which when be brawled she should hold still in her mouth, and that as often as he chid; she did so two or three times with good success, and at length, seeing her neighbour, gave her great thanks for it, and would needs know the ingredients, she told her in brief what it was, fair water, and no more: for it was not the water, but her silence which performed the cure. Let every froward woman imitate this example, and be quiet within doors, and (as Marius Aurelius prescribes) a necessary caution it is to be observed of all good matrons that love their credits, to come little abroad, but follow their work at home, look to their household affairs and private business, be sober, thrifty, wary, circumspect, modest, and compose themselves to live to their husband's means, as a good housewife should do. Howsoever 'tis good to keep them private, not in prison.

Whoever guards his wife with bolts and bars
May be a learned man but sure's a fool.

[MENANDER]

These cautions concern him; and if by those or his own discretion otherwise he cannot moderate himself, his friends must not be wanting by their wisdom, if it be possible, to give the party grieved satisfaction, to prevent and remove the occasions, objects, if it may be to secure him. If it be one alone, or many, to consider whom he suspects or at what times, in what place he is most incensed, in what companies. Nevisanus makes a question whether a young physician ought to be admitted, in cases of sickness, into a new-married man's house, to administer a julep, a syrup, or some such physic. The Persians of old would not suffer a young physician to come among women. Apollonides Cous made Artaxerxes cuckold, and was after buried alive for it. A gaoler in Aristaenetus had a fine young gentleman to his prisoner; in commiseration of his youth and person he let him loose, to enjoy the liberty of the prison, but he unkindly made him a cornuto. Menelaus gave good welcome to Paris a stranger, his whole house and family were at his command, but he urgently stole away his best-beloved wife. The like measure was offered to Agis, King of Lacedaemon, by Alcibiades an exile, for his good entertainment; he was too familiar with Timaea his wife, begetting a child of her, called Leotychides, and bragging, moreover, when he came home to Athens, that he had a son should be king of the Lacedaemonians.

If such objects were removed, no doubt but the parties might easily be satisfied, or that they could use them gently and entreat them well, not to revile them, scoff at, hate them, as in such cases commonly they do; 'tis an human infirmity, a miserable vexation, and they should not add grief to grief, nor aggravate their misery, but seek to please, and all means give them content, by good counsel, removing such offensive objects, or by meditation of some discreet friends. In old Rome there was a temple erected by the matrons to that Viriplaca Dea, another to Venus Verticordia, whither (if any difference happened between man and wife) they did instantly resort: there they did offer sacrifice, a white hart, Plutarch records, without the gall (some say the like of Juno's temple), and make their prayers for conjugal peace: before some indifferent arbitrators and friends, the matter was heard between man and wife, and commonly composed.

In our times we want no sacred churches or good men to end such controversies, if use were made of them. Some say that precious stone called beryllus, others a diamond, hath excellent virtue, to reconcile men and wives, to maintain unity and love; you may try this when you will, and as you see cause. If none of all these means and cautions will take place, I know not what remedy to prescribe, or whither such persons may go for ease, except they can get into the same Turkey paradise, where they shall have as many fair wives as they will themselves, with clear eyes, and such as look on none but their own husbands, no fear, no danger of being cuckolds; or else I would have them observe that strict rule of Alphonsus, to marry a deaf and dumb man to a blind woman.

If this will not help, let them, to prevent the worst, consult with an astrologer, and see whether significators in her horoscope agree with his, that they be not in signs and quarters of hostile aspect and command, but in such as are good and mutually loving, otherwise (as they hold) there will be intolerable enmities between them: or else get him the Seal of Venus, a characteristical seal stamped in the day and hour of Venus, when she is fortunate, with such and such set words and charms, which Villanovanus and Leo Suavius prescribe from the magic Seal of Solomon, Hermes, Roguel, etc., with many such, which Alexis, Albertus, and some of our natural magicians put upon us: that a woman shall not commit adultery, take a lock of her hair, etc., and he shall surely be gracious in all women's eyes, and never suspect or disagree with his own wife so long as he wears it.

If this course be not approved, and other remedies may not be had, they must in the last place sue for a divorce; but that is somewhat difficult to effect, and not all out so fit. For as Felisacus urgeth, if that law of Constantine the Great, or that of Theodosius and Valentinian, concerning divorce, were in use in our times, we should have almost no married couples left. Try therefore those former remedies; or, as Tertullian reports of Democritus, that put out his eyes because he could not look upon a woman without lust, and was much troubled to see that which he might not enjoy, let him make himself blind, and so he shall avoid that care and molestation of watching his wife.

One other sovereign remedy I could repeat, an especial antidote against jealousy, an excellent cure, but I am not now disposed to tell it, not that like a covetous empiric I conceal it for any gain, but some other reasons, I am not willing to publish it; if you be very desirous to know it, when I meet you next I will peradventure tell you what it is in your ear. This is the best counsel I can give; which he that hath need of, as occasion serves, may apply unto himself. In the meantime, ye gods, avert such a plague from the earth. As the proverb is, from heresy, jealousy, and frenzy, good Lord, deliver us.